CHAUCER'S PEOPLE

Everyday Lives in the Middle Ages

LIZA PICARD

WN
WEIDENFELD & NICOLSON

First published in Great Britain in 2017
First published in paperback in 2018
by Weidenfeld & Nicolson
an imprint of The Orion Publishing Group Ltd
Carmelite House, 50 Victoria Embankment
London EC4Y 0DZ
An Hachette UK Company

1 3 5 7 9 10 8 6 4 2

Text © Liza Picard 2017
Maps © John Gilkes 2017

A CIP catalogue record for this book
is available from the British Library.

ISBN (paperback) 978 1 78022 890 7
ISBN (audio) 978 1 4091 7087 7
ISBN (ebook) 978 0 297 60904 9

Typeset at The Spartan Press Ltd,
Lymington, Hants

Printed and bound by CPI Group (UK) Ltd,
Croydon, CR0 4YY

MIX
Paper from
responsible sources
FSC® C104740

www.orionbooks.co.uk

Liza Picard was born in 1927. She is the author of many acclaimed works of social history, including *Elizabeth's London*, *Restoration London*, *Dr Johnson's London* and *Victorian London*. She read law at the London School of Economics and was called to the Bar by Gray's Inn, but did not practise. She worked for many years in the office of the Solicitor of the Inland Revenue before retiring to become a full-time author. She lives in London.

Praise for *Chaucer's People*

'Liza Picard, a chronicler of London society across the centuries, now weaves an infinity of small details into an arresting tapestry of life in fourteenth-century England. Her technique – pursued with the verve and spirit for which she is already justly admired – is to celebrate Chaucer's pilgrim portraits by resituating them within an enlarged field of medieval practices and assumptions... Picard concludes with a speculative Chaucer continuation... Most notably, she – a woman who has herself lived long and thought much – creates an inner monologue for the Wife of Bath, who, after visiting the shrine, drifts into a Molly Bloomian soliloquy, reflecting on the pros, cons and possible personal advantages of taking the veil. As in the rest of the book, we here encounter not presumption but homage, an enthusiast enacting her respect for Chaucer's enduring and indelible accomplishment'

Paul Strohm, *The Spectator*

'Chaucer's pilgrims are the first historical characters who feel like real people, and now Liza Picard makes their world as vivid and three-dimensional as the merry band themselves. *Chaucer's People* is a holiday in the complex, joyful, indelicate medieval world – an approachable, engaging and highly recommended account of an England which is long gone, but whose spirit lingers'

John Higgs, author of *Watling Street*

'As you read this book, Chaucer's writing gains a depth and pungency it usually lacks... Sometimes these snippets, in their oddness, distance the toiling pilgrims from us. At others, they bring them much closer... There is a Chaucerian pleasure in plain sentences, plainly written. This is more almanac than argument, but no less enjoyable for that. If you were to reread *The Canterbury Tales*, you'd get so much more from it with this at your side ... And there are some excellent titbits'

Catherine Nixey, *The Times*

'Wonderfully readable and full of delights ... It buoyed me up with its brilliant insights, many of them entirely new to me'

John Simpson, BBC World Affairs Editor

'An absorbing and revealing companion volume to *The Canterbury Tales*'

The Oldie

'Engaging and fun ... The premise of this entertaining book is to provide historical context for the multitude of figures in Geoffrey Chaucer's *Canterbury Tales*. It is well researched and packed with intriguing nuggets – from the etymology of the word "haberdasher" (from an old Icelandic word meaning a pedlar's sack), to the story of Richard Steris, "one of the cunningest players at the tenys in England", and a wonderful selection of medieval recipes ... Picard provides a wealth of detail both about the occupations of the various characters, and the wider contexts in which they operated. The section on the overwhelmingly complex nature of medieval law is particularly clear and effective'

Hannah Skoda, *BBC History Magazine*

'Chaucer's fourteenth-century story collection *The Canterbury Tales* is a classic hook on which to hang an exploration of the Middle Ages, and this take pleasingly spirals outwards to cover the characters (the nun, the knight, the miller) and the lives they would have led'

History Revealed

'Instructive fun ... The writing is always lively, and there are excellent colour illustrations'

Dr G. R. Evans, *Church Times*

'Brings to life the social history of a period we still know little about. A jolly good read for historians'

This England

To John, with love

CONTENTS

The Religious Life

The Armed Services

LIST OF ILLUSTRATIONS

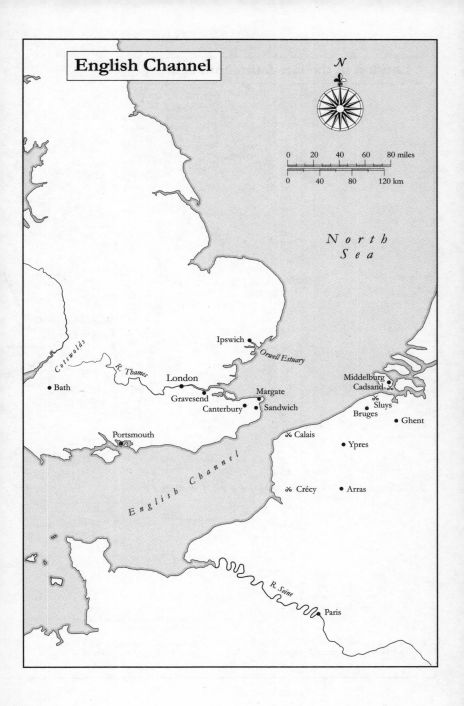

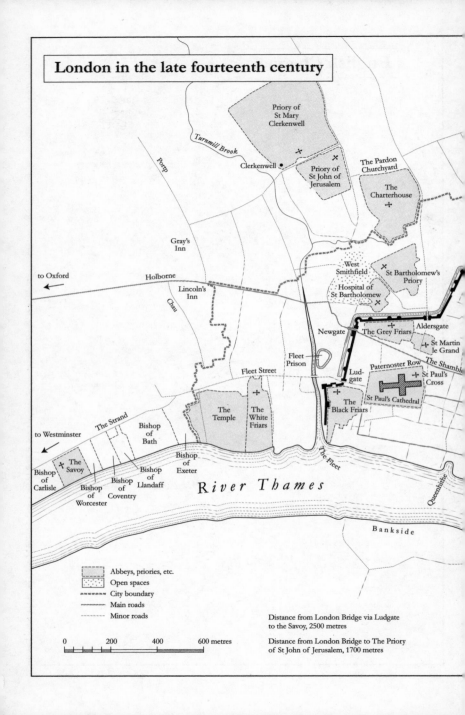

London in the late fourteenth century

Priory of St Mary Clerkenwell

Turnmill Brook

Potop

Clerkenwell

Priory of St John of Jerusalem

The Pardon Churchyard

The Charterhouse

Gray's Inn

to Oxford

Holborne

Lincoln's Inn

Chau

West Smithfield

St Bartholomew's Priory

Hospital of St Bartholomew

Newgate

The Grey Friars

Aldersgate

St Martin le Grand

The Shamble

Fleet Prison

Paternoster Row

St Paul's Cross

Ludgate

St Paul's Cathedral

Fleet Street

The Temple

The White Friars

The Black Friars

The Strand

to Westminster

Bishop of Bath

Bishop of Exeter

The Savoy

Bishop of Carlisle

Bishop of Worcester

Bishop of Coventry

Bishop of Llandaff

The Fleet

River Thames

Quenhithe

Bankside

Abbeys, priories, etc.
Open spaces
City boundary
Main roads
Minor roads

Distance from London Bridge via Ludgate to the Savoy, 2500 metres

Distance from London Bridge to The Priory of St John of Jerusalem, 1700 metres

0   200   400   600 metres

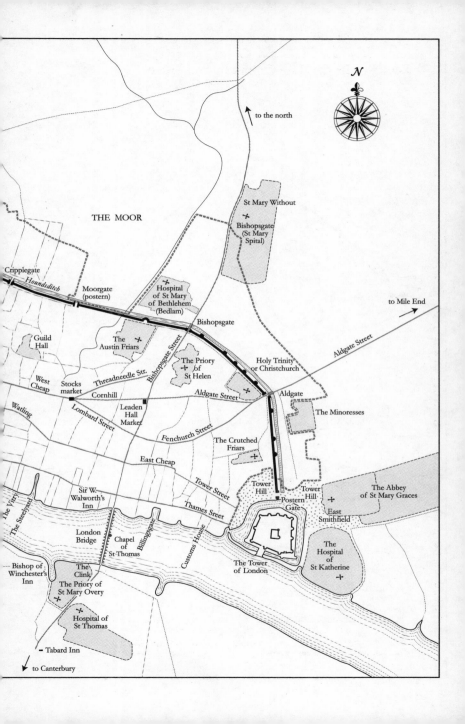

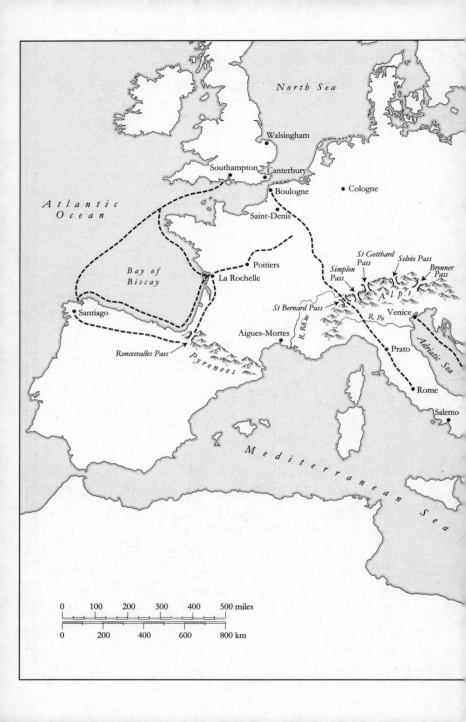

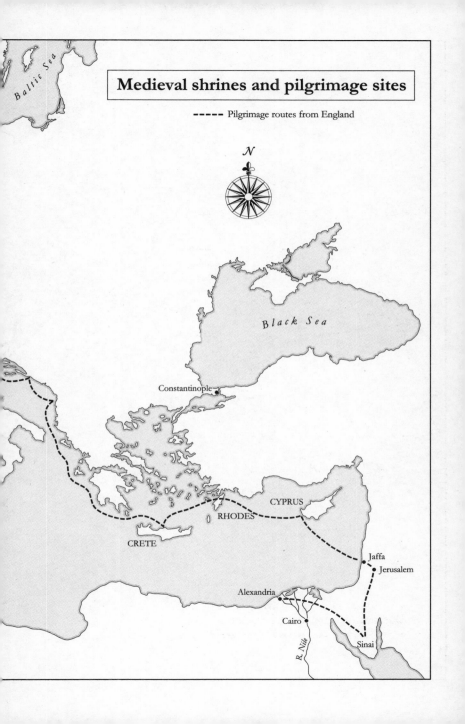

INTRODUCTION

Geoffrey Chaucer was born, probably, in 1340, and died, definitely, in 1400, by when he had seen a war, a pandemic, a rebellion, and a regime change.

The war was England versus France. It began in 1337 and went on for more than a hundred years, in fits and starts. When it was over, it was called the Hundred Years War. While it was going on, it was called the French War.

The pandemic was a plague known as the Black Death, or the Great Pestilence. In 1348 it killed about half the population of England.

The rebellion of 1381 was the protest by peasants against the burden of taxation. It was not just peasants who rebelled, and they had other grievances besides taxation.

The regime change happened in 1399, when Henry Bolingbroke (see Appendix A) took over the throne from his cousin Richard II (r. 1377–99), and became King Henry IV (r. 1399–1413).

People don't change. Their surroundings may change, and their perception of the past and the future, but we share the same impulses and hopes. Chaucer created his pilgrims in the fourteenth century. Here is one view of how they look, six centuries later. All I've done is to supply some background.

He wrote in Middle English, which has developed into the language we speak. Sometimes he's easily understandable, sometimes I've modernized him. I hope I've made the right choices.

I have used the edition of *The Canterbury Tales* published by Penguin Books in 2005, edited by Jill Mann. I am deeply indebted to her for her permission to do so. Her notes have been invaluable.

I owe huge thanks to Gosia Lawik, of that wonderful institution the London Library. She has patiently and efficiently dealt with my requests for books, and offered suggestions of her own about medieval sources, which have been more than I deserved, and always enlightening. My dear son John has saved me from some medical howlers and encouraged me when I needed encouragement, as well as disentangling the computer tangles in which I excel. My editor Simon Wright has by his gentle, perceptive suggestions kept me from many a blatant error and divagation. I must also say 'thank you' to my friends who have put up with many a chunk of medieval history when they just called by to exchange the time of day.

I have been surprised by the wealth of original sources available, in particular the annals of the City of London, and the many chroniclers of their times. Account books for various enterprises have survived, in surprising detail. Perhaps my favourite is the careful record of expenditure incurred by Henry Bolingbroke, just a few years before taking over the throne as Henry IV. He had gone on a pilgrimage to the Holy Land, and he had collected some inconvenient mementos on the way, as one does on holiday trips. It can't have been easy, travelling with a leopard and a parrot. The very last entries in his treasurer's account of expenditure were a mat for the leopard, and '£6 for a cage for the popinjay, plus 1 sh for a cord for hanging it' (the cage, not the popinjay).

Ealing
2017

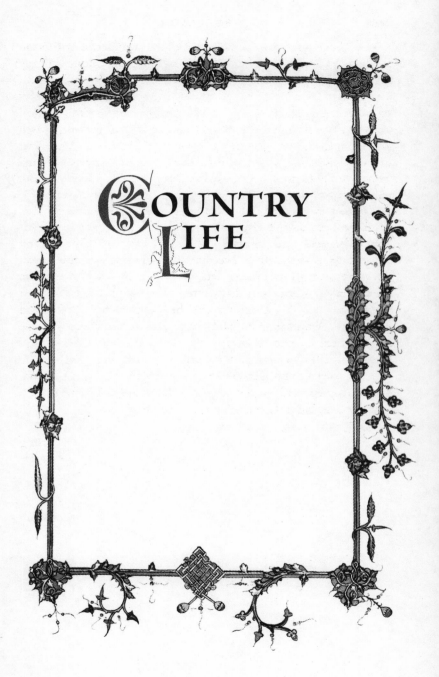

COUNTRY LIFE

I THE WIFE OF BATH

She really came from 'beside Bath', probably one of the Cotswold villages, not Bath itself, but she has gone down in history as the Wife of Bath, and it seems pointless to correct her address now.

Her Appearance

She was certainly eye-catching. 'Bold was her face, and fair, and red of hue.'[1] She had an elaborate wimple round her face and head, and a wide-brimmed hat on the top of it, as big as an archery target.

'Her hose were of fine scarlet red.'[2] Scarlet was the finest kind of wool cloth you could buy; the word did not at that time mean a colour. But hers were dyed red, another indication of her status since red was an expensive dye. Hose in those days were made of cloth, preferably cut on the cross or bias which would give them a little elasticity, but they had to be 'full straight [tightly] tyed', by garters below the knee, for women. They were made of one piece from the knee down to the instep, with a seam up the back, and pieces let into the sides of the foot and the sole. It seems obvious to us that knitted hose would have been so much more comfortable, but knitting had not yet taken its place among fashionable garments. Hose are always shown in contemporary pictures as smoothly encasing the leg, which I assumed was an artistic licence until I caught sight of a modern young woman whose jeans were tighter than skin-tight, and certainly encased her legs smoothly, leaving little room for wrinkles.

The Wife's 'moist' new shoes were of soft tanned leather – she clearly had no intention of walking anywhere. We are not told much about what else she wore, but it was no doubt in the forefront of fashion for long-distance riders. She did wear a 'foot mantle about her hips large, / And on her feet a pair of spurs sharp'.³ The foot mantle was a kind of deep bag usually covering a rider's clothes up to knee-level or beyond, to save them from the dust and mud of the journey. But she must have had her feet out of it, to show off her elegant red hose and her new shoes.

The Wool Trade

English wool, especially from the Cotswolds and Norfolk, had been prized in European trade circles for many years. The Italian textile merchants regularly sent agents over to England to bargain for the best wool. (They sometimes found English place names difficult: for example, 'Cotswold' turned into 'Chondisgualdo'.) The significance of the Wife of Bath lay in the simple fact that she was a weaver – and such a skilful weaver that she outdid the weavers in the long-established Continental cloth centres of Ypres and Ghent.⁴ Chaucer's audience well knew the importance of those cities. Flanders ran a smouldering trade war with English weavers. For many generations England's prosperity had rested on the export of raw wool – hence the Lord Chancellor sat, until recently, on a woolsack, England being still devoted to its history of even half a millennium ago. Suddenly, in historical terms, everything changed. Wool was processed in England and exported to the great fairs in the Low Countries as woven cloth.

There had been weavers in England for many years. London weavers were the first of any trade to get a royal charter, in 1155, giving them a monopoly of weaving in London, Southwark and the district within five miles. But the weavers were never able to compete with the twelve 'Great Companies' such as the Drapers'. They were mostly small master craftsmen working at home, on piece-work rates, converting yarn supplied by the purchaser of their product. For the whole trade to change from producing wool to weaving cloth meant a vast national reorganization. A numerous and skilful work force had to be recruited and trained from scratch, to carry out the many processes between the sheep's back and the merchant's counter. The wool had to be washed and dyed, unless this was done after the cloth had been woven. The wool from different sheep had to be blended, and combed or carded to get the fibres to lie parallel to each other. Spinning it on a distaff was thought to produce a stronger thread, but a spinning wheel worked much faster. The warp – the long threads that bore the weight of the fabric – had to be wound onto reels and then onto the loom. Only then could weaving begin. One person could work a narrow loom, throwing the shuttle across with his right hand and catching it at the other side with his left, but a broad loom needed two weavers. Six spinners were required to supply one loom. A medieval loom was an intricate, complicated piece of machinery that hardly changed until the factories of the Industrial Revolution.

Once the cloth was woven, it had to be cleaned, in fuller's earth or stale urine, to remove grease and dirt. Then it was rinsed again and pounded, by hand, feet or a water-powered mill, to close the weft up more tightly. Then it was stretched on a tenter-frame, and rubbed with teasels (the seed pods of a plant, with prominent hooked thorns, often to be seen nowadays in roadside ditches) to raise the nap. These teasels were so essential to the weaving process that their export from England to Flanders was forbidden when the Flemings threatened to buy them all up and prevent competition from English weavers.

Successive English kings had tried to galvanize their subjects into the weaving trade by importing skilled Flemings, to show them how. Flemish weavers even enjoyed favourable tax treatment. Rumour had it that Edward III (r. 1327–77) employed secret agents in the Low Countries, to attract skilled weavers to England by pointing out the contrast between the wretched conditions in Flanders, under the harsh rule of the Counts of Flanders, and the prospect of happiness in England. But the immigrant Flemings were bitterly resented by the English weavers. They had to be protected by repeated proclamations forbidding 'hurt or insult to the men and merchants of Flanders'. Nevertheless, by 1376 the English guild alleged that most of the weaving in London was done by these foreigners.

So to say that the Wife of Bath was a 'weaver' meant much more to Chaucer's audience, used to exporting sacks of raw wool for generations back, than may be apparent to us at first sight.

Matrimony

'Husbands at church door she had five, / Withouten [not counting] other company in youth[.]'⁵ That's a fair total for any woman – and 'welcome the sixth, when that ever he shall'.⁶ She began her marital career at twelve, the earliest that a woman could legally marry. Of the five, 'three of them were good, and two were bad. / The three men were good, and rich, and old'⁷ – prime qualifications for a gold-digging wife. The fourth was a 'reveller' – 'That is to say, he had a paramour. / And I was young, and full of ragerye [high spirits], / Stubborn and strong, and jolly as a [mag]pie'.⁸ The predictable upshot was that they quarrelled bitterly and violently. She went off to Jerusalem on one of her many pilgrimages and got back just in time for his funeral.

Her fifth husband, Janekin, was a 'clerk of Oxenford'. She took him 'for love, and not for riches'.⁹ He was a disaster. She had noticed him at her fourth husband's funeral. '[M]ethought he had a pair / Of legs and of feet so clean and fair, / That all my heart I gave unto his hold [into his possession]'¹⁰. He was only twenty, and she was perhaps twice his age; but the real cause of their fighting was his favourite reading – all about husbands ill-treating their wives. In a stand-up fight, she hit him, and he punched her back so hard that he knocked her unconscious and injured her ear. She had been deaf ever since.

All of the Wife's five weddings had been 'at church door', outside the church. This didn't mean that they lacked validity. What made a marriage legally binding was not any religious ceremony, but the exchange of vows between the parties. If each party took the other, there and then, to be their spouse, they were married. If there was some condition such as that they *would* marry at some future time, or if one party had already promised to marry someone else – a 'precontract' – there was no marriage. Because of the social and legal rights and duties implied in marriage, it would be as well to exchange their vows before witnesses who could, if some legal query arose later, testify that the vital words had been duly spoken, but the presence of witnesses did not add to the legality of the marriage.

The parties could choose to marry in some faraway place, or a family home, or even in the local inn, but it would be prudent to conduct the exchange of vows in a public place, among people who knew them both and would know whether either of them was already married, or had precontracted to someone else. In those days it would be unusual to travel far from your birthplace, and plenty of people would know the man and woman from their childhood onwards. They would speak up if needed. The church door, which often served the purpose of a community noticeboard, would give the proceedings some publicity and dignity. The parish church normally had a porch outside the south door, big enough to shelter the happy couple and at least some of their friends. It was also usual for the husband to follow his vow with some words corresponding to the later 'With my worldly goods I thee endow', setting out exactly what he gave her there and then, and what she would get if he died leaving her a widow – another good reason to have witnesses there.

But once the vital vows had been exchanged, they could adjourn into the church for a blessing if they wished. Their parish priest would have been impatiently waiting to take a part, and a fee, in the proceedings. Or they might follow up the ceremony with a feast, held in the churchyard – a convenient open space – or the village square, or the village inn. The priest might earn an additional fee by blessing the happy couple's marriage bed, among bawdy ballads and jokes.

There may have been a certain disapproval of serial marriages, in some quarters, to which Chaucer gives the Wife the answer. The Apostle Paul, she remarked crushingly, 'was a maid', i.e. a virgin, so he would hardly know what he was talking about when he recommended celibacy.[11]

All this was related to her fellow-pilgrims at the top of her voice – like many deaf people, she tended to shout – before she even got started on her 'Tale'. She blamed her rampant libido on her birth sign; there was nothing she could do about it. She had been born

under the zodiac sign of Venus, so she 'followed aye mine inclination, / By virtue of my constellation. / That made me [so that] I
could not withdraw / My chamber of Venus from a good fellow'.[12]

Sex is an important part of marriage, as the Wife well knew.
Her first three elderly husbands may not always have been able to
rise to her full-blooded sexuality. 'I set them so to work, by my
faith, /that many a night they sang "Weilawey!"' Marriage implied
a bargain. The wife owed her husband a duty to be cheerful and
obedient. The husband owed his wife an obligation to satisfy her
sexually. After all, why else had God, that wise Creator, given men
their dual-purpose penises, which could both urinate and pro-
create? 'Now wherewith should [man] make his payment, / If he
ne [didn't] use his sely [blessed] instrument?'[13]

One way or another the Wife was certainly the head of her local
community. This was made clear every Sunday at church. She
would be there, dressed in all her finery, with maybe ten pounds
in weight (I think Chaucer is exaggerating here) of elaborate head-
cloths wrapped round her head. It was the custom, at that time,
for people attending Mass to take their offerings up to the altar
personally, in order of rank. If anyone dared to precede her, 'so
wrath [angry] was she / that she was out of all charity' – in a filthy
temper.

There was a certain amount of clashing of status cymbals in
church, nevertheless. Parsons in London churches had been refusing
to take farthings in the offertory. In 1382 the mayor and aldermen
directed that 'no one is to give more than a farthing at a mass, and
he who receives the offerings has to give change for a halfpenny';
if not, the offeror 'shall depart without making any offering whatever'. (Imagine the jingle of small change as the celebrant moved
along the line of reverent parishioners.) Prosperous people had been
giving 'large sums of money' to the church, at baptisms and marriages. The 'ordinary classes' had tried to emulate this when they
couldn't really afford it. Henceforward the maximum gift was to
be 40 pence for a baptism and half a mark (6s 8p) for a marriage,
except for close relatives.

Pilgrimages

Pilgrimages were a splendid way of enjoying the English spring. As well as this pilgrimage to Canterbury, the Wife could visit other English shrines, such as Walsingham in Norfolk, where there was a phial of the Blessed Virgin's milk and a model of her Holy House.[14] But foreign travel beckoned. 'Thrice had she been at Jerusalem ... At Rome she had been and at Boulogne, / At Galicia she had been, and at Cologne[.]'[15]

Jerusalem

Take Jerusalem first. Enter Margery Kempe (1373–1438), a real person, although more difficult for us to imagine than Chaucer's fictional Wife of Bath. She enjoyed, or suffered from, such religious fervour that she spent her time in floods of tears, 'cries and roars', as she talked with the Lord, who probably didn't get much of a word in. This made her an unacceptable fellow-traveller to the band of English pilgrims destined for Jerusalem in 1409, but she managed to survive being deserted by them in foreign lands. On her return she dictated her book. If you can skip her religious soliloquies, it gives a unique account of a pilgrimage to the Holy Land. Twenty-three years had elapsed since Chaucer began to write his *Canterbury Tales*, but I doubt whether things had changed in the interim.

She set out from Yarmouth, the nearest port to her home town of Lynn (now King's Lynn), for the Netherlands in 1409. Thence overland, through what is now Germany to Bologna and Venice, where she stayed for thirteen weeks, presumably to organize the sea voyage to the Holy Land. She would need to assemble her proper pilgrim's kit – a staff with a metal point, useful for walking in mountains and fighting off fierce dogs; a soft leather pouch or 'scrip' for immediate necessities and the small amount of money she was allowed to take; the 'sclavein', a long tunic of coarse cloth (Chaucer's pilgrims don't seem to have bothered with these rules), and a broad-brimmed hat turned up at the front. (Was the huge hat worn by the Wife of Bath a gesture towards that?) Although

the general idea of a pilgrimage was that the soul should profit
from the physical exertion of the journey and the visits to holy
places and relics, not all pilgrims travelled so austerely. In 1384 three
Italians took with them several mattresses, a large number of shirts,
a barrel of good wine, a Bible in several volumes and more reading
matter, a silver cup and 'other delicate things'.

The Venetians operated regular package tours to the Holy Land,
at a fixed price. The sea voyage from Venice to the disembarkation
port in Palestine, stopping at intermediate ports to load fresh supplies
and to trade, could take nearly five weeks. Passage in a small boat was
cheap but very uncomfortable. Margery was divinely guided to book
her passage in one of the large oared galleys, the luxury liners of the
time. The fleet of Venetian galleys sailed every March, and, in a good
year, again in September. They were not as comfortable as we would
expect on a luxury liner. 'When it was time to make her bed' Margery
found that a priest had stolen one of her sheets and someone had
hidden her clothes. The pilgrims disembarked at Joppa (also called
Jaffa: today part of Tel Aviv), where they were met by local officials
who exacted the first of many tolls payable to the Mamluk Turkish
state. With a two-day stopover on the way, they were escorted up to
Jerusalem, where they paid another toll, and began a well-organized
tour of the holy places. Margery was so overwhelmed by her first
sight of Jerusalem that she fell off her mount – luckily not far because
it was only a donkey. Pilgrims were not allowed to ride horses in Palestine, so many a noble knight had to humble himself on a donkey
or a mule. Fortunately a kind fellow-pilgrim picked Margery up and
'put spices in her mouth to comfort her'.

Having paid her entrance fee, she was allowed into the Church of
the Holy Sepulchre, which seems at that time to have included not
only the chapel that visitors would be shown nowadays, but also the
Mount of Calvary, rising 15 feet above the floor with another chapel
on its summit, all roofed over, and another structure supported on
arches, revered as the site where Jesus was nailed to the Cross. Margery stayed there for twenty-four hours, 'from evensong-time till the
next day at evensong time... Then the [Franciscan] Friars lifted up
a cross and led the pilgrims about from one place to another where
our Lord had suffered... every man and woman having a wax

candle in their hands' while the friars gave a running commentary. At the Mount of Calvary Margery for the first time 'might not keep herself from crying and roaring' in ecstasy, a habit that did not endear her to her fellow-pilgrims. Then on, to 'Jesus Christ's grave'. They were shown the marble slab where Jesus's body was laid when it was taken down from the Cross. They walked the Via Dolorosa that pilgrims still walk today (it has been rerouted through the crowded streets of Jerusalem). One day 'they went forth all the forenoon till they came to Mount Sion', where pilgrims believed that the Last Supper had been held, and where the Holy Ghost had descended on the apostles after Christ's death. Then 'she went to the place where Our Lady was buried ... Afterward she rode on an ass to Bedlem [Bethlehem] where she saw the crib where our Lord was born'. By now her fellow-pilgrims were heartily sick of her crying and roaring, and went off to the River Jordan without her. She got there anyway, where 'the weather was so hot that she thought her feet should have burned for the heat that she felt'. Sandals were little protection. Then they all went off to 'Mount Quarantine', the hill where Jesus was tempted by Satan for forty (quarantaine) days and nights; then to Bethany, where John the Baptist had been born and Martha and Mary had lived, and Lazarus had been buried, 'and she stood in the same place that Mary Magdalene stood when Christ said to her "Mary, why weepest thou?"' (John 20:15).

Margery spent three weeks in Jerusalem and the surrounding district. She may have been lucky: by 1458, when we can consult another first-hand account, thirteen days was the usual allotment, making for a very crowded itinerary. Then she decided, or was divinely inspired, to go to Rome next, before returning home. Being who she was, she was undeterred by having little money and no knowledge of any language but English.

Rome

Rome was next on the Wife of Bath's itinerary too. We have a vivid picture of the Rome the Wife visited, in the form of a doggerel poem in Middle English titled *The Stacions of Rome*, dated about 1370: a sort of medieval Baedeker and publicity brochure.[16]

> There were no need to men in Christianity
> To pass into the holy land, over the sea
> To Jerusalem, nor to Katherine [in Sinai] –

Rome was where they should come.

The tour begins with St Peter's Church, where there were a hundred altars:

> Among these altars, seven there be
> More of grace and dignity.
> The altar of the vernicle is one,
> Upon the right hand, as you shall go [in].

(The vernicle, or shell, was already the symbol of St James of Compostela.) The Wife will have been irritated to find that the seventh one, dedicated to the Holy Cross, was for men only; 'no women shall come'. But then her spirits rose as she made her way round St Peter's, let alone making a quick call into the myriad other churches in and near Rome. Each one purveyed pardons, also called indulgences. Some gave only modest numbers, a hundred at a time. They were probably the early ones, before the papacy had spotted the commercial potential of multi-pardoning. Several could be relied on for 14,000 pardons a go – 14,000 years off the eternity you might otherwise spend in purgatory: well worth the effort. An energetic pilgrim visiting all the named churches could clock up about 132,000 years; and there was no reason why he or she should not do the rounds again, for another 132,000 years, which should surely be enough. (The inconsistency of lessening an infinite number by a finite number never seems to have troubled the medieval pilgrim.) Some churches gave special rates to any pilgrim from overseas. Sundays and Wednesdays were good days, as you often got better rates then than on other days. It was worth planning your schedule carefully.

Then the pope hit on another great commercial wheeze. One of his predecessors had declared 1300 to be a 'jubilee year', to be repeated every hundred years. Anyone who came to Rome in that jubilee year could claim twice the normal rate of pardons. The pandemic of 1348–9 had such a devastating effect on the tourist trade that the Roman shopkeepers implored the current pope to declare another jubilee year in 1350, which he did. Anyone coming to Rome in 1350 could be sure of a plenary pardon – forgiveness for all his sins. A once-in-a-lifetime trip to Rome in a jubilee year, braving the risk of infection, was a sound spiritual investment.

As well as pardons, there was a wealth of holy relics in Rome. They were important to the medieval mind, as we shall see when the Pardoner comes along. The Byzantine emperors had amassed a huge collection of relics by the time their capital was sacked by the Crusaders in 1204. Professional relic-merchants moved in. Anyone who was anyone, and especially any newly founded abbey or monastery, had to have as many relics as they could lay their hands on, whether by fair means or, regrettably, by foul. Stealing relics was far from unknown. By 1215 the market had reached such a pitch that they were being stolen all over Europe. Men were taking bites out of withered bits of holy flesh, to be spat out and sold whenever they could find a buyer. The Lateran Council of 1215 decreed that any relic had to be enclosed in a reliquary, for safe keeping, and was never to be removed from it. This gave rise in its turn to the demand for jewel-encrusted reliquaries, which could be as small as a hollowed gem, or as huge as an elaborate tomb, or even a whole chapel such as the French king built to house the crown of thorns. The tomb of St Thomas Becket in Canterbury Cathedral was 'entirely covered with plates of gold' before Henry VIII's commissioners implemented his policy of 'dissolving' – winding up – the monasteries and swallowing their wealth. 'The gold is scarcely visible beneath a profusion of gems, including sapphires, diamonds, rubies and emeralds... exquisite designs have been carved all over it.' It took twenty-three carts to carry away the jewels and precious metals from the tomb to Henry's treasury.

The best relics, of course, were parts of the body of a saint or martyr. According to *The Stacions of Rome* the Wife could see St Christopher's arm – perhaps the very one that Christ sat on as a baby, when St Christopher carried him across a river. A more recent arm had belonged to St Thomas Becket of Canterbury; there it was, along with some of his brains and the blood-spattered robe he had worn when he was murdered only two hundred years ago. In the 'Pope's Hall', the Lateran Palace of the popes before St Peter's basilica was built,

> Of Peter and Paul their heads be here
> Well enclosed under the High Altar
> And other relics, many [a] one.

This was not too far from the truth. The heads of Saints Peter and Paul had been found under the High Altar in the Chapel called Sancta Sanctorum, in the Lateran Palace, as late as 1365. (I do not know by what process of identification they were authenticated. Were they clearly marked, like lost property in a railway office?) Who knew what other miracle-working relics might still be discovered?

Meanwhile, one of Mary Magdalene's feet was displayed in St Peter's Cathedral, and St Julian's jaw, still with some teeth. Christ's swaddling clothes were there, and some of the hay he had lain in, on the manger. One of the nails that had nailed him to the Cross was there, with the sponge soaked in vinegar which he had been offered on the Cross, and the paper on which Pilate had written 'Here is Jesus, the King of the Jews'. The table on which the Last Supper had been served was there, with the tablecloth. The very best of all, of course, would have been some body part of Jesus himself, but none was available, since he had risen to heaven in his complete body, as had his mother Mary, later. But all was not lost: the only bit of his body that stayed on earth when he rose up to heaven was the foreskin that had been cut off when he was circumcised as a baby. There it was. At least four other pilgrimage sites also claimed to have the holy foreskin; but Rome's had the strongest claim to authenticity, since the tiny piece of withered skin had been spirited from Jerusalem by an angel, who gave it to the great Emperor Charlemagne, who gave it to the pope. There was a phial of his mother's breast milk there too. (One cannot help wondering why, let alone how: had she been expressing it? But it crops up in several other holy places.)

Compostela

The Wife of Bath had also been to Santiago de Compostela, in the north of Spain. Despite the claims of Rome, let alone Jerusalem, Compostela had by adroit publicity established itself as the premier pilgrimage destination of the Middle Ages. St James (Iago in Spanish) was one of the twelve disciples. According to legend, after the death of Jesus, James had gone to Spain to spread the Christian gospel, but he got nowhere with the Spaniards of the time so he returned to Jerusalem, where he was martyred in AD 44. Some time later, a coffin containing his uncorrupted body was found on the seashore of northern Spain, near Compostela, whither it had been transported by angels. The church to house this holy coffin was begun in the late twelfth century. It attracted papal and royal patronage. By the time the Wife of Bath got there Compostela was a well-organized tourist site. Pilgrims congregated in the courtyards flanking the church – by now a cathedral – where they could buy the cockle-shell emblems showing that they had indeed made the journey to St Iago's tomb. They could also buy medicines for their ailments and aching feet – whether miraculous or charlatan, only time would tell – and replacements for their equipment, and food and drink for their stay and their homeward journey. There was a permanent fair in the courtyard, noisy, international and often drunk. There is not much of the medieval building to see now, since successive builders have engulfed it in waves of Renaissance and baroque architecture and décor. The simple, majestic church that welcomed the Wife and her fourteenth-century companions must have been awe-inspiring. Perhaps it even induced the Wife to stop talking.

Cologne

Beside Rome, Jerusalem and Compostela, Boulogne and Cologne were small beer. Cologne was the improbable site of the relics of the Three Kings, the Magi. Wherever they had ended their long journey home, their holy bones had – like so many others – ended up in Constantinople (now Istanbul) four hundred years later. In

1162 Frederick Barbarossa had acquired them and installed them in a magnificent tomb in Cologne Cathedral.

Sinai

The only major foreign shrine the Wife had so far missed was the reputed burial place of St Catherine, in distant Sinai. That journey took many days of arduous travel, constantly in danger from armed bandits and risking death from starvation and thirst. Not many embarked on it. It was where Moses received the Ten Commandments, and saw the burning bush (Exodus 3:1–21). There had been a sanctuary there since at least the fourth century. It made its name when some enterprising members of its community identified bones found on the top of a nearby mountain as the skeleton of St Catherine, miraculously transported there from her martyrdom in Alexandria. In his *Travels* Sir John Mandeville described the saint's alabaster tomb in tantalizing terms: 'the monks' prelate moves the bones of the body with a silver instrument, and a little oil, like sweat, comes out . . . and they give a little of it to pilgrims. After that they show the head of St Catherine, and the cloth it was wrapped in when the angels brought the body up to Mount Sinai, and there they buried it with that very cloth, that is still bloody and always will be. And they also show the burning broom [bush] that Moses saw.'

The Pilgrimage Ways

The great pilgrimage routes across Europe to the major shrines were well established by the fourteenth century. Innkeepers had set up shop on the way, and religious houses provided hospices for true pilgrims. But it would still be handy to have a guide, who could not only lead the way but also, most importantly, negotiate rates of exchange. In 1462 thirty-nine different currencies were involved in the journey between England and the Holy Land, and the position was probably the same in Chaucer's time.[17]

If the Wife had been to Jerusalem three times, she probably knew the way as well as anyone. She 'had passed many a strange stream ... she knew much of wandering by the way'.[18] Streams and rivers had to be crossed by fords or ferries, for which tolls were payable unless the local community or a nearby monastery had undertaken their maintenance, as a mercantile or religious gesture. Bridges, such as the one over the Rhône at Avignon, were few and far between. Often a journey was best accomplished by a mixture of river or sea transport by barge or ship, and land travel on horseback or on mules or donkeys.

The pilgrim routes attracted predators. Whenever the war between the French and the English was in temporary remission, bands of unemployed soldiers roamed the land north of the Alps looking for booty on which to sustain themselves until the next campaign, and the territory between the Alps and Rome was infested by bandits. It was as well to travel in a band. When the Wife went on her travels she had probably taken an entourage with her, as the Prioress did in the General Prologue. In the jubilee year of 1350, Beatrice Luttrell set off for Rome, as did countless others, with a 'damsel' or waiting-woman, a chaplain, a yeoman and a groom. Some pilgrim bands were armed. When Margery Kempe asked a disabled Irishman she had met to escort her from Jerusalem to Rome, he told her to rely on her countrymen – who had already deserted her – because 'thy countrymen had bows and arrows' which he had not.

For Compostela, the road lay over the Pyrenees, where unpredictable snows could obliterate the path in blizzards. An unwary step could land a pilgrim in a drift from which his only hope of rescue lay in his companions. Had they heard his cries, in the piercing wind? Would they turn back to look for him? Fortunately, they mostly did, being imbued with Christian charity. The monks at Roncesvalles, just off the summit, would give the weary pilgrims shelter and a degree of care when they struggled to the gates of the monastery.

The Alps were a daunting barrier confronting the pilgrim setting out for Rome or the Holy Land. The choice of pass probably depended on the weather conditions. The Great St Bernard, the Stelvio, the Brenner and the Simplon Passes were all known in the Middle Ages, but they were passable only on foot or on a mule, during the short season when snow did not preclude travel. Part of the St Gotthard Pass consisted of a wooden way for men and pack animals, hanging from the wall of a granite defile by chains. Hannibal and his elephants managed to cross the Alps into Italy, but which pass they used is debated. If pilgrims got lost on the way over the St Bernard Pass, the only help they could count on was the rescue service of 'marroniers' provided by the monks of St Bernard's monastery at the top of the pass. Marroniers didn't come with attached brandy barrels. There were hospices along the routes, run by monks, like service stations on a motorway, where travellers could have their mounts reshod, attended to or exchanged for others, and they themselves could rest or even, if the worst came to the worst, be buried in consecrated ground – always for a fee, of course.

Some pilgrims bound for the shrine of St James in Compostela preferred to go all the way by sea, rather than taking the long trek through France and over the Pyrenees. They might suffer five days or more of acute discomfort as they coasted round the Bay of Biscay in a small, crowded flat-bottomed ship, but God surely took that into account when they arrived. In the same volume as *The Stacions of Rome*, considered above, is a hilarious ditty, again in Middle English, from the time of Henry VI, i.e. 1421–71, but I doubt if much had changed since Chaucer's time. It is entitled 'The Pilgrims Sea-voyage and Sea-sickness':

> Men may leave all games
> That sail to St James!
> For many a man it [is] gramis [troublesome]
>   When they begin to sail
> For when they have take[n to] the sea
> At Sandwich or at Winchelsea
> At Bristol, or wher[ever] that it be,
>   Their hearts begin to fail.

After various commands to the crew, incomprehensible to the wretched passengers as well as to us, except when the passengers are rudely told to get out of the way, the captain foresees a storm, so he orders the cook to prepare a meal for him and the crew.

[Meanwhile] the pilgrims lie,
And have their bowls fast [beside] them
And cry after hot malmsey [shout for hot red wine]
   Their health for to restore.
And some would have a salted toast,
For they might eat neither sode [boiled meat] nor roast . . .

Some laid their books upon their knee
And read, so long as they could see.
'Alas! My head will split in three!'
   Thus sayeth another, certain.

But the shipowner arrives, and tells his carpenter to make some
cabins 'here and there' – but they must have been below decks.

A sack of straw were there right good [would have been a
    good thing]
For some must lie in their hood [wrapped only in the long
    head-covering they wore]
I had as rather be in the wood [on the deck?]
   With no meat or drink.
For when that we shall go to bed
The pump was near our bed's head,
A man were as good as dead
   As smell thereof the stink!

Perhaps things were not always so bad. The pilgrim ships were
licensed by Venice, which surely imposed minimum standards of
accommodation if this profitable trade were to be preserved. There
are records of licences to just one Venetian family, to carry about a
hundred pilgrims, in 1382, and seventy and sixty-four in 1384. There
must surely have been many more.

Paperwork

The shrines did not necessarily make huge amounts from the pilgrims flocking to them. The performance of their monastic duty to give hospitality consumed much of the offerings they received.

In 1220, the year when the sumptuous tomb of St Thomas Becket was completed, the cost of hospitality incurred by Canterbury Priory exceeded the amount of the pilgrims' offerings; not by much, but neither figure could be safely predicted, a situation which would give a modern accountant a severe headache. What the owners of the shrines gained, as well as, no doubt, heavenly approval, was power and influence in ecclesiastical circles, which could be invaluable. It is difficult to guess how much a pilgrim would expect to pay for his journey. There may be a clue in one of the stained-glass windows in Canterbury Cathedral. After a series of tragedies, a man and his wife vowed to go on pilgrimage to the tomb of St Thomas. Somehow they kept postponing the journey, and things went even worse for them. Finally all is forgiven, but not before they had given the four silver pieces they had originally pledged, and much more. A pilgrim was expected to be as generous as his or her means would allow.

The first step was to obtain a special licence, or passport, from the Crown, giving permission to leave the kingdom. Married women had to carry with them their husbands' formal consent to their leaving the matrimonial home, but surely the husbands didn't charge for that. Once the licence was granted – for a fee – the pilgrim would sort out his or her travel money. In 1368 four pilgrims aiming for Santiago de Compostela had £4 'in exchange', that is, in the form of a letter of exchange payable at Calais, plus 20 shillings each for expenses. This does not seem very much, considering that they would be expected to pay for their board and lodging at the various hospices run by religious orders on their way, as well as incidentals such as blacksmiths to shoe their horses or mules, or the cost of exchanging or selling their own mount for another if it could not go any further, let alone the entrance fees for every shrine. Bequests directing the beneficiary to make a pilgrimage to a specified shrine, and to pray for the testator's soul there, give us some guide, but they varied widely in amount. The journey to Compostela was assessed at anything between £2 and £20 (for money values, see Appendix C). Two testators directing their legatees to make the journey to the Holy Land each left 60 *scudi*, a Florentine currency convenient for the Venetian entrepot. But Margery Kempe, and no doubt countless others, relied on the Christian charity of those whom she met on the way, and her faith was on the whole justified.

Vicarious Pilgrimages

It would of course be most effective, and augur well for your after-life, if you walked to a holy shrine barefoot, and prayed there for redemption on your knees. But suppose that in some particular financial or personal crisis you had vowed to make a pilgrimage to a particular shrine in the future, in return for immediate divine help; suppose, too, that the crisis had been satisfactorily resolved, but your vow still hung over your head; and that now was not a convenient moment to be away, just as trade was looking up and the market was buoyant; or that somehow there had never been time to redeem your vow before you were called away by death. The answer was to find a substitute to make the pilgrimage, and pray the prayers, on your behalf, leaving you to get on with your life, or rest unworried in death.

Your substitute would expect some reward, as well as the costs of his travel. Maybe he could also make a bit on his expenses, if he travelled carefully. Better still, he could collect a portfolio of gifts and bequests from several people, all to the same shrine. He could make a comfortable living by travelling to and fro on the pilgrimage route, duly praying for the souls of his various employers, getting to know the best local hostelries and the cheapest blacksmiths, and perhaps pocketing an occasional commission on the side . . . Maybe he took the opportunity to pray for his own soul too while he was there.

The obvious difficulty was that there was no means of check-ing whether your substitute had done his bit, as promised. If you stayed in your London counting house and sent someone else to Compostela for you, you wouldn't know what had been credited to your account in heaven until you got there – if you did.

Did the Wife of Bath benefit spiritually from her travels? Chaucer leaves us in doubt.

II THE PLOUGHMAN

The Poor Parson, of whom Chaucer approved, had come with his brother, a ploughman 'that had ylad [carried] of dung many a fother [cartload]'.[1] This seems a curious distinguishing feature to choose. He probably smelled a bit, but then most medieval people did, if our sensitive noses were to get near them.

His Appearance

He was dressed in a tabard, the simplest of garments, being two pieces of fabric joined on each shoulder. A sumptuary law of 1363 had enacted, perhaps optimistically, that 'carters, ploughmen... and all other keepers of beasts... attending to husbandry shall not wear any manner of cloth but blanket or russet, of wool, worth not more than 12 pence, and shall wear girdles of linen... and they come to eat and drink in the same manner that pertains to them, and not excessively'. But enforcement of these sumptuary laws was always a problem, and the 1363 law was almost immediately repealed.

Agricultural Methods

Dung was a vital element of medieval agriculture. It was a precious way of returning to the earth what growing crops had taken out of it. For dung you have to have animals, and for animals you have to have grass, and some other fodder grown on arable fields. A complicated, totally organic system of rotating grass and other crops operated, depending on local conditions.

The English climate varied, from the cold northern counties to the warm south-west. The soil varied too, from the thin, stony ground of the north where little could be grown but heather and oats, to the fat lands of the south where wheat would flourish. Life in the northernmost counties could be disrupted by the Scottish raiders. In the remote areas of Yorkshire the Cistercian monks developed a thriving wool industry, where little land was under the plough and few labourers were needed. The south coast was prey to French raiders who sailed in on the high tide, destroyed and pillaged everything in sight, and sailed out on the ebb tide. Chaucer's pilgrims came 'from every shire's end',[2] so we can only guess where the Ploughman came from.

An agricultural settlement would usually have the 'Lord's Hall' – what we would think of as the manor house – at its centre. The hall might be inhabited by its owner or, more probably, by a tenant of his. Nearby, there would be living quarters for the *famuli*, the permanent skilled staff such as the ploughman, the carter, the dairywomen and the various animal herders. The ploughman would turn his hand to other tasks when the autumn and spring ploughing was done; 'He would thresh, and thereto dike and delve [make ditches and dig]'.[3] All these skills were important to the well-being of the land. Threshing was a seasonal activity in which anyone available was expected to join. Ditches, as well as providing drainage, were often used as boundaries between plots. As to delving, the medieval spade hadn't changed its shape since Adam used it after his expulsion from Eden, although it might have acquired an iron sheath along its edge.

There would be one or more barns, for storing grain until threshing time came, and for housing animals in winter. There was usually a mill, powered by water if there was a handy stream, or by wind, on whatever high ground there was. A pond for ducks and fish was useful. There might be a smithy. Iron shoes for horses, and sometimes for oxen, had been common since the eleventh century, and they needed frequent replacement. Iron ploughshares needed frequent repair. The kind of plough that Chaucer's pilgrim used could have been a 'wheeled plough', which could be set to plough at any given depth, which was ideal for light, well-drained soil; or it could have been a 'swing' plough, for heavy soils or very uneven ground. Either kind needed two men to operate it, the ploughman who steered the plough and the driver who controlled the animals. Power was provided by pairs of oxen, sometimes as many as eight, making a long train that needed plenty of room to turn. Horses were increasingly used. They were faster, but they cost more to feed. Some teams combined oxen and horses. By the end of the fourteenth century oxen still provided the normal pulling power for a plough, and for heavy wagons ('drays'), but horses were gradually gaining on them, and were invariably used for harrowing, for pulling the two-wheeled carts in which produce was taken to market and as pack animals for smaller loads. One advantage of oxen was that they could be eaten at the end of their useful lives, whereas there was an English taboo against eating horseflesh.

The lord's demesne, his landholding, might extend to over a thousand acres, including woods and pasture, meadows and waste ground. The lord might farm it himself, or, increasingly, lease it out. Traditionally it would be worked by the villeins, who held their land subject to the lord's customary right to call on them for 'boon-work' whenever he summoned them, regardless of their own needs to get in their own harvest while the summer weather lasted. With luck a villein might have a family who could look after his holding while he worked on his lord's land. His obligation was part of his entitlement to his holding, not part of his status as slavery had been. If he left his land and went to live in a city for a year, he became a free man. A serf could also shed his servile status if he could find an apprenticeship in the city. Both villeinage and serfdom were becoming rarer as the century wore on.

The land round about the manor house was divided into two, or sometimes three, fields. Every year some land was left fallow, with no crop growing on it other than grass. This rested the soil, and provided pasture for the farm animals. The remaining land was parcelled out in strips or 'selions', usually following the lie of the land, each strip being roughly as much as a plough team could plough in a day. If there was a stony, arid area that no one wanted, and a lush area down by the stream where crops would flourish, the villeins would decide how to allot the available land equitably, in a

highly organized cooperative system, recorded and enforced in the
manorial court. The system had served them well for generations.
Exchanges and sales were often agreed so that the allotted strips
were next to each other, making a compact holding, sometimes up
to 30 acres, although a more normal holding would be less.

Wheat was cut with a sickle, about halfway up the stalk, laying
the ear-heavy stalks on the ground in handfuls, to be bound by
the women and older children into sheaves, which were stood
in shocks to dry. One binder was needed for every four reapers.
Wheat straw was useful for animal and human bedding and animal
feed. Oats and barley were mown with scythes, close to the ground,
but leaving many grains for the gleaners coming to pick up what
they could find once the harvest was done. If the labourers were
paid, they were paid in kind, and because it was so easy to steal a
sheaf, any payment in the form of sheaves had to be done by the
landholder or his agent, in person, by daylight, at the barn door –
not in the field. The rector took his tithe by sending his servants to
take every tenth sheaf, or every tenth shock. Beans were gradually
becoming known as good fodder for animals, and sometimes as
food for the poorer peasants. The admirable nitrogenous nature of
legumes was not yet known, but surely some observant peasants
must have noticed that ground which had supported a crop of
beans was more productive than before.

Once the harvest had been safely gathered in, the parson would
announce the day when the stubble could be pastured. Once again,
there were careful regulations. Sometimes tethered animals were
allowed in first, for instance a mare with her foal. Each kind of
animal took its turn – first horses, then oxen, then cows. Sheep
came last because they cropped so close that they wouldn't have
left anything for the other animals. Then the peasants' wives, and
their geese and poultry, came to pick up ('glean') whatever was left.

This peaceful way of life was abruptly shattered by two events:
the Great Pestilence in 1348–9, and the Peasants' Revolt of 1381.

The Great Pestilence

We lack accurate mortality figures for the Pestilence, named by the Victorians the Black Death. Historians have agreed that perhaps a third, or even half, of the population of Europe died. Meticulous record-keeping, and the enforcement of the countryside laws, became faint memories. Human corpses lay unburied. England became a ghastly expanse of death. Henry Knighton, an Augustinian monk who died in 1396, included in his chronicle of England an account of the Pestilence, which he must have witnessed. It makes bleak reading:

> In that year [1348–9] and the following year there was a general mortality throughout the world. It first began in India, then spread to Tharsis, thence to the Saracens, [i.e. the Middle and Near East, down to the shores of Palestine] and at last to the Christians and Jews ... In that same year there was a great murrain [disease] of sheep everywhere in the realm ... in one place more than 5,000 sheep died in a single pasture ... sheep and oxen strayed through the fields and among the crops and there was none to drive them off or collect them, but they perished in uncounted numbers ... for lack of shepherds ... After the Pestilence many buildings ... fell into total ruin for lack of inhabitants; similarly many small villages and hamlets became desolate and no homes were left in them, for all those who had dwelt in them were dead.

It was impossible to summon Parliament immediately, so Edward III, 'considering the grievous incommodities which of the lack of Ploughmen and such Labourers may hereafter come', issued a royal ordinance freezing wages at their pre-Pestilence levels, and compelling workers to remain in their pre-Pestilence employments. Two years later the Commons passed the Statute of Labourers, on the same lines as the ordinance. Blaming the labourers for being so selfish as to refuse to work except for grossly inflated wages 'in the interests of their own ease and greed', the Commons, uninfluenced of course by their own 'ease and greed', laid down maximum rates of pay for various categories of workers.[4] Daily rates were prescribed for various trades. The wages of *famuli* such as ploughmen were fixed at pre-Pestilence levels. Their contract of employment was to last for a whole year and they were forbidden to leave before it expired. Stringent enforcement provisions required recalcitrant labourers to be put in the stocks – every village was ordered to build some – and then sent to gaol. Special justices were to be appointed to see that the statute was observed.

But as the surviving peasants awoke from the nightmare of the Pestilence, they found that for the first time in their history they had power. No matter what laws were passed by the landowners sitting in London as Members of Parliament, the hard fact remained that the same men had to think of their landholdings outside London, where the harvest had to be gathered, the flocks and herds tended, the land ploughed and the corn sown – otherwise their income would be nil. The labourers could dictate their own terms. If they felt ill-treated, they could always leave, no matter what the law said. They would easily find work elsewhere, on terms that suited them. By 1359 wage levels seemed to have settled at only a little above the statutory limits, but relations between employer and labourer would never be as they had been before the Pestilence. Discontent simmered below the surface.

In 1377 there was a 'Great Rumour' among some peasants that 'The Book of Domesday' absolved them from 'all manner of service'. They even clubbed together to pay a lawyer to get a formally certified, or 'exemplified', copy of the relevant extracts. They contended that the manors where they held land were part of the 'ancient demesne of the Crown', therefore they were not obliged to pay the disputed dues. It was an attractive argument, but it failed. 'Exemplifications' of the Domesday Book went the rounds for years afterwards, acquiring almost magical force – but not in a court of law. Discontent was fanned by a series of poor harvests.

The Poll Tax

All this time, the war with the French continued. With their gift for catchy titles, the Victorians called it the Hundred Years War, but no one who didn't live till the centenary of its outbreak knew it was to last for a hundred years, just as no one living in Chaucer's period knew they were living in the 'Middle Ages'. It was known at the time as the French War. Chaucer's contemporaries may have lacked the daily news bulletins that we enjoy, but they understood enough of the conduct of the war to be increasingly critical of it. Edward III's army was by then largely composed of professional, paid soldiers, so he needed huge amounts of money in his war chest.

In 1341, the year after the king had formally claimed the crown of France and raised the tempo of the war, Parliament had granted him, on the traditional lines, a fifth of the value of 'all moveable goods of England, and the custom of wools, and the ninth sheaf of every manner of corn'. Happy in the glorious victories of Sluys (1340), and Crécy (1346), the Commons were content to vote further imposts as the war ground on. But in 1371 a new form of tax was imposed. The French War had resumed, after a lull, and a huge sum of money, £ 50,000, was needed fast, to finance the war effort. The traditional system was too slow, so a new 'parish tax' was tried, to raise the much-needed funds. Every parish in England was assessed to a certain sum, which should meet the crisis. Every resident in the parish was to pay a proportion of the parish assessment. Unfortunately, the experts got the number of parishes wildly wrong, and had hastily to correct the figures. Instead of only 22s 3d per parish, which might have been tolerable, the proper amount turned out to be 116s per parish. (Even modern Treasuries can be fallible.) There was widespread evasion. The official idea was that 'the parishioners of each parish of greater value shall be aiding and contributory to the parishioners of the parishes of lesser value' – perhaps a pious hope, since there were no clear rules as to how this should happen. In practice, it didn't.

In 1379 a different and novel formula was tried, a graduated poll tax. Dukes were assessed at £6 13s 4d, earls and the mayor of London at £4, 'the great merchants' at £1, down through the ranks of the nobility and gentry and the professional classes, to 'each married man for himself and his wife, who do not belong to the above-named estates, above the age of sixteen, except veritable beggars, 4 pence, and each single man and woman above sixteen [many of whom had never been taxed before] 4 pence'. It, too, was widely evaded.

But the poll tax of 1380 was a step too far, for those at the bottom of the pile. 'Every lay person, males and females, of whatever estate or condition, who has passed the age of fifteen years', except beggars, was to pay 12 pence, *three times* the amount due under the first poll tax. 'Suitable persons' were to be commissioned to collect the money. The more affluent would surely help 'the less'. Payment was required in two instalments: two-thirds by the end of January 1381, the rest by June. The tax was imposed specifically to fund a planned expedition into Brittany, and for the defence of the realm, and for 'keeping of the sea'. But the Brittany expedition was a dismal and costly failure, the defence of the realm did not justify expensive campaigns overseas, and the sea round the south coast was so poorly 'kept' that the French and their Spanish allies could raid English coastal settlements with impunity. To crown it all, the collectors were perceived as letting the rich go tax-free, extorting money from the poor who could ill afford it, and pocketing the money themselves.

The Rebellion of 1381

The events of the summer of 1381 were recorded by various chroniclers, at the time or soon afterwards, from their various viewpoints. Unfortunately no chronicle survives from the standpoint of the rebels themselves. They were not in the habit of writing chronicles. Various historians have pored over these chronicles ever since. Space prevents me, fortunately, from a multi-page version of my own. It isn't possible to splice together the various chronicles into a coherent whole. There is ambiguity about dates, times and places which could spark endless discussion. And it may not always be wise to trust paintings of the 1381 events, which may depict how the painter imagined them, rather than what actually happened.

Medieval figures have to be treated with circumspection. 'Many thousands' might just boil down to 'quite a lot'. And these revolting English 'peasants' – the word didn't come into circulation until later – were not like the French tatterdemalions who had tried to resist similar burdens but had been firmly squashed by their overlords a few years earlier. These were solid, self-respecting men and women who owned some sheep and a cow and perhaps a carthorse, and could make their own livelihoods from the land they cultivated; or they were skilled small artisans in a town, lacking the wherewithal to become members of the prestigious guilds, but still deserving of respect. They were often joined by the small landholders in their district, and even by some priests. What follows is my own assessment.

The conflagration flared in an Essex village, Fobbing, on a small inlet on the Thames estuary, east of Tilbury. On 1 June 1381 Thomas Brampton, the local landowner's steward, 'who was regarded as a great magnate in that area ... had summoned ... a hundred of the neighbouring townships [in the context, communities], to pay their dues ... all the people gave answer that they would not pay a penny more because they already had a receipt from him for the said subsidy. On this, Thomas menaced them strongly.'[5] The inhabitants of Fobbing and two other villages still refused to pay, and 'would not be arrested, but tried to kill Thomas and the two sergeants' (his escort). In the general mayhem that followed, Brampton managed to escape to London but the crowd caught three of his clerks and 'cut off their heads, which they carried about with them for several days, as an example to others; for it was their purpose to slay all lawyers and all jurors and all the servants of the King whom they could find'. The rioters, who by now, according to the chronicler, numbered 50,000, took to the woods and razed the countryside. 'They burned or destroyed the houses of all who would not join them.' News of the uprising spread rapidly north as far as Lincoln, and west into the counties round London.

Meanwhile events in Kent followed a similar course. In January 1381 a Commission of Inquiry had been given three months to report on the receipt of the poll tax in Kent. By 20 May collectors had been appointed for Canterbury. All might have been well if Sir Simon Birley had not upset the applecart. By some historical accident, serfdom had rarely existed in Kent, but after the Pestilence the landlords of Kent had been able to impose 'a second serfdom'. Their tenants could not leave their land without the landlord's permission, for which they had to pay in hard-earned cash, and they could be forced to work for the landlord at harvest and other farming crises, when they needed to cultivate their own holdings. In May 1381 Birley sent his minions to Gravesend, to arrest one Robert Belling, alleging that he was an escaped serf from one of his estates. The peasants refused to stand by and let this happen. Pausing only to storm the gaol in Maidstone, they frightened the governor of Rochester Castle into freeing Belling. Some of the rebels went home, job done. Others, led by Wat Tyler, went on to Canterbury, where the rebellion turned violent and bloody. Suspected enemies were killed and their properties destroyed. The abbey's library was broken open, legal documents of title were burned. The next day several hundred men led by Wat Tyler took the road to London.

Not much is known about Wat Tyler. He may have been an archer who had fought in the French War. He certainly had the gift of leadership. Some of his followers were armed with bows and arrows; others had grabbed sharp billhooks, iron-edged spades or long-handled pitchforks. Most of them were accustomed to local responsibilities as bailiffs and constables and the many other village offices, or had done their military service, and knew the value of concerted action. They hated the collectors, and all other government servants, for their perceived corruption. They hated the large ecclesiastical landowners such as the prior of Canterbury for trying to preserve the servile status of their workers. They hated lawyers for their obfuscatory denials of the people's rights. Above all they hated serfdom. The Londoners among them hated foreigners, especially the Flemings, who had been given unfair trading privileges by the king.

John Ball, a radical priest from Essex, took as his text two lines from a popular song of the time:

> When Adam delved and Eve span,
> Who was then the gentleman?

None of the rebels was in it for the money. Compared to the medieval treatment of besieged enemy towns, where the occupants were mercilessly slaughtered if they failed to surrender, these fighters were indeed gentlemanly. At one stage the king's mother crossed their path. She could have been captured and held for ransom, or worse; but they let her pass with only a few ruderies. The rebels' watchword was 'With King Richard and the true Commons'. They had faith in their young king, who would surely see the justice of their cause.

And it seemed to them, at first, that he did.

The long reign of his grandfather, Edward III, had descended into squalor and corruption. His father, the famous Black Prince, had died an unglamorous death from dysentery, the scourge of medieval armies, in 1376, just a few months before Edward's death in 1377. Richard succeeded to the throne at the age of ten.

In June 1381, most English soldiers were abroad fighting the French, or in the north of England fighting the Scots, under the king's uncle and mentor, John of Gaunt (see Appendix A). Armed opposition to the rebels was out of the question. But Richard had the benefit of advice from a powerful trio: his mother Joan of Kent, a formidable lady; Simon Sudbury, the archbishop of Canterbury who was also the chancellor of England; and Brother William Appleton, a friar. His presence is surprising. He was the principal medical adviser to John of Gaunt, and bound to follow him everywhere, in peacetime and in war, for the whole of his life, so one would have expected him to be at his master's side. Perhaps his employer knew he could trust Appleton to represent his views, and to give effective advice, while he was unavoidably absent in the north. These three convened in the Tower of London, with other nobles, to agree a strategy. We can only infer what that strategy was by looking at how it was implemented. Time would be gained by offering mediation. If this failed, Richard was to meet the rebels in person, and promise them whatever they demanded. They would disperse back to their homes, where they could be picked off one by one. Richard's every move was carefully choreographed.

The Kentish rebels paused at Lambeth long enough to burn the muniments in the archbishop's library, and marched on to Black-heath, on the south side of the Thames. The next day they listened to yet another rousing sermon by John Ball. The rebels from Essex and the Home Counties encamped on the north side of London. Sympathetic Londoners joined each camp.

On 12 June the bishop of Rochester urged the Kentish rebels to go home, but without success. On the morning of 13 June Richard took to a barge to parley with the Kentish rebels, downriver at Greenwich. But neither side would leave its safe stance to talk, so Richard went back to the Tower.

Later that day the Kentish rebels, pausing only to 'pull down a house of ill fame near London Bridge which was in the hands of Flemish women... surged on to the bridge to pass into the city, but the mayor was just before them and had the chain drawn up and the drawbridge lifted to stop their passage. And the commons of Southwark rose with them and cried to the keepers of the bridge to lower the drawbridge and let them in, or otherwise they would be undone. And for fear of their lives the keepers let them enter.'[6] At the same time the Essex contingent with their allies swarmed into London through Aldgate, where Geoffrey Chaucer must surely have watched them from his lodgings over the gate. Both bodies of rebels set about methodically achieving their aims. They killed any Crown servant they could find. They opened the prisons, freeing the prisoners and killing the gaolers. Some of them diverged northwards, to the priory at Clerkenwell, the headquarters of the Knights Hospitallers who owned the site at the Temple occupied by lawyers. They set fire to it, 'causing it to burn by the space of seven days together, not suffering any to quench it'.[7] Others kept along the river, to the Temple, where they 'went into the Temple Church and took all the books and rolls and remembrances [records] which were in the hutches [chests] of the apprentices of law in the Temple, and carried them into the highway and burned them'.

Some of them took the nearest route west along the river, through Ludgate and past the land gates of miscellaneous bishops' palaces, till they came to the Savoy, John of Gaunt's magnificent palace.[8] 'They broke open the gates and... took all the torches they could find and set fire to all the sheets and coverlets and headboards of great worth, for their whole value amounted, it was said, to 1,000 marks... [they made a huge bonfire and] found three barrels of gunpowder, which they took to be gold or silver, and they threw them on the fire and this powder blew up high'.[9] The magnificent building remained a derelict wreck for centuries. 'They would fain [have] had the Duke of Lancaster [John of Gaunt] but as grace was he was not to be found.'[10] Here the ethos of the rebels shines out. The palace was full of portable treasures paid for by the honest sweat of the peasants. Nothing was stolen. 'One of their companions they burnt in the fire because he minded to have reserved one goodly piece of plate.'[11] Everything was destroyed. Jewels that couldn't be burned were ground to powder or thrown into the Thames.

There were two arranged meetings between Richard and the rebels. The first was east of London at Mile End. Richard invited the rebels to put their demands in writing. By now Wat Tyler had been elected as the head of the whole rebellion. 'He required that no man should be a serf... but should give 4 pence rent for an acre of land, and that no one should serve any man but at his own will, and on terms of regular covenant.'[12] Richard appeared to listen. He announced the end of serfdom, and promised 'justice'. Meanwhile other rebels entered the Tower of London and found the archbishop in the chapel there, with Brother Appleton. The Chapel of St Peter ad Vincula in the Tower was tiny, up narrow winding stairs. This was not the dignified martyrdom of St Thomas Becket. The archbishop tried to escape the mob of peasants, but they caught him and bundled him down the stairs and out into the yard, and on to Tower Hill. In the words of a chronicler, 'at Tower Hill they beheaded Master Sudbury, then archbishop of Canterbury and chancellor of England, and Brother [i.e. Friar] William Appleton, a grey friar, he was physician to the duke of Lancaster... many men of law, Flemings and other aliens as they came to hand, they were beheaded in various places'.[13]

The other meeting with the rebels was a few days later. The prearranged plan to defuse the tension came into operation. While London ran with blood behind him, Richard went to Smithfield. (This was not west Smithfield near St Bartholomew's Hospital, but east Smithfield, adjoining the Tower.) A royal show of force might have inflamed the rebels, so it was a sensible decision to escort the young king with the mayor of London, William Walworth, accompanied by his sword-bearer and a few other notables. The Londoners in the crowd knew Walworth as the man who patrolled their streets to check on fair trading regulations. The young king's mother, unaware of the fate of her co-advisers, proudly watched her son's performance from the sidelines, sitting in her 'whirlicote' (carriage).

The rebels were led by Wat Tyler. When the royal party arrived,

> Jack Straw [a name often given to Wat Tyler] spoke to the King as [if] it had been to his fellow: and John Blyton that bore the Mayor's sword of London bade him doff his hood while he spoke to the King; wherefore Jack Straw waxed [grew] angered and made to cast his dagger to Blyton. And then William Walworth... drew his baselard [dagger] and smote Jack Straw on the head, and with that, Rauf Standish, that bore the King's sword, [struck] Jack Straw through the body with a sword: and then he fell down dead. And anon [afterwards] his head was smitten off and set on a pole.[14]

His death had not been part of the plan.

We can turn to the *Chronicles* of Jean Froissart (1337?–*c*.1404). Often relying on earlier chronicles, and not always accurate, he nevertheless gave a vivid account of events in England, France and the Low Countries in the fourteenth century. He always had an eye for dramatic detail. When the rebels in the front row of the crowd saw their leader fall, 'they began to bend their bows and to shoot'. The rustle as they did so must have been the only sound. They were too close to miss. For interminable moments, bloody regicide and massacre hung in the air.

Then Richard retrieved the remnants of the plan. He spurred forwards and 'did cry that no man should do them [the rebels] bodily harm'. He 'benevolently granted their requests and made a clerk write a bill in their presence in these terms: Richard King of England and France gives great thanks to his good commons, for that they have so great a desire to see and maintain their king: and he grants them pardon for all manner of trespasses... done up to this hour, and wills and commands that everyone should quickly now return to his own home: he wills and commands that everyone should put his grievances in writing, and have them sent to him; and he will provide, with the aid of his loyal lords and his good council, such remedy as should be profitable both to him and to them, and to the kingdom. He put his signet seal to this document in their presence.'[15] They believed him. They turned and peacefully made for home.

If this were a stage drama, the last scene would have shown the king telling Walworth to put on a helmet. Walworth was puzzled. 'The King replied that he was greatly obliged to him and therefore was going to confer on him the order of knighthood. And the mayor answered that he was not worthy nor able to have or keep up a knight's estate, for he was but a merchant and had to live by merchandise; but at last the King made him put on the helmet and took a sword in both his hands and dubbed him knight resolutely and with great goodwill.'[16] (Walworth must have been wearing body armour but had taken off his helmet in deference to the royal presence.) So Walworth rose a proud and, one hopes, a happy man.

But there was more to come. The forty royal clerks who Richard had told the rebels would be set to writing out charters of manumission (freedom from servitude) were indeed busy; but on 2 July the charters were revoked, as was the general amnesty proclaimed by Richard. The best thing for the rebels to do was to sue for the royal pardon, as quickly as possible. By October, letters of pardon began to flow from the royal chancery. By December Parliament had settled the terms that rebels could expect – including the price. They could cost from 25 to 30 shillings, considerable sums in those days. Two men each paid £40. But the market steadied at a mark – 16s 4d – and after a year they were issued free. Some men who had never gone near the rebellion bought pardons, just to forestall any evil-wisher's launching unfounded legal proceedings against them which would have cost time and money to defend.

So finally this extraordinary episode could be laid to rest. Poll tax was never tried again, until the Conservative government imposed it in 1990, when it was so unpopular that, once again, it provoked riots and had to be withdrawn.

When Richard made such glowing promises to his rebellious subjects, was he aware that they would be revoked as soon as the rebels had left for home? Was he duplicitous? Or naive? He was undoubtedly brave. But the respect for the royal family must have taken a hard knock.

When Chaucer began to write the *Tales*, he had recently moved out of London to Kent. When he began to read them to his audience, the events of 1381 were perhaps six or seven years in the past. But such earth-shattering events won't have been easily forgotten. By the time Chaucer's audience contemplated the Ploughman, what did they see in his background? Nothing untoward, it seems:

> His tithes paid he full fair and well,
> Both of his propre swink and his catel.[17]

His 'propre swink' would be the profit from the work ('swink') he had put into his land, from a good harvest. His 'catel' would be his livestock, which would have increased naturally over the year. So he paid his dues to the Church, and even went further in Christian charity, giving his labour freely:

> For Christ's sake, for every poor wight [soul, man]
> Withouten hire [without payment], if it lay in his might [power].[18]

But Chaucer makes no mention of the rebellion. Why not? We can only guess. This silence, about the drama that had unfolded so recently, must surely have made his audience reflect on the justice of the peasants' claims and the turpitude of the king. Perhaps it was safer to rely on his audience's reaction, without expressing his views in words: a Chaucerian technique?

III THE MILLER

Full big he was of brawn and eke [also] of bones...
He was short-shouldered, broad, a thikke knarre [thick-set]...
His beard as any sow or fox was red,
And thereto broad as though it were a spade.
Upon the cop [tip] right of his nose he had
A wart, and thereon stood a tuft of hairs,
Red as the bristle of a sow's ears.
His nostrils black were and wide...
His mouth as great was as a great furnace.[1]

His Appearance

Why this dwelling on his physical appearance? Indeed, what was he
doing in the cavalcade of pilgrims at all?

His big red beard and, presumably, red hair too meant, to anyone
in Chaucer's audience, that he couldn't be trusted. From a *Book of
Courtesy* published in 1460 but dealing with long-established custom,

> In never house where a red[-haired] man be
> Nor woman of the same colour, certainly
> Take never thine inn, for no manner need,
> [don't stay in an inn where a red-haired person is,
>   no matter how badly you need it]
> For those be folk to hold in dread.[2]

This prejudice dies hard. It can have a positive side. When I was a
student in Gray's Inn in 1948, a swarm of bees settled in one of the

bomb-damaged buildings. The official bee-handler summoned by the Metropolitan Police gave his enthralled audience of students the lowdown on bees' intelligence, as he scooped the bees by handfuls into an insecure-looking cardboard carton to take home with him by Tube. Among many insights, he told us that bees will never sting a red-haired woman. At that time, long ago, my hair was red, but I have never put this immunity to the test.

The Miller's wide black nostrils were shared by evil-doers in medieval illuminated manuscripts and books. Certainly an upturned nose showing black nostrils looks unattractive, but it may be too long a shot to accuse the Miller of downright wickedness on this score alone.

Chaucer's Miller, no matter how unattractive his appearance, was likely to be a powerful man in the community: one not to be trifled with by anyone. You would need to think twice before accusing him of cheating, by stealing corn or by taking three times the proper amount, as he did; 'and yet he had a thumb of gold, pardee [by God]!'.³ This seems to be just another Chaucerian jibe. Chaucer chose him to lead the cavalcade out of the inn yard, playing his bagpipes and no doubt regaling his companions with his fund of rude songs and dirty jokes. The Prioress and her entourage must have kept well clear of him.

The Mechanism of a Mill

Chaucer's Miller was very strong: 'At wrestling he would have always the ram [i.e. the prize].'

Millers certainly needed strength, whether they ran a watermill or a windmill. Either building was made largely of wood. Oak was preferred. The power source might differ but the mechanism was basically the same: two stone discs stacked horizontally, power being applied to rotate the upper stone, the 'running stone'. Some elaborate gearing was needed to convert the vertical force of a waterwheel through 90 degrees into horizontal energy to rotate the running stone. The waterwheel outside the mill building was connected by a shaft to a 'trundle-wheel' on the same axis, inside the building. The trundle-wheel meshed into a 'lantern pinion' wheel at right angles to it, by cogs. The lantern pinion turned the spindle ('the stone-spindle'), which went through the (static) lower stone, to the upper, running stone, which it turned. Crab-apple or holly wood had been found best for the pegs in the cogwheels. The stone-spindle was made of iron, which needed constant replacing. The gearing of a windmill followed the same principle as a watermill.

The grain was fed in from a hopper, through a hole in the middle of the running stone. A carefully designed pattern of grooves in the working surface of each stone carried the grains to the edge of the stones, gradually crushing them so that they emerged as flour, which was collected in a bag or chest below the stones. The quality of the flour could be adjusted by fractionally raising or lowering the running stone: a tricky operation, since if the gap between the stones was too narrow they might impact on each other and could break. If the gap was too wide the grains would not be evenly ground, and the running stone would roll them rather than grind them, producing poor-quality flour.

Each stone might weigh up to half a ton, and measure up to 56 inches in diameter. The best were imported from a quarry near Paris, where the stone was particularly hard and suitable for grinding. The next best, which was not so hard, came from Cologne. The problems inherent in a cargo of millstones in a choppy North Sea or English Channel must have been appalling, but the trade flourished. Cheaper English stones could be bought from rocky places such as the Peak District. The cost of millstones has been computed at 28 shillings, averaged over the whole of England, varying from nearly 60 shillings in East Anglia to 7 shillings in the north of England, probably doubling after the Pestilence of 1348. If a stone fractured it could be mended by sticking the pieces together with plaster of Paris and binding them, like a cartwheel, with an iron brace. Routine maintenance and repairs could be done by skilled carpenters or blacksmiths, but the regrinding of the stones themselves was left to an experienced millwright. They would all need regrinding every few years, to deepen the grooves. This involved disengaging the lantern pinion so that the running stone could be carefully levered off and turned over – one reason why a miller needed huge strength.

Wind and water are free, but they don't always crop up in the right place. East Anglia's flat plains were ideal for growing crops, but the rivers pursued their tranquil course to the sea without much of a gradient, and never a waterfall. This could be remedied by forcing the water into a narrow channel and letting it build up until it poured fast over the waterwheel. 'Leets', as these were called, could be as long as a mile. Alternatively the water could be collected in a reservoir beside the mill and released when sufficient pressure had built up, which was the more usual method. Either could be constructed by local unskilled labour, perhaps supervised by a mason, who would maintain the stone walls of the leet. Mill-ponds had the advantage of sheltering fish and eels, thus providing two of the elements of medieval diet – fish and bread – at one sweep, although what the fishes felt as they revolved in the wheel is not known.

The God-given power of wind was spasmodic and unpredictable. In most winds, the running stone might rotate between 100 and 140 revs per minute.[4] A windmill worked best in a wind of 18–23 miles per hour (force 5 on the Beaufort scale). It could function in winds of 8–12 mph (force 3) up to 25 mph (force 6), but by 40 mph the sails would have to be stopped. The problem was to keep the sails facing into the wind, to maximize their strength. One solution was to enclose the millstones and the gearing in a separate wooden shell at the top of the building which could be turned round on a central pivot, a massive timber post going right through the middle of the building to the ground, where it was steadied by a framework of supporting timbers – hence their name, 'postmills'. This was another call on the miller's great strength. It was not until the next century that someone invented a subsidiary wheel at ground level that ran in a groove round the mill building, so that a horse harnessed to the ground-level wheel could pull the sails up above, into the wind. Until then the miller might use a winch, or sheer brute force.

But the problem of braking a windmill remained. When the miller needed to stop the mechanism of a watermill he could divert the water into a sluice flowing past the mill without much trouble, but it was more difficult to brake a windmill. The sails could be 20 yards and more long. The wind was caught by canvas tied to the sails or woven through a framework attached to them. This had to be done at the start of every day that the mill was working, and undone, 'reefed' like a ship's sails, at the end of the working day. If the wind suddenly strengthened, the miller might have to part-reef the sails to slow them down. If the wind changed direction, the miller would have to turn the mill to catch the new wind. If he needed to halt the sails altogether he could turn the mill out of the wind, but if he adjusted it too far the wind would blow onto the back of the sails and could blow them out. A miller running a windmill needed great physical strength and split-second judgement.

The Peasant and the Miller

Watermills had been around for many centuries. The Domesday Book of 1086 listed 5,624 watermills but not a single windmill. As the feudal system developed, it loaded many burdens onto the backs of the villeins and the 'unfree'. In an era when bread formed the major part of the diet, the peasant who grew enough grain to feed his family was dependent on a miller to turn his grain into flour for bread-making. The lord of the manor took advantage of this by enforcing his 'suit of mill'. The peasant had to use the lord's mill, even if it was not conveniently near, and even if the lord charged an exorbitant fee. How strictly the suit of mill was enforced varied from manor to manor and it faded away towards the end of the century, but while it applied, disputes were settled in the manorial court, where the peasant rarely won.

As he queued up with his sacks of corn, waiting his turn at the mill, it must have been exasperating to watch some favourite of the lord jump the queue and go 'hopper-free' in front of him. When it was his turn he faced another blow: 'multure'. The miller was never paid in cash, only in kind, taking a certain proportion of the corn in payment for his services. He used a special wooden dish, in which the corn had to be level, not heaped, but this was notoriously open to abuse and overcharging. Different customers paid different amounts of multure. Serfs and other 'unfree' men paid up to a twelfth part of their harvest to the miller; freemen got away with only one-twentieth, and 'foreigners' who were friends of the lord of the manor might pay much less. Considering that the peasant also owed a tenth of his income to the Church, his laboriously gathered corn shrank alarmingly before his family got their daily bread, in the words of the Lord's Prayer.

The Profits of a Mill

The miller could sell surplus corn in a neighbouring market. He would need some cash for those replacement millstones, even if he could pay the blacksmith and the carpenter in corn. Many water-mills were leased out to entrepreneurs who installed a miller as an employee, with probably a boy to help him, paying a lump sum upfront to the lord of the manor for a lease of perhaps twenty-one years or more, balancing the probable repair bills against the profit to be made. Some such leases provided for the maintenance and replacement bills to be shared between lessee and lord. In those days, some way of investing profits from trade was useful, in the absence of banks and stocks and shares. Sir John Pulteney (d. 1349), a notably rich City man, had two mills in Smithfield in his port-folio, as well as twenty-three manors in five counties.

Watermills could be used for purposes other than grinding grain. One of the more laborious stages in producing cloth was 'fulling', working the woven cloth in water so that the weave closed up and the cloth became stronger. A wearying business, treading wet, heavy cloth in water up to your thighs. Someone must have realized that the power engendered by a waterwheel could be applied to full-ing as well; but the idea never took on, generally. Fulling mills remained rare.

The Weather

To any miller, knowledge of weather-forecasting was vital. The weather in Chaucer's time was, as usual, variable. There was an earthquake felt in London in 1345, and another in Canterbury in 1382, in the middle of a synod convened by the archbishop of Canterbury to discuss Wycliffe's heresies; it 'portended the puging of the kingdom from heresies' by a divine fart. What clearer indication of God's view of him would you need? There were two more *terrae motus* noted by a monk, in Latin of course, in 1385. A *stella comata*, a star with hair, surely a comet, was seen in 1340 and again in 1367, which was a bad year when the Black Death recurred: 'many men and beasts were infected with pox wherethrough they died'. There were frequent storms, with 'violent lightning which smote men, beasts, trees and houses'. The hailstorm and bitter cold of 'Black Monday', 14 April 1360, were one reason why Edward III decided to make a temporary peace with France. Two years later a storm-force gale lasting four days blew down 'pear-trees and plum trees, [while] beeches and broad oaks turned upward their tail [roots]' – a sure sign of God's wrath at man's pride.[5] These gales may have given rise to the new fashion for weather vanes, often gilt, on church towers and domestic buildings, catching the sunlight as they swung. A dolphin swam up the Thames as far as London Bridge in 1392, which was interpreted as forecasting storms, which did indeed follow within the week.

In Lincolnshire, the Reverend Father William Merle was keeping meticulous meteorological records for the period 1337–43, which show what could be done without modern methods. According to him, rain could be predicted by the way salt absorbed the increased humidity in the air and liquefied. The sound of bells carried further in damp weather. Even 'the activity of fleas and the extra power of their bites' was duly noted by the reverend father. The autumn of 1342 was so mild that 'in certain places the cabbages blossomed'.

Modern research methods using polar ice cores show that somewhere in the world, in about 1258, there must have been one of the greatest volcanic eruptions of the past two millennia. The vast cloud of volcanic dust it generated changed the climate worldwide for centuries. Vineyards which had been productive in the English climate until about 1350 failed. From 1350 to 1360 summers were wetter and winters colder. By 1370 the succession of wet summers had raised food prices to famine level. The 1380s saw a period of warm, dry summers, just as Chaucer recorded in his Prologue to the *Tales*, writing in 1386.

An impersonal seismic upheaval, at an uncertain date in an unknown distant land, and a tempest showing God's wrath – which would have seemed the more probable, to medieval men?

IV THE REEVE

The Reeve was a slender, choleric man.
His beard was shaven as neigh [close] as ever he kan [knew how];
His hair was by his ears full round yshorn [cut];
His top [the top of his head] was dokked [cut short] like a
    priest biforn [in front].
Full long were his legs, and full lean,
Like a staff – there was no calf ysene [seen].[1]

Of the four humours (see p. 125), choler could indicate a short
temper, but there's no further mention of that. He wore a long
coat of blue or dark cloth tucked up into his girdle like a friar's
robe. He seems to have been bareheaded, which was unusual for
that time. So he might, at a cursory glance, have been taken for
some kind of cleric, in holy orders – which would be misleading,
from the business methods Chaucer goes on to describe. A rusty
sword hung by his side; again, a puzzling cross-reference to some
kind of military man. It wasn't usual for ordinary people to wear
swords, rusty or otherwise; knives, yes, but not swords. Perhaps the
tucked-up gown and the almost-tonsure and the useless sword bore
some medieval resonance lost to us now.

The Reeve rode a good 'pomely grey' (dappled) farm horse called
Scot – no double entendre there – and he came from Baldeswell,
in Norfolk. Norfolk people were popularly supposed to be either
stupid or devious. The Reeve was certainly not stupid. He had
trained as a carpenter in his youth. His home was 'shadowed with
green trees', and 'full fair upon a heath', which seems to denote
a house sufficiently out of the village to have its own grounds,

extensive enough for trees. He always rode last in the cavalcade of pilgrims. He was probably enjoying the chance to see the farming methods of another county in peace, without any responsibility.

Medieval Land Tenure

To appreciate the role played by a reeve, it may help to look briefly at the system of land tenure in medieval England. When Duke William, called the Bastard in his native Normandy because of some doubts about his parents' marriage, landed on English soil in 1066 and proclaimed himself king, the Norman knights who had come with him expected fitting rewards. He set up the feudal system, giving them estates in his new realm in return for their obedience and loyalty ('fealty'). If he needed them to fight for him again, he would call on them; meanwhile they could live as they liked on their newly acquired lands. Two and a half centuries later, the idea was losing its original strength but still persisted – land was held subject to feudal dues. The landholder to whom the king had granted land, the 'tenant in chief', could assign parts of his land to his tenants, who again were subject to various personal duties to him: a chain of bargains, from the king down to the merest peasant, or 'villein' (think 'villager', not 'villain'), who held his land subject to obligatory 'boon-work'. The landholder might have several estates scattered through the country. He would need someone to look after his interests if he lived on another of his estates, or while he was away on pilgrimage or serving the king. He might appoint a bailiff, or he might use a local man who had proved to be intelligent and honest and had already been elected by the villeins on the estate, or 'manor'. This was the reeve.

He had to see that all the miscellaneous feudal dues were correctly paid. In addition, he was responsible for all kinds of minor decisions governing the day-to-day life of the community. When harvest time came round, it was he who decided who had to do their boon-work and who had a valid excuse. If anyone pleaded ill health, the reeve might allow him to join the band of gleaners when the corn had been cut – a valuable perquisite. It was for him to decide when a field had to be cleared, so that the farm

animals could be allowed in to graze on the stubble; and when that
date had been announced from the pulpit, he had the authority to
decide the order in which each kind of animal could take its turn,
and implicitly who in his community did best out of the grazing.
He had to check that all the pigs roaming about had their noses
properly ringed, to stop them from churning up the ground.

For all this he would get no salary, other than a remission of
the rent or services that he paid for his own holding. He would
be elected by the peasants and had to retain their goodwill, while
answering to the lord of the manor, whose interests might conflict
with theirs.[2]

On some estates the lord appointed his own agent, who would
be called a bailiff or steward, to perform the same functions as a
reeve. Both reeve and steward would be expected to render annual
accounts to the lord of the manor. Where these survive they can
show life on a country estate in fascinating detail. Since it would be
worth the reeve's while to have his accounts accepted by his lord,
he might employ a clerk to prepare them, working from his own
records – much like employing an accountant to prepare a modern
tax return. The number of men able to write business letters,
draw up accounts and draft simple title deeds and contracts had
developed since the late thirteenth century. The reeve himself may
have been illiterate, but he would produce the collection of tallies
that had accumulated during the year, and he could often rely on
his memory.[3] Before the advent of universal education, memory
tended to be longer and more accurate than now, when everyone
can depend on written or electronic notes.

Estate Accounts

The accounting year usually ran from Michaelmas, 29 September.
By then it should be possible to assess the income from the harvest
and sales of livestock, and set it against the cash expenditure on
renewing livestock or replacing machinery such as ploughs or
millstones, and factoring in debts owing to the estate. Final figures
would be agreed between the reeve's clerk and the lord's auditors,
after discussion and wrangling over each item. They could go into

astonishing detail, for instance the numbers of peacock feathers gathered during the year, or the number of goslings and ducklings on the day of the auditors' visit – all entered under 'poultry'. As the cash economy took hold after the Pestilence, even cockerels and hens could be rented out for 6 pence a head.[4] The language was the Anglo-Norman French current in the lord's circle, occasionally supplemented by the local Anglo-Saxon where the clerk was lost for an elegant Anglo-Norman word. The figures were in Roman letters (i, ii, iij, iv or iiij, v, vi or vj, vij, viij, ix, x and so on; the 'j' in a group of letters replaced the final 'i').

A sophisticated system of double-entry book-keeping was increasingly current in the counting houses of city merchants, using the new Arabic numerals, but country estate accounts were simple cash accounts, usually written in Latin and still using cumbersome Roman numerals. To give you a flavour of them, here is an entry of debts still owed to one reeve at the year's end in 1349, for which he was responsible to his lord. He seems to have been unlucky in supplying farm produce to the Court or to the royal provisioners, who were notoriously bad payers: 'summa xxxix l xvs iiijd', which included 'Edwardus Rex pro ix qr [quarters] avenarum [of oats]'. The summa, or total, was £39 15s 4d, 'l', sometimes written as 'li', standing for *libra* or pounds, the 's' for *solidi* or shillings and the 'd' for *denarii* or pence.

Here is another list of debtors who owed money to this unfortunate reeve:

Dominus Edwardus Rex Anglie [the king]
Domina Philippa regina [the queen]
Dominus Edwardius princeps Wallie [Edward, prince of Wales]
Johannes Comes cornubia [John, duke of Cornwall]

– all lumped together as 'de antiquo xv li vjs xd' (carried forward, £15 6s 10d).

So accounts were no simple matter. The reeve's clerk may have attended one of the courses on business methods and estate management run by Thomas Sampson and his competitors in Oxford during the second half of the fourteenth century.[5] Sampson is known to have written a mass of teaching material, such as nine treatises in Anglo-Norman on letter-writing, eight similar treatises in Latin, fifteen treatises on conveyancing, three on wills, two on holding courts, three on the office of coroner, an explanation of legal terms, and five treatises on household accounts, four in Latin, one in Anglo-Norman, with a useful Anglo-Norman–English vocabulary. Copies of all these were on sale. In addition, anyone who managed to grasp the salient points of his oral lectures would be well qualified to act as clerk for a whole district of reeves. There were various earlier treatises on the market, concerned primarily with the general running of an estate but incidentally giving information about keeping accounts. The lord is recommended to look through the accounts himself, not to leave this tedious business to employees. Reeves are told to record their notes on parchment rather than on such temporary material as wax tablets, which could all too easily be erased and the proper entries lost for ever. Various treatises warned against sly tricks of reeves hoping to deceive the auditors, such as inflating the number of barren ewes if some lambs had somehow gone missing.[6]

Chaucer's Reeve can be set against that background: 'There was no auditor [who] could on him winne [get the better of him].' Chaucer gives him a detailed testimonial.[7] Ever since his lord was twenty, the Reeve had looked after the estate. He knew how to check on barns and corn bins. He knew the crop yields in years of drought and rain. He was wholly responsible for his lord's sheep, his cattle and dairy herd, his pigs, horses, livestock and poultry. He kept the estate accounts accurately, according to his contract with his lord. He knew the frauds and tricks of every bailiff, herdsman and other farm servant; they feared him like death. He knew how to please his lord tactfully. He made presents and loans to his lord out of his own resources, and earned his thanks, while retaining the status of a servant, entitling him to some benefits in kind. And yet – and here's the Chaucerian twist – 'full rich he was stored privately'.[8] How he had managed to build up a private cash hoard while keeping impeccable accounts and busily detecting everyone else's fraud, we are left to wonder.

The Villein

A villein's life was entangled in a web of feudal dues. When he took on a holding, he paid the lord of the manor an entry fee. The holding might be as much as forty acres, with a house and some farm buildings. When the newly entitled villein had had a chance to look around, he found that repairs were needed to his house and the fences round his fields. If he used wood from his lord's woods – and there was no practical alternative – he would be liable for house-bote and haye-bote. He needed winter fuel – wood from the lord's woods involved payment of fire-bote. The house was unlikely to have an oven to bake bread – the lord charged for the use of the estate oven. When he needed his corn ground into flour, he had to use the lord's mill and pay for the privilege. If the villein's daughter became pregnant while unmarried he might have to pay leywrite on her behalf. If she did marry, her father had to pay merchet to the lord. If he kept pigs, as most villeins did, he would pay pannage for letting them feed in the lord's woods. If he wanted to sell his livestock, he paid a toll to the lord. When a villein died, the most valuable thing he had owned – usually a horse or his best ox – went to the lord as 'heriot'. Since his second-best chattel went to his parish priest, death was a financial blow as well as a bereavement, but if the surviving family members could raise the cash, they often bought back the horse or the ox from the lord. Most irksome and most resented of all was boon-work. If sowing and, especially, harvesting were urgent while the weather lasted, the lord's fields took priority, which must have been maddening. All the other dues tended to fade away with time, or change into money payments, especially after the Pestilence of 1348. But the boon-work was the last to be commuted for cash. It was a major grievance, and one of the causes of the 1381 revolt.

V THE FRANKLIN

White was his beard as is the daisy.
Of his complexioun [temperament] he was sangwin
    [sanguine] . . .
An anlaas [a two-edged dagger] and a gipser [an ornamental
    purse] all of silk
Hung at his girdel [belt], white as morning milk.[1]

No matter how hard one looks at Chaucer's Franklin, there is no
discordant bitter twist, as with so many of the other pilgrims.

He was 'sangwin'; of the four 'humours' (see p. 125), his domin-
ant humour was blood. His face was red, his beard pure white, and
he must have been a cheerful sight compared to the morose Reeve,
whose humour was choler. There were two sides to his character.
His main characteristic was his love of pleasure, to be shared with
his guests.

Hospitality

To live in delight was ever his wone [custom],
For he was Epicurus' own son,
That held opinion that plein delight [unalloyed pleasure]
Was very felicity perfect.

'Saint Julian was he in his country', St Julian being the patron saint
of hospitality. He began the day with a 'sop in wine'. Before the era
of breakfast as we know it, this was normal, for those who could
afford it – a piece of bread dipped in wine. Then his days were

spent in a constant round of entertaining. His was a well-organized household, always prepared with a splendid meal, no matter how short the notice. Bread, ale, wine – all were superb. There was always a fish pie or a meat pie ready. 'It snowed in his house of food and drink.' The menus for dinner and supper changed with the season. Partridges were fattened, fish swam in the fish pond; he would never be caught out by a meatless day when fish was the obligatory main dish. The cook had to have all his utensils ready, and a stock of good tasty sauces. The Franklin's table stood ready in his hall for guests all day, instead of being folded away when the meal was over, as was the usual custom. That was where he would dine, with any number of guests – not hidden away in a private room, in the 'modern' fashion deplored by Langland's Piers Plowman:

> Wretched is the hall, each day of the week,
> Where the lord nor the lady likes not to sit.
> Now hath each rich [person] a rule – to eat by himself
> In a private parlour, so as to avoid poor men,
> Or in a chamber with a chimney [fireplace] and leave the
>   chief hall
> That was made for meals, for men to eat in.[2]

We are not told, but we can take it as read, that the 'poor men' and beggars might well congregate at the Franklin's door at meal times, hoping justifiably for 'crumbs from the rich man's table'.

His Status

There was another side to him. The status of a franklin was fluid, between the upper peasantry and the lower nobility. He might not own extensive estates, but the land that he did hold was free of feudal obligations. He was a familiar and a vital part of rural society. Perhaps the later term of 'squirearchy' would have suited him, if it had been invented in time. Most legal business was conducted in London, but the life of a medieval village or small township needed some legal input, and this was the Franklin's sphere.

Justice of the Peace

At sessions there was he lord and sire[.][3]

'Sessions' were courts presided over by justices of the peace, originally the 'Keepers of the King's Peace'. By the end of the thirteenth century the unpopular justices in eyre, who had been seen, and resented, as part of the central regal authority, were replaced by two or three of the most respected men of the county, of whom the Franklin was surely one. Their jurisdiction gradually widened until by 1334 they could hear cases of felony and trespass. After the Great Pestilence of 1348 they were given the impossible task of enforcing the Statute of Labourers, an attempt to keep wage rates down to the pre-Pestilence levels.

As a justice of the peace, he was told (and had to swear to it):

you will serve the king and his people well and truly as a justice of the peace... and conceal the counsel of the king, and will do right as far as you are able to all, both to the poor and to the rich, and that you will take no gift from anyone to do wrong or to delay justice, and that neither for the great nor for the rich, nor for hatred, nor for the estates of any person, nor for benefit, gift or promise of anyone made to you or that could be made to you, either by art or by design, interfere with or postpone justice contrary to reason and contrary to the laws of the land but without regard to the aforesaid laws. So help you God and his saints.

Perhaps the emphasis on *not* taking 'gifts', i.e. bribes, implies that corruption among justices was widespread, despite any attempt to eradicate it. It was certainly perceived as such by the 1381 rebels.

The sessions sat once in every quarter – hence 'quarter sessions' – with occasional intermediate petty sessions if needed. Chaucer's Franklin must have chaired his local sessions by sheer force of character. One would have expected one of the professional lawyers to take the chair, but the Franklin was 'lord and sire' in his own court, sitting in his own hall, helped by his knowledge of local wrongdoers. No doubt he disposed of the day's business briskly, as he looked forward to the next meal which he had invited his fellow-justices to share.

Sessions had not always gone so smoothly. In 1336 John Whittlebury, 'Keeper of the peace in the county of Rutland', sent an urgent plea to the king for protection. He and a colleague had heard a case against a gang of thugs who had terrorized the local people. The four ringleaders, who were brothers, and their followers were 'accustomed to beat, trample and wrong the [local] people daily. And nightly [they] are at the tavern and then go with all their unruly crowd around the vill [the village]... and break the doors and windows of the good people of the vill, and beat the good men and women in their own dwellings, against the peace, so that no man of the vill is so bold as to carry out the [legally required] watches in order to maintain the peace.' Whittlebury and his colleague, with considerable courage, had gone twice to the vill in question, 'to inquire upon the complaints that we have heard... the said [brothers] have come with force and arms with all their unruly crowd against the peace before us, and have so threatened to beat and trample the juries [who were an essential fact-finding part of the judicial machinery] that no man either dares to appear before us or indict them, and us they have openly threatened of life and limb... we are in great danger'. The gang arrived at Whittlebury's manor one night while he was asleep. They caught his son and two servants and beat them up and threatened to kill Whittlebury, 'and ever since, they [Whittlebury and his family] have expected it daily. So he prays remedy to our lord the King that they will send two serjeants-at-arms of the king's household to arrest [the wrongdoers] wherever they may be found, for no man of Rutland dares either to indict or arrest them... and to send them to the Tower of London, because the sheriff of Rutland dares not hold them.' Help was sent, but too late. Whittlebury already lay dead.[4]

Knight of the Shire

The Franklin was also a knight of the shire. This did not mean that he had been knighted. Ever since the 1230s the knights of the shire had formed part of the king's Great Council, which became known as the Parliament – a forum for discussion, from the French for talking, *parler*. The common people of the realm were represented by two elected members from each of the thirty-six shires, the shire knights, and two elected by each of the hundred or so cities and boroughs. The other members of the Council were the hereditary peers, the 'temporal lords', and the archbishops, bishops and abbots, the 'spiritual lords'. In 1341 the Council was formally divided into the two chambers that exist today, the House of Lords and the House of Commons.

Like present-day MPs, the shire knights were paid their travelling expenses, depending on the length of their journeys – a knight from Northumberland claimed for seventy-five days, compared to a knight from Kent who could get to Westminster and back in sixty-one days. (Perhaps he lived in the very furthest part of Kent, but it still seems a remarkable amount. Was there a certain degree of corruption in the matter of MPs' expenses, even then?) They also got accommodation expenses for their stay in Westminster, where Parliament usually sat. Knights of the Shire were paid 4 shillings a day, which must have added up to a tidy sum if they found themselves a bed with a friend or relation. Their colleagues, the citizens and burgesses, got only half that. But they all had to turn up, once summoned, unless they could prove a valid excuse such as illness.

By the 1340s the Lords totalled about seventy, far outnumbered by the Commons. It was the Commons who controlled the purse strings. Whenever the monarch needed money, for the necessary expenses of his government, the medieval civil service or his military campaigns, let alone his own expenditure, which could reach scandalous heights as he lavished lands and money on his favourites, he had to ask Parliament, and the Commons could impose conditions on him.

Chaucer must have been an obvious choice for the electors of Kent in October 1386, given his long Crown service and his intimate knowledge of its finances. The 1386 session of Parliament was dramatic. The nineteen-year-old king sat enthroned, with his full, splendid regalia. England was as usual facing foreign invasion, this time from the Low Countries. The chancellor, Michael de la

Pole, who was a favourite of the king, asked for a grant of tax for the defence of the realm. But the Commons presented 'grave complaints' against the chancellor, and asked for him to be arrested, which he was. He was later released on bail, but the Commons had shown its strength. When all parliamentary business had been concluded and the House was getting ready to go home, the king rose and 'protested in person that nothing that had been done therein should redound to the further prejudice of himself or his crown'. It was a sad comedown from the valour and dignity he had shown just five years earlier, when he confronted the rebels in Smithfield. The growing tension between the king and Parliament culminated in his deposition in 1399.

Sheriff

> A sheriff had he been, and a countour;
> Was nowhere such a worthy vavasour.[5]

We glimpsed a sheriff in the sad story of John Whittlebury. His local sheriff should have arrested and imprisoned those wrongdoers, but lacked the strength, moral or physical; help from the central power was needed. Sheriffs had been unpopular in earlier times – hence the wicked sheriff in the Robin Hood legends – but their power had been curtailed until they became merely the instrument of central government machinery in the provinces, charged with summoning the Knights of the Shire to Parliament, and so on.

A 'vavasour' was a splendid fellow, a good chap – whatever contemporary slang term would apply. In the eighteenth century it would apply to a typical country squire. But the 'countour' is a little more puzzling. A 'countour' was an advocate such as a serjeant-at-law, with the exclusive right of audience in the higher courts. This, patently, the Franklin was not. Perhaps in this context Chaucer meant that he was an able, though unqualified, lawyer. Maddening to have this puzzle sprung on us at the very last moment; perhaps Chaucer himself might have amended it when he checked over his manuscript.

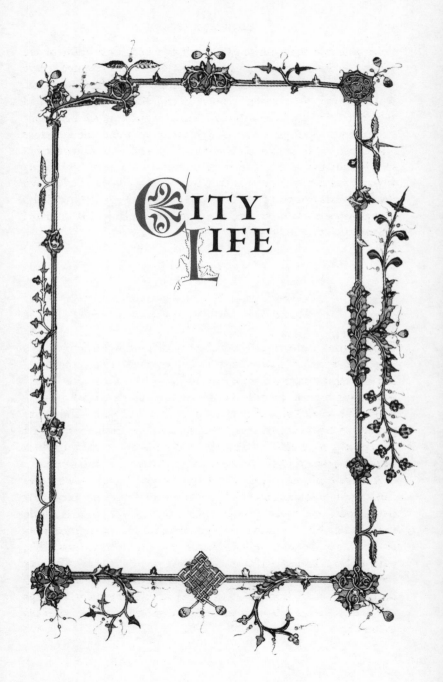

CITY LIFE

VI 'MINE HOST'

Great cheer made our Host us everyone...
He served us with vitaille [food] at the best;
Strong was the wine and wel to drinke us leste [gave us
    pleasure]...
A large man he was, with eyes stepe [prominent];
A fairer burgeis [citizen] was there none in Chepe
    [Cheapside].[1]

This was the only pilgrim who could be identified with a real person, Harry Bailly, an innkeeper in Southwark. Chaucer gave him a really good write-up, for the benefit of those in his audience who might be looking for a good place to eat or stay in Southwark. It was he who suggested the idea that each pilgrim should tell a 'Tale' or story, on the way to Canterbury and another on the way back – the framework of all the *Tales*. He volunteered to be their guide on the way to Canterbury, and to judge whose Tale was the best. There were thirty-three pilgrims, including Chaucer himself and the Host. If each of them had told only one Tale they would have made a longer book than Chaucer managed to finish. Perhaps he would have amended the plan of two stories per head, if he had ever got round to checking his manuscript.

Travel in England

There was a network of tracks and minor roads criss-crossing England. Local markets were rarely more than a day's ride away. The miller took his surplus meal there, and looked out for good quality imported millstones. The farm bailiff or steward could sell livestock not needed for breeding, and buy new stock to improve his herd. There would be a local distributor of necessaries such as salt, and iron for mending ploughshares.

There was also constant long-distance traffic. Friars were on their way to the friaries to which they had been assigned. Monks were regularly called to attend chapter meetings at their motherhouse in Rome, or Cîteaux in France. The monarch and his territorial magnates arrived in one of their several castles and stayed until the cellars were empty and the cesspits full, before moving on to the next. The fellows of Merton College in Oxford regularly set off for the North Country to inspect the landed property left to the college by benefactors. Merchants would make for the London market to buy luxury goods in exchange for their wool or wool cloth. After the declaration of the French War, conscripted men, requisitioned supplies and war material were constantly on the move to the embarcation ports on the south coast.

In AD 410 the Roman army had pulled out of England. Their superbly engineered road system had been centred on London. The main Roman roads can still be identified on any modern map. For example, the road between Dover and London, via Canterbury, lies as if ruled with a straight edge. But in places the Roman roads fell into disrepair. The Anglo-Saxons who took over when the Romans had gone saw no need to spend funds on their upkeep. Fallen timber might block the way, a dam might create a marsh, livestock could see greener grass on the other side. The system was patched up here and there by charitable bequests to improve local roads and build bridges, but it remained at best uneven.

Rivers were a vital element in the landscape. They could impede the traveller, who would be deflected to the nearest ford or bridge; or they could be used, if they flowed towards his or her goal, as the Thames flowed from the Cotswolds through Oxford to London.

Knowledge of the best route to follow would be handed down from traveller to traveller, father to son, mendicant friar to a younger brother. There were no guide maps, except for one astonishing survival, known by the name of one of its early owners as the Gough map. It shows and names every settlement, no matter how small. London is given special treatment. The main Roman roads appear. Rivers are given prominence. Their source is meticulously shown, as if significant; maybe this was to indicate the place from where riverine transport could be looked for. Bridges and fords can be identified. The whole map was made of parchment from two separate lambskins, making it almost 46 x 22 inches. The effect is of a gigantic game of snakes and ladders, the snakes being rivers and the ladders being the distance between points, given in miles on straight red lines. It is believed to have been made in 1370. By whom or why is still a mystery.

Introducing his pilgrims, Chaucer tells how 'from every shire's end / Of England to Canterbury they wende',[2] but we know of only three starting points. The Wife of Bath came from a village near Bath. She could have used the Thames for most of her journey to London. The Shipman came from Dartmouth; the river Dart wouldn't have been much use to him because it flows south and east, but perhaps he came round the coast to Portsmouth before taking to horseback. The Reeve came from 'Baldeswelle' (now Bawdeswell) in Norfolk, which was well served by Roman roads.

Southwark

Southwark was a natural place for inns. Just as there was a real Harry Bailly, there was a real Tabard Inn. John Stow, writing his incomparable *Survey of London* in 1598, had access to records that didn't survive for later historians. In his section on Southwark he quoted Chaucer's Prologue in his list of inns, of which the Tabard was 'the most ancient'. In 1381 twenty-two innkeepers were registered for the poll tax there. Travellers converging on London from the south and west, and Continental visitors from Dover or the 'long ferry' from Gravesend, would need somewhere to leave their horses and pack animals, before crossing London Bridge and venturing into the crowded streets and lanes of the city. Horses need stables, and blacksmiths to renew their shoes, and farriers to medicate them, as well as feed and water, grooms and stable boys. Chaucer's group may not have been the only guests in Harry Bailly's inn that night. In addition there would be the kitchen staff to produce the 'vitaille at the best', and wine cellars, and storehouses, and probably a brewery for beer, and a bakery unless he bought bread in. So medieval inns were considerable enterprises, more like motorway service stations than the quiet local 'pub' of our day.

Southwark had a very mixed population. It increasingly attracted small businessmen who were reluctant to pay the steep fees charged by the livery companies for admission to the freedom of London, which they needed if they were to open retail shops within the city limits. There was a leper hospital there, sited away from the city's main population but convenient for sufferers to beg alms from passing travellers. Leprosy was a dreaded disease in the Middle Ages for which there was no cure. It was thought to be caught by merely breathing the same air as a leper, so the only 'treatment' was isolation outside the city limits.

Presumably lepers were barred from the precincts of the bishop of Winchester's town house, or palace, at the northernmost boundary of his diocese, touching the south bank of the Thames. The bishop's diocese included the Hospital of St Thomas the Martyr, a hospital for the sick poor founded by the Augustinian canons (monks) in the twelfth century, probably as part of their Priory of St Mary Overie, St Mary's 'over the water'. (The hospital still exists, on a slightly different site.) Three earlier churches on the site had been destroyed by fire. The first, according to legend, had been built in the seventh century by a ferryman, in gratitude for the profits of his trade, since there was then no other way to cross the river. The present building was built in 1220 in the Gothic style, making it the earliest Gothic building surviving in London. It is now the Cathedral of Southwark.

The Stews

The Augustinian canons must have been taken aback by the other tenants of the bishop – the prostitutes known as the Winchester Geese. 'Ordinances touching the government of the stewholders in Southwark under the direction of the bishop of Winchester' had been in force since 1161, 'stewholders' meaning the men who owned the 'stews', the brothel-keepers. The Crusaders had brought back with them the idea of taking a hot bath and 'stewing' in it, but the baths somehow morphed into brothels, just as our 'massage parlours' may well have begun by offering innocent massages. The ordinances, which were alleged to be founded on the 'Old Customs' already existing, were stern and detailed. They found it necessary to forbid stewholders to admit any 'woman of religion or any man's wife', so to describe a woman as a 'single woman' carried the implication that she was a prostitute.

A table of fines was laid down. 'If a woman of the bordel [brothel] hinders any man from coming and going, or if she draws any man by his gown or by his hood' she was fined 20 shillings. The same amount was payable for plying her trade if she had 'any sickness of burning'. (Gonorrhoea? Any other sexually transmitted disease? And what happened to her subsequent clients? Medieval medicine was not sufficiently evolved to follow them.) A man was entitled to a whole night's worth – if he was short-changed, she would be fined 6s 8d. The same fine was payable if she was in the area between sunset and dawn the next day, while the king was in Westminster holding Parliament or Council. The brothels had to shut on holy days, which occurred frequently in the medieval calendar. So a hopeful punter would be wise to check carefully where he, the king, Parliament and the Church stood before making for the stews. Pity the country MP, down from the provinces and hoping while he was there to enjoy the bright lights of London and Southwark – he might be sorely disappointed.

The majestic machinery of the law was brought to bear on the trade. All legal disputes had to be settled in 'the lord's court', and the stewhouses were to be inspected by his bailiff and constables every quarter. How much all this was actually enforced is shrouded in doubt, as so often happens with well-meaning legislation. A prostitute who argued with her stewholder risked arrest, a fine of 20 shillings and being put 'thrice upon the cucking stool', followed by banishment. A cucking stool was not the same as a 'ducking stool',which meant only dowsing in water; cucking involved immersion in mud and filth.[3] If she 'makes affray' it could be worse – three days and nights in prison, as well as a fine. But the law did go some way to protect these women. A stewholder was not allowed to lend a prostitute more than 6s 8d, preventing her from running up impossible debts to him, and if the periodical inspections found any woman compelled to prostitute herself against her will she was freed. Each prostitute paid 14d a week for her room. Neither she nor her stewmaster was allowed to offer food or drink.

Southwark didn't hold a monopoly over stewhouses. The trade flourished in other districts, such as Cock's Lane and Gropecunt Lane. Nor was the trade limited to English whores: Flemish women invaded the territory, just as their men successfully competed with English weavers. The Flemings attracted both trades by their known expertise. Hoping to cash in on that, some English prostitutes adopted as a trademark the Flemish name of Pernell, a version of Petronella, the Dutch form of Peronell, the Old French word for a whore. The Flemish women incurred the wrath of the 1381 rebels, who diverged from their objective of sacking John of Gaunt's Savoy Palace just long enough to wreck a Flemish brothel. By 1393 the mayor of London had to issue an ordinance 'Concerning Street Walkers by Night and Women of Ill Repute'. It blamed the many 'broils and affrays' on 'common harlots, at taverns, brewhouses of hucksters and other places of ill fame', and especially on 'Flemish women who profess and follow such [a] shameful and dolorous life'. They were all to 'keep themselves to the places thereunto assigned... the stews on the other side of the Thames and Cocks Lane'. But where and how both streams of women were recruited remains a mystery.

It's difficult to imagine the buildings where all this was going on. They were sufficiently substantial to attract investment by the king, the bishop of Winchester, the prioress of Barking and the mayor of London, William Walworth, who so distinguished himself in 1381. But clearly these houses, called 'great houses' in the ordinances, were not like the sordid back alleys of modern-day Soho.

The Wine Trade

The Gascon merchants, who had long enjoyed the fiscal privileges granted by Edward I (r. 1272–1307), were squeezed out of the English market when the French War began in 1337. The Vintners'

Company, which included wine importers and innkeepers or 'taverners', took their place, with an effective monopoly of the wine-importing trade with Gascony. This was formally recognized by royal charter in 1364.

Law-abiding shippers would land their cargo at the Vintry, the quay owned by the Vintners. Other shippers, of whom Chaucer's Shipman may well have been one, perhaps used the small ports and landing-places on the south and east coasts on dark nights, in the best smuggling tradition. Statistics are lacking.

Judging by the number of writs and regulations on the subject issued by the mayor and aldermen of the city, there seems to have been an almost neurotic insistence on quality control – or perhaps an incorrigible practice of selling bad wine. Vintners and innkeepers were always being reminded that they had to allow their purchasers to go into their cellars and watch the wine they had ordered being drawn from the right barrel. By 1352 innkeepers were prohibited from hanging a curtain over the door to the cellar. 'So that the purchasers may see whence the wine is drawn ... one of each company may see that the vessel into which the wine is drawn is clean and from what cask the wine is drawn', which must have delayed the start of the party. When it did arrive, the wine was not in a glass bottle (not invented till the eighteenth century) but in a leather bottle, or pewter or earthenware tankards.

One innkeeper who was found guilty of selling bad wine was 'condemned to drink a draft of his own wine, the remainder to be poured on his head, and he was to forswear the calling of vintner unless he obtained the King's favour' and was pardoned; which he was, three months later. But he deserved some sympathy. The barrels in which wine was imported were not airtight, so that it was almost impossible to prevent wine turning into vinegar within two or three years. The careful ageing dear to the modern oenophile was not feasible. New wine was better than last year's vintage, and probably much better than that of the year before. Wine older than that might well have to be poured away.

Up to mid-century the controlled prices were 6 pence a gallon for 'rhenish', from the banks of the Rhine, including Alsace or 'Oseye' wine – what we might think of as 'fine wine' – but only

4 pence a gallon for 'Gascon' or Bordeaux wine, which formed the bulk of the wine trade. After the beginning of the war with France prices went up, although demand stayed remarkably constant. One had to drink something, after all; ale was for the commonalty, and water was unsafe. In 1365, if you felt like a sweet wine, generally known as malmsey, instead of a tankard of rather sour red, you would have had to find one of the only three taverns 'assigned for the sale of sweet wines, the profits of which were to be devoted to the repair of the City's walls', where the prohibitively high prices were set by a vintner who had cornered that market. But he came unstuck, and after 1376 you could buy sweet wine in any tavern. Sweet wines were imported from Malvesyn (Madeira), Romanye (Romanée-Conti), Candy (Crete) and other Mediterranean countries.

The usual subjects for discussion in modern pubs are sport, including football, cars, football, jobs, women, football and 'in-house' games such as darts. It was much the same in the inns and taverns of Chaucer's time. Sport included football, cock-fighting and wrestling, which could be carried to fatal lengths. There was even tennis. The execution of Richard Steris for treason was widely regretted, because he had been 'one of the cunningest players at the tenys in England, for he was so delyvyr [agile?] that he would stand in a tub that should be near breast high, and leap out of the same, both standing at the hows and at Rechace [sic], and win of a good player'.[4] For 'cars' read 'horses'; there must have been talk about their respective merits and prices. Inns and taverns were useful places in which to hear of job opportunities, and perhaps to meet possible employers. The barmaids were, naturally, beautiful, and sometimes available for more than serving drinks. In quiet corners there would be a group playing backgammon or shove-ha'penny or its predecessor, and another gambling with dice or knuckle-bones. There would be the usual crooks bent on fleecing foreign tourists and innocent countrymen. There might be a friar, seeking converts and contributions and playing his 'hail fellow well met' act. The hubbub of voices included regional accents from distant parts of England. But there would be no fighting or brawling – customers had had to leave their weapons with the innkeeper as they came in. And he must have called the medieval equivalent of 'Time, gentlemen, please' to remind drinkers that they had to be off the streets by the time the curfew bells rang from St Martin's le Grand and other churches.

Alehouses

At the other end of the social scale from Harry Bailly's Tabard Inn were the alehouses, kept by brewers (men) and brewsters (women). They had to sell ale by the regulation gallon, pottle and quart, respectively 8, 4 and 2 imperial pints. A gallon of the best ale cost one and a half pence, the cheapest three-quarters of a penny, which doesn't look too bad when a master tiler's mate working on London Bridge was paid 4d a day. Langland gives a vivid picture of an alehouse of his day. Gluttony, personifying one of the deadly sins, is on his way to church on a Friday, when Beton the Brewster greets him and invites him in to try her 'good ale'. 'Have you any hot spices?' he asks. She has pepper and peony seeds, and a pound of garlic, and a farthing's worth of fennel seed 'for fasting days', in case he wants to disguise the smell of food or drink on his breath before taking Holy Communion. The rules required Communion to be taken fasting, but he doesn't look like a man who would be overly bothered by breaking them. So in he goes, and meets a crowd of drinking cronies:

Cesse the Souteresse [female shoemaker] sat on the bench,
Wat the Warner [warren-keeper] and also his wife,
Tim the Tinker and two of his lads,
Hick the Hackneyman [horse hirer] and Hugh the Nedlere
     [needle seller],
Clarice of Cock's Lane [see above] and the Clerk of the church,
Sir Piers of Pridie [Pray to God], and Pernele of Flanders
     [see p. 66],
Davy the Dykere [Davy the ditcher], and a dozen others –
A fiddler, a rat-catcher, a Cheapside scavenger,
A roper [ropemaker] a redyngkyng [lackey] and Rose the
     Dish-seller,

Godfrey of Garlickhythe [a London riverside parish] and
   Griffith the Welshman
And a number of old-clothes men[.][5]

There was a butcher there too, an ostler and a cobbler. They all greeted him and stood him a drink. Two of them began some drunken game involving bartering their clothes and betting, leading to much drunken laughter and brawling. In the end Gluttony passed out. His wife and his maidservant managed to get him home, where he nursed his hangover throughout Saturday and Sunday. When he came to, his first words were: 'Where is the bowl?'

VII THE MERCHANT

Chaucer's Merchant must have been recognized by many of his audience. He rates only fifteen lines in the General Prologue, and four of them are taken up by a description of him, with his 'forked beard' and his Flemish beaver hat – clearly expensive headwear. But:

> His resons [remarks] spoke he full solemnly,
> Sowninge alwey the th'encrees of his winning[1]

– he went on and on about the profits he made. For all his self-advertising he had a high reputation, with his 'bargaines and with his chevisaunce' (borrowing or lending money). Chaucer ends his portrait with a very half-hearted tribute: 'For sooth, he was a worthy man withall.' But we never find out what the Merchant dealt in when he wasn't wheeler-dealing.

The Financial World

The financial life of London was booming. The basic tools had been in place for some time. Those cumbersome Roman numerals had given way to Arabic figures in most contexts, which facilitated the system of double-entry book-keeping imported from Italy. In practised hands abacuses, known as 'tables' or 'counters', could manipulate figures with the speed of light. Gradually, independent advisers infiltrated the market, displacing the Church officials acting for the pope who had monopolized the financial world before then. Italians from the north of Italy dominated the field at first. They were generally known as Lombards, and they tended to congregate in a street that became known as Lombard Street, the centre of London's financial life until very recently.

Usury, more kindly called lending money at interest, could present problems. The Church disapproved of it and labelled it as sinful. But the world of commerce moved on, including lending at interest. St Thomas Aquinas (1225–74), that agile philosopher, found the way round this dilemma. Suppose A lent £10 to B, to be repaid in thirty days. By the thirty-first day, B had not paid. He let a whole month elapse before he paid up. During that time, A could have used the £10 to make other bargains: he 'suffered damage' by missing them. B should compensate A for this damage. Such 'compensation' should not be confused, for a moment, with 'usury'. The party 'damaged' by such delay might even accept a gift to compensate him with a clear conscience. The moneylenders who took a poor man's pots and pans as pledges for a debt the man could never repay were the real, sinful usurers.

Bills of exchange for foreign transactions had been in use since the previous century. Normally the system worked well. The alternative, payment in cash, would have involved heavy costs in providing an armed escort for the chests of bullion, let alone insurance premiums of up to 5 per cent of the value of the consignment against robbery or piracy on the high seas. Instead the seller could accept a document signed by the purchaser, acknowledging the debt. That document could be negotiated for goods in Bruges or elsewhere, or sold on to another merchant. An example from the Court of the Mayor of London: in 1364 Vane Camby, a Lombard silk merchant, complained that he 'had bought a letter of exchange in London for £30, from Nicholas Sardouche of Lucca [surely his name was really Nicolo Sarduccio? but he appeared as Sardouche in all the records], which letter was payable to him or his attorney [authorized agent] at Bruges in the form of 200 scudos, each scudo being worth 3 shillings; that he had given the said letter to his attorney . . . [who] had been refused payment in Bruges'. The case was adjourned for evidence to be obtained from Bruges.

Thus encouraged, some English businessmen went into the moneylending business with enthusiasm. Gilbert Maghfeld was a prominent London merchant in the 1390s, an alderman and several times a sheriff of London. But he became spectacularly unstuck. He went bankrupt in 1397. His account books make fascinating reading. His clients included scores of fellow-merchants from London and other English towns, besides merchants of Prussia, La Rochelle, Bordeaux, Italy and Spain, two men of law, six bishops, the mayor of London, the earl of Derby (see Appendix A), the duke of Gloucester, the king himself and several knights and squires of the royal household, including Geoffrey Chaucer, who borrowed 26s 8d for only a few days.

English merchants operating in the financial market were up against formidable competition. In 1365 Nicholas Sardouche stood surety for a fellow Lombard merchant in the sum of £1,000, an immense sum in those days. Four years later he was involved in major litigation. He was accused of having rigged the market in silk. It began when two 'silk women' complained to the Mayor's Court that Sardouche had bought up 'all the silk he could find' in London, causing the price of silk to rise from 14 to 18 shillings per pound, and pricing them out of the market. Even worse, he went on to contact all 'aliens' (foreigners, probably fellow-Luccese) bringing silk to London, and got them to sell at this inflated price by spreading a rumour that the price was due to rise even further. This was the root cause of the silk women's complaint. Sardouche admitted that he done as they alleged, but pleaded – in terms all too familiar nowadays – that 'he didn't know he had done wrong'. He was now prepared to sell at 16 shillings, so surely all could be forgiven?

But as the hearing went on more scandals emerged. Sardouche admitted that he had weighed silk worth £2,000 on his own scales, instead of the official scales, and that he had evaded customs duty on £1,000 worth of imports from Flanders. Worst of all, he had smuggled into London enormous quantities of luxury goods. One cargo, worth £4,000, included 'gold of Cyprus' (a fine silk fabric woven with gold thread), cloth of gold, silk fabric and thread, pepper, ginger and wax. Another cargo worth £6,000 included more fine silk fabric, ribbons from Venice and Damascus, saffron, sugar and 'brasil', a wood originating in the East Indies used to dye a deep red. (The Portuguese later named their new colony in the western hemisphere after it.) He had also illegally exported gold and silver in the form of coinage and bullion. In view of all this evidence the case was adjourned to a higher court, the King's Bench, Sardouche standing bail in £21,600, the amount of his frauds. The case became a tussle between the royal power and the City jurisdiction. Somehow Sardouche managed to obtain a pardon for 'all his misdemeanours' on payment of the risible sum of £200, with a royal writ of protection from further proceedings thrown in. His luck ran out two years later, however: he was killed in a brawl by two understandably irate members of the Mercers' Company in 1371.

The case throws light on the luxuries that the rich Londoner might spend his money on. There are other glimpses of conspicuous consumption. In 1361 the vintner Henry Picard was reported as having 'in one day sumptuously feasted' four kings – his own monarch and the French king, who was a royal captive, and the kings of Scotland and Cyprus, with the prince of Wales 'and many other noblemen'. Alas, this may be only legend, but it remains good as a symbol. In 1345 the debts due to Henry Picard are said to have amounted to £23,000, an unthinkable sum in medieval money, and he was at the back of most of the syndicates of oligarchs manipulating the London market.

Apart from moneylending, how else could a merchant invest his profits? Land was, as always, a good investment, especially land within London, where it could be bought free of villeinage burdens. Brothels, mills and fisheries were all reliable profit-makers. Sardouche's exploits showed the profits to be made from importing fine textiles, even after paying customs. Precious stones would find a ready market, especially pearls from the Persian Gulf and Serendip (Sri Lanka), which could be threaded into ropes or sewn onto garments. Diamonds came in from Golconda in India, rubies, emeralds and sapphires from India and Myamar (Burma), lapis lazuli from Afghanistan – all handled by successive traders on the long series of ways known as the Silk Route, between the Far East and the Mediterranean coast at Venice or Constantinople, where Venetian merchants sent them on their way into the markets of Europe.

But not all profits found a safe haven. When the king suggested that his loyal London subjects might like to lend him £5,000, they asked to be excused. They did eventually come up with the £5,000, because the king held the whip hand. He could always 'seize the franchise and the liberty of London', as he did in 1393; the City had to pay £10 million to get them back. Richard also had a nasty habit of issuing blank charters, for which the City had to pay £1 million. (These figures come from a contemporary chronicler and look suspiciously inflated. It is safe to say that they were very large, and correspondingly resented.) The relationship between the Crown and the City gradually stabilized, each realizing that it could not do without the other.

The Wool Trade

English wool had long been prized on the Continent. In Anglo-Saxon days, England had exported slaves, tin from Cornwall and copper from the Midlands. But Archbishop Lanfranc persuaded William the Norman that slavery was unchristian and should be abolished, and the demand for English tin and copper diminished when new mines were discovered on the Continent. Wool remained the premier exportable commodity. Edward III ordered that his Lord Chancellor should sit on a woolsack in the new Parliament, to remind all and sundry of the importance of wool to the English economy.

The small sheep that endured the hard conditions of the Welsh Marches, Shropshire and Herefordshire produced short, strong wool, good for heavy cloth. Bigger sheep with longer wool cropped the lush grass of Norfolk and the Cotswolds, where the Wife of Bath lived. Their wool could be woven into strong, smooth fabric such as the 'worsted' still used for men's suiting, named after the village of Worsted near Norwich where it was produced in the Middle Ages. By 1350 wool accounted for 92 per cent of the value of the English export trade.

Chaucer's Job

The wool customs department was headed by the collectors, powerful figures in the London world. Chaucer served under them as a mere 'controller'. He hadn't followed his father into the wine trade, preferring a post in various royal households, the civil service of the day. By 1374 he seems to have settled comfortably into a job as Controller of Customs of Hides, Skins and Wools in the port of London, with rent-free lodgings in Aldgate. The job carried a regular salary, which was augmented by an annuity from John of Gaunt. He was required to write up his records himself to prevent fraud, and to act in person, except for the times when he went abroad on royal service, when he was allowed to appoint a deputy. His office, the Customs House, was on the Wool Quay on the Thames, a pleasant walk from Aldgate. His jurisdiction extended downriver as far as Tilbury and Gravesend. He had a staff of underlings, including searchers in London and Gravesend with the power to seize uncustomed goods and prevent the export of bullion and the import of counterfeit money. Another minor controllership of the Petty Customs, covering most other kinds of merchandise except wine, came his way in 1382. All seemed set fair. But the factional convulsions and internal strife in the City suddenly coalesced into disaster for him in 1386. His controllerships ceased, he was turned out of his lodgings and he had to leave London for Kent. The Kent move gave him a brief entrée into national politics when he was appointed a knight of the shire (see p. 56); but for one born and bred a Londoner the abrupt change, let alone the dip in income, must have been unwelcome.

The Staple

The export of all this wool was so profitable that the rapacious English monarchs, perennially short of cash, fixed on it as a cash cow; but how best to milk it? One expedient adopted by Edward II (r. 1307–27) was to compel English exporters to use eight 'Staple' towns, including Bristol, Norwich and London, giving them in return preferential treatment over foreign merchants. Meanwhile the foreign wool merchants, resenting this discrimination, bought up all the teasels, madder, woad and fuller's earth they could find, all essential to weaving, so the monarch forbade the export of such things. I don't know who won that round, but *plus ça change*, in a war of sanctions.

The Ordinance of the Staple was given statutory approval in 1353. The mayor and ministers of the Staple had jurisdiction over offences against the ordinance, with power to arrest offenders and even, up to 1363, to execute them. The law they applied was the international mercantile law, excluding the English common law. In 1378 the Staplers built their London headquarters, Staple Inn, at the eastern end of Holborn. It still exists, behind some heavily restored 'sixteenth-century' shops.

The customs checks in London and other Staple towns in England were not infallible. The system had flaws, and was not too difficult to evade. The next idea in the royal mind was to establish one centre where all wool exported from England would be taxed before it could be sold. Bowing to various pressure groups, Edward III fixed the Staple in Low Country towns such as Bruges and Antwerp. The two ideas – an English base or a Continental base – fluctuated from time to time. In 1340 the Staple was fixed in Bruges, shifting slightly to the port for Bruges, Middelburg, in 1348, when the waterway between Bruges and the sea silted up. Bruges was an international money market and commercial hub where the English merchants could buy the luxuries that Nicholas Sardouche had so spectacularly dealt in, paying for them by bills of exchange. In 1399 the Staple settled permanently in Calais, then an English possession.

Financing the Wool Trade

The wool trade also functioned as a channel for long-term commercial loans:

> The great landowner usually disposed of his crop by contracting for it directly with an export merchant. In such cases the exporter or his agent would ride round to the monasteries and big houses,

view their crop when it was ready or contract for it in advance. It was to facilitate transactions such as this that lists were circulated among business firms containing details as to monastic houses with wool to sell and the quantity and quality which each produced... In most cases the wool was disposed of by advance contracts, and this was always the practice of monasteries, who often sold their wool for two or three years and sometimes for as much as fifteen and twenty years ahead... In almost every case the merchants paid large lump sums in cash in advance... these were really loans made on security of wool, which converted the transactions into credit deals. This characteristic direction of credit from buyers to sellers was a reflection of the economy of the age, when merchants, especially great foreign firms, were rich in liquid capital, and the agricultural producers poor in it.[2]

Once a bargain had been concluded, many things could go wrong. Langland's Piers Plowman dreamed about a merchant who suffered agonies of anxiety whenever he sent his servants, or an apprentice, to Bruges or Prussia to do business for him; his only recourse was to trust in God.[3] Chaucer's Merchant doesn't mention divine help, but was equally anxious about the sea passage between Middelburg and the River Orwell, in Suffolk:

> He would the sea were kept, for any thing,
> Betwixen Middelburgh and Orewelle.[4]

The estuary of the River Orwell begins at the harbours of Harwich and Felixstowe, now a huge container depot, and leads inland to Ipswich, a centre of the medieval wool trade. In 1372 the English had been heavily defeated in a sea battle off La Rochelle, leaving English coasts open to enemy attack and the seas between Suffolk and Flanders infested with pirates. It took fifteen humiliating years for the English to remedy this by the victory of Cadzand in 1387, just after Chaucer had begun to write the *Canterbury Tales*. By then the Staple had moved to Bruges, so safe passage to it was vital. No wonder the Merchant, and doubtless many of Chaucer's audience, had been worried.

The physical complexity of transporting a cargo of wool from its producer in England to its final buyer in Pisa is well illustrated by a transaction noted by a Florentine merchant employed by a Lombard bank in 1336. The chain began at a wool fair in the Cotswolds. All the Italian merchants, such as the Bardi, a powerful banking family from the north, sent their agents to negotiate the best available price. The wool was packed into gigantic sacks weighing 26 stones, each containing the wool from around two hundred sheep. One such sack filled a cart. In London the carts were emptied into ships that had brought wine from Gascony and were returning to their home port. The ships unloaded their cargo of wool at a port on the River Dordogne, Libourne. The 'swain' who had come with the woolsacks from London handed them over to the innkeeper in Libourne. His responsibility ended there. The innkeeper weighed the wool and unpacked each of the huge sacks into two bales that could be carried by pack animals. He arranged for them to go on to another innkeeper at Montpelier, who in turn arranged the next stage, down to the mouth of the River Rhône at Aigues-Mortes. There they were loaded onto the first available galley for shipment to Porto. The Bardi merely paid the succession of innkeepers for their storage and incidental expenses.[5]

As to the finances of the bargain, only mercenary soldiers insisted on being paid wholly in cash. One optimist offered his troops payment partly in cash, for spending in this world, and the rest in indulgences (see p. 12), for use in the next world, but his offer was not accepted. The system of bills of exchange was not proof against fraud. Langland's Piers Plowman dreamed about a merchant who

> ... with Lombard's letters ... carried gold to Rome,
> And took it by tally here, and told them there, less.

This may not be altogether clear to the modern eye, but that international trader was up to no good.[6]

The Bardi and another Italian banking family, the Peruzzi, largely financed the English state by lending Edward III enough to pay for his Continental wars, taking as security the customs revenue from the wool trade. By the early 1340s Edward had ruined them, largely by his habit of ignoring his obligations to repay his debts on time. He also raised money on his 'Great Crown', for which another Italian, Simon de Mirabello, charged him 35 per cent interest. When the Italian sources dried up, Edward III's successor Richard II turned to domestic ones. In 1350 the Drapers' Company lent him £4,000 on the security of that useful 'Great Crown', and another £20,000, again on the security of the customs revenue from the wool trade.

The Foreign Money Market

Chaucer's Merchant also boasted of making a profit from juggling foreign currency rates. There were many different currencies in Europe, all accepted in major trading centres such as London and Bruges. When the future King Henry IV went off to Prussia and the Holy Land in 1390–93, his treasurer kept exact accounts of all expenditure by his master and his very considerable entourage. It involved eleven different currencies, from Italian ducats through to Spanish gold florins, Prussian pfennigs, Bohemian penc, Hungarian florins, Austrian florins, Venetian ducats also changeable in Friuli and Rhodes, Milanese pichoni and French francs.[7] He didn't go through Luxembourg, which was lucky for him, since the currency 'in Luxembourg is a bad alloy, but it looks like a sterling [silver]: / The mark [imprint] on that money is good, but the metal is feeble.'[8] That explains why merchants always had a pair of scales handy, to check the weight of any currency they were offered, as well as a mirror to reflect light onto their ledgers.

For this kind of speculation speed of communication was vital. The fastest transport was still the horse. Crossing the Alps could be slow, especially in winter, but a messenger from Lombardy to London could make up time over the plains of France until he reached the Channel, where he might be further delayed by contrary winds. A horseman could generally cover 30 miles a day, but it would be prudent to expect the journey between Naples and London, for example, to take anything from twenty-seven to seventy-five days. It made more sense to gather the latest commercial news at one of the great international fairs such as Bruges or Frankfurt, where fellow-traders from all over Europe could catch up on the going price of slaves from Romania, and the latest arrivals in Venice from the East via the Silk Route.

Sardouche's case is fascinating, not only as an example of how to succeed in medieval business, but as a spotlight on the kind of luxury goods traded in Chaucer's London. Textiles from north Italy and beyond headed the list, then pearls – *apparently* not handled by Sardouche. Other exotic imports were ostrich feathers – another mercer's stock listed sixty of them, valued at £25, his most valuable item – and coconut shells for mounting in silver. Spain exported the soft white soap favoured for its benefit to complexions, as well as sword blades from Toledo and ivory tusks from the Barbary (north African) coast.

The Hanseatic League

Merchants from Cologne had long enjoyed trading privileges in London. In 1194 Richard I had used them to import grain from the Baltic, to alleviate a crop failure in England. By 1281 they had been joined by merchants from Hamburg and Lübeck to form the Hanse, or League, of Almain. (Almain and Allemands were the medieval words for the region and its inhabitants that later became Germany and Germans, Allemagne and Allemands in French.) By Chaucer's time their privileged trading and tax position had enabled them to acquire a prime site called the Steelyard, with its own loading wharf on the Thames, storehouses and living accommodation, a garden and a vineyard, all walled against armed attack. It was probably only the walls that saved the Allemands from the mayhem that overwhelmed other 'aliens' in 1381.

They had a practical monopoly of the import of grain, the timber and cordage needed by English shipbuilders, the alum vital to the textile industry, wax, zinc and copper to make brass, and the many kinds of fur that formed such a part of medieval wardrobes. Their trading contacts stretched from Novgorod to Constantinople. The Allemands were not popular with native-born

Londoners. By 1351 the quarrels between them and the London
merchants had reached such a pitch that the mayor issued a writ
authorizing the seizure of all their goods. How strongly this was
enforced is unclear, but it took a year for the king to repeal it. Six
years later the London merchants again appealed to the king for
help, voicing the familiar complaint that 'foreign merchants who
took their gains out of the country were more free than themselves'. In 1388 eighteen Hanse merchants were arrested in London,
in reprisal for the arrest of seventeen English merchants who had
been refused free entry to Hanseatic ports. The friction between
the Hanseatic merchants, backed by the Crown, and the London
merchants, backed by the City, lasted far longer than Chaucer's
time. The Hanseatic League retained many of its privileges until
the seventeenth century.

The Great Companies

The medieval trade companies are properly referred to as guilds or
'misteries', from the Latin *ministerium*, a trade or craft. ('Mystery'
is derived from the Latin *mysterium*, Greek *musterion*, a secret thing
or ceremony – which explains many apparent misprints.)

They had begun as early as 1155, when the London Weavers got
their formal charter. A steady stream followed, of some trades well
known to us such as the Goldsmiths, from 1180, and the Butchers,
from 1331, and others less well known, such as the Hurrers, who
made caps. Some drew up ordinances which they presented to the
mayor and aldermen for formal recognition. Some petitioned the
reigning monarch for formal charters. Some are very much alive
today, such as the Mercers, who made their own ordinances in 1348
and whose present charitable activities include St Paul's School and
St Paul's Girls' School. By 1377 there were more than fifty misteries
in London.

Their primary object was to protect their trade from competition:
a 'members-only enclosure'. Trade secrets were jealously guarded.
Some people were totally excluded, such as villeins and aliens, but
most admitted women. Once in, a member could count on the
support of his fellow-members. If a member fell on hard times,

he could draw on the mistery's funds for a modest pension. When he died his fellow-members would see him to his grave, and if his resources didn't stretch to a proper funeral they would provide one, with a fitting funeral feast afterwards. They might even look after a member's widow. Most misteries were centred on a church, where they worshipped together in state on the anniversary of the church's patron saint. Since members of one trade tended to congregate in one district, this might be – but was not necessarily – the local parish church of most of the members. As well as the annual procession in honour of the saint, there would be meetings to elect the ruling body of Masters. A handsome feast would be laid on, to which members could bring their wives or other 'demoiselles or compagnons'.

Their administrative organizations were roughly similar. In 1347 the Mercers resolved that 'in order to nurture unity and friendship between them and for the communal advantage of the mistery, four persons of the said mistery should be elected once a year to rule and govern the said mistery. And that everyone who is of the same mistery shall be obedient to them.' These elections were carried out with elaborate ceremonies:

> On Monday at night when supper is done and wafers and hippocras [sweet, highly spiced wine] set on the tables and especially on the high table, then must the three Wardens be ready in the parlour with three round garlands of gilloflowers [carnations] on their heads. [Each Warden has a 'personable' man in front of him holding a standing cup of hippocras] . . . The Clerk of the company . . . shall go foremost of all before the three wardens, with a goodly standing cup . . . full of hippocras in his right hand and a diadem of gilloflowers on his arm . . . And so to pass through the midst of the hall in good order, the three wardens following him with their garlands on their heads and their men before them with their cups in their hands full of hippocras . . .

They all bow to the elite on the high table, and exchange speeches and more toasts. Then the most senior member there

take[s] the diadem crown garland and put[s] it on his head a little
and so conveys it from him to the next that sits by him and so
from one to another until it has perused all the . . . worshipful
there . . . and last of all it shall be conveyed to the Master of the
Company and when he has received it and put it on his head
awhile, he shall cause it to be conveyed unto him that he is
minded to chose Master of the company in his room.

The retiring Master and the next Master toast each other, and
they all go through just the same rigmarole with the 'Uppermost
Warden', then the second Warden, then the last of the four Wardens. By now the garlands must be getting rather the worse for
wear, also the Wardens. But the retiring Wardens were sufficiently
sober to hand over any cash in hand, and the accounts, which were
kept in detail, down to the last farthing.[9] Surprisingly, they were
still wrestling with those Roman numerals as late as 1457.

On the surface, one might suspect that membership of a mistery
was merely an excuse for conviviality. A deeper purpose was not
so apparent. The law forbade land to be held in perpetuity, 'in
mortmain' (in a dead hand), without changing ownership, on
which occasion fees and charges would have been payable to the
Crown. If the Masters of a mistery bought land on which to build
a hall, or as an investment, there was a danger that their successors
would succeed to the title to that land without paying the requisite
fees. The Church, being eternal anyway, was allowed to do this,
but it was not, understandably, popular with the monarch. The
Second Statute of Mortmain of 1391 compelled corporations such
as the misteries to buy a royal licence to allow them to hold land
in mortmain. In 1397 the Mercers paid out £6 9s 6d for such a
licence.

The ruling monarchs were all in favour of these well-organized
misteries. They were sitting ducks for taxation, and found it difficult, but not impossible, to refuse the Crown's constant requests for
loans which might never be repaid. To show there was no ill feeling,
Edward III became a brother of the Linen Armourers, later called
the Merchant Taylors, Richard II was a member of the Mercers'
Company and also the Skinners', who controlled the fur trade.

All these misteries were the progenitors of the livery companies, which still have a pronounced influence in the life of the City of London. By 1385 the top twelve were:

the Mercers
the Linen Armourers, later called the Merchant Taylors
the Grocers, formerly called the Pepperers
the Drapers
the Fishmongers
the Goldsmiths
the Skinners
the Vintners
the Haberdashers
the Salters
the Ironmongers
the Clothworkers

of whom the first eight were predominant. They each had their own liveries, distinctive robes and headwear which they wore on formal occasions. This livery was often changed, so that only a rich man could afford to keep up with the latest fashion diktat. The Goldsmiths wore 'red barred with silver and powdered with trefoils' when 140 of them rode out to welcome Edward III's new bride in 1328. When King Richard II arrived from France in 1392 the Mercers went to greet him in a new livery of baudekin, a richly embroidered silk fabric, originally with a warp of gold thread. Froissart described how, when Henry IV went to Westminster Abbey to be crowned in 1399, he was escorted by all the companies of London in their liveries and with the banners of their trades, which must have been a colourful sight.

Apprentices

Admission to a mistery was normally through apprenticeship. The terms of the apprenticeship were written in a formal Deed of Indenture, stating the length of the term. In a typical deed of 1382 binding an apprentice to a goldsmith, the apprentice was 'not

[to] commit fornication either in his master's house or elsewhere, should not marry, nor get engaged without his master's permission'. He was not 'to play at tables [backgammon] or chess or other forbidden games or go to taverns except on business for his master', which all seems a hard regimen for a young adolescent growing to maturity: it would hardly suit modern youth. The minimum age for entry was twelve years, but most were older and often had already been partly trained. Most misteries required an apprentice to serve at least seven years, but individual bargains were often for longer. The Goldsmiths kept their apprentices for as long as fourteen years.

The master would be paid a premium fixed by the mistery, notionally covering the cost of the apprentice's upkeep during the term and a fee for instruction. It could be considerable, as much as £40 to become a Mercer, but in times of scarcity, as after the Great Pestilence, apprentices were taken on for £1 or less. An apprentice would begin as a guileless boy. He often came from a part of England far from the hubbub of London, and he would find it hard at first to understand the London dialect. The Mercers, for example, took apprentices from Norfolk, a centre of the wool cloth-weaving trade, where the local speech was slow and deliberate. The lad would move into his master's household and learn from him. To begin with, the relationship was one-sided, the master teaching him and using the lad's labour for trivial tasks, but as the years wore on the apprentice became more useful and the master could relax and even go on pilgrimages, like Chaucer's Merchant, leaving his apprentice to look after the shop. By his final year he could be entrusted with cash to conclude bargains in his master's name, and to travel abroad for him.

But relationships between master and apprentice were as varied as any human relationship. There was a constant stream of cases about apprenticeships in the Mayor's Court. Sometimes the master complained that the apprentice had run away, back to his home, and a messenger had to be sent to fetch him, or the local mayor was asked to find him and send him back to London. This often happened when the apprentice was within a year or two of completing his term and could set up his own business in a small provincial centre where his London expertise, no matter how incomplete, impressed his clientele. Sometimes the master himself disappeared, to escape his creditors, fleeing overseas or into a sanctuary such as St Martin's le Grand, leaving the apprentice high and dry. He was usually found articles with another master in the same trade, to serve out the rest of his term. There were many reported cases of bad treatment by the master or mistress. In 1364 'Agnes' was told that she must 'instruct her apprentice in a proper manner, and not beat her with stick or knife'. In 1369 the father of Alice complained that Elis Mympe, embroiderer, to whom his daughter had been apprenticed, was beating and ill-treating her and failing to provide for her. In 1365 a goldsmith had to swear that he would teach his apprentice the trade which he practised, and stop sending him into the country to thresh his corn. In 1366 an apprentice complained that instead of his master teaching him the trade of draper, he had 'turned him into a houseboy, thus wasting his time, wherefore he prayed to be discharged from his apprenticeship', which the court granted. In 1372 two brothers, William and Thomas Swale, both apprenticed to John Sharpe, complained that he 'had been for a long time in Newgate [prison] and his wife had fed them insufficiently, beaten them maliciously', even blinding one brother in his left eye. The court exonerated them from their apprenticeship. Quite what they could do next was not for the court to suggest.

An apprentice could be treated as a chattel, to be disposed of like any other inanimate object. When a master died he could leave his apprentices' terms to his widow. In 1366 Thomas Bunny pleaded that in 1362 he had bound himself apprentice to serve Thomas Rose, sheath-maker, for four years. Rose 'sold his estate in [Bunny] to a woman who kept stews on the far side of London Bridge. She set him to all manner of grievous work, such as carrying water ... and while thus employed he fell down and received a permanent injury. Further, she incited her paramour to beat and ill-treat him, and when he fell sick of ill usage she turned him out. Later, when he was able to work a little, his mistress wanted him to return and carry out his covenant.' The court exonerated Bunny from his apprenticeship articles.

A master might have several apprentices, at different stages of learning. In 1385 a vintner sent two of his apprentices, a senior one and a beginner, to Bordeaux to buy wine, with 205 marks in gold. Sad to relate, the young one let his master down badly by stealing the money. He admitted the theft and was sent to prison. The Mercers' records include the future mayor Richard Whittington, who had four apprentices in 1391, while a fellow-Mercer had ten. The usual number seems to have varied between two and five. To house ten boys and young men must have involved quite a substantial and noisy house, unless that master boarded some of them out.

When a master died leaving a senior apprentice, it often happened that the young man stepped into his master's shoes – not only into his bed, as his widow's second husband, but into his status in the mistery to which he belonged, thereby cutting short the unexpired part of the apprenticeship: a bargain advantageous to both parties. Marriage was generally seen as a business transaction, and the widow and the apprentice had been living in the same house together for some years so that neither was surprised by the habits of the other. Short of marriage, there were cases where an apprentice was appointed as the trusted executor of a deceased man's will, or the guardian of his children.

There was a high drop-out rate. No more than one-third of apprentices to the tailoring trade, for example, ever completed their terms.

Chaucer could hardly include an apprentice among his pilgrims: they would all be looking after their masters' businesses. But they were a very real presence in any London crowd.

Journeymen

Once the apprentice had served his term and satisfied his master that he was properly experienced, he could become a journeyman. (The word doesn't denote a commercial traveller, but someone who is paid by the day, 'journée' in Anglo-Norman.) He would be allowed to trade in London, but he was more likely to join a master, perhaps his own old master, as an employee until he could afford to set up on his own. This was the normal way of life for those who had completed their apprenticeship and had been admitted as freemen of London. The mega-rich at the top of the mistery system, such as Henry Picard, were few and far between.

VIII THE FIVE GUILDSMEN:
the Haberdasher, the Carpenter,
the Weaver, the Dyer and the Tapicer

It's not clear why Chaucer picked out these five guildsmen for mention. He gave them no individual characters. None of them got a chance to tell a Tale. They allow Chaucer to have a crack at City of London aldermen; perhaps that's why he included them. Maybe he just stuck some pins into a list of misteries and took the first five.

Before considering their joint significance, they need to explain what they each did for a living.

The Haberdasher

The etymology of this odd word can be traced to an Icelandic word *haprstask*, meaning pedlars' wares, or the sack in which the pedlar carried them.[1] The Company of Haberdashers was originally part of the powerful Mercers' Company. It included the Hurrers, or Cappers, who made and sold caps and hats, and the Milliners, who imported fashionable small wares from Milan. Its first ordinances were promulgated in 1371, but 'haberdasherie' had been included in a list of miscellaneous items chargeable to import duty as long ago as the reign of Henry III (r. 1216–72). It seems to have extended to what an American would call 'notions': all sorts of eye-catching small wares that were generally below the notice of the Mercers, but were nevertheless profitable, such as pins, caps, hoods and stockings. There was constant friction between the Haberdashers and the Mercers, since the boundaries of their trading spheres were not always clear. One difference was undeniable: to become a freeman of London as a Haberdasher would cost only 20s, whereas the Mercers charged anything up to £40 for the same thing.

The Carpenter

He belonged to one of the Great Companies, so it's surprising to find him lumped in with the other four Guildsmen. When most buildings were based on wood frames, the carpenters functioned more as general building contractors than as men you might ask to put up a shelf. As early as 1212 their craft had been subject to building regulations that required, for example, that roofs should be covered with non-flammable materials such as stone or tiles, not thatch, and that privies had to be sited well within the plot boundary. Judging by the repetition of these rules over the years, they don't appear to have been strictly observed. To maximize the living space by 'jettying' or extending the building past the plot boundary by means of protruding beams was likewise forbidden. In 1343 the residents of houses in a fashionable quarter of London near Gracechurch Steet complained that 'the shadows under a house built on beams [i.e. jettied] were the resort of bad characters, who sprang out on passers-by and robbed them'. The owner was ordered to demolish his house and pay a 40-shilling fine for contempt as well. But jettying survived until the Great Fire in 1666, which destroyed all the wooden houses of London.

The best timber for building was oak, but it was already running short in England and some had to be imported from the Baltic. Elm had a tendency to split, but was useful for underwater work such as piles into the Thames waterside, and drains.

A famous medieval mason and architect, Henry Yevele (d. 1400), was the project manager of a huge undertaking, raising the ceiling of Westminster Hall by two feet. Under his supervision Hugh Herland, carpenter, installed the great hammer-beam roof that can be seen today. It is 92 feet high in the centre, weighs 660 tons and has the widest unsupported span in the country. Fifty-two massive oak trees were used in its construction, each tree needing two carts and sixteen horses to transport it to the work site in Farnham, more than thirty miles from London. There the roof was prefabricated and then dismantled, every piece numbered so that it could be correctly reassembled. Once more it was transported by horse-drawn carts across country to Ham, and then by barge down the Thames to its present site. Herland was so well respected that he was entertained at the high table of New College, Oxford University.

We have the full text of a building contract in 1410, which is interesting although strictly beyond Chaucer's period. A carpenter undertook to build three shops, with living accommodation above them, in Friday Street, a prosperous district of London. The buildings are to have some built-in furniture. The ground-floor shops are to have 'stalls' (counters), and 'partitions'. On the first floor were to be

> a hall, larder and kitchen... in each hall they shall make benches and reasonable [appropriate] screens... with reasonable and suitable windows... which floor shall be suitably jettied... and on the second floor [they] shall make... a principal chamber and a foreign [a privy projecting from the main building]. And the second floor in front shall be made with a ceylingpiece [a horizontal beam projecting slightly from the front of the building]. And [they] shall make in each house two flights of stairs good and sufficient.

The ceiling height of the ground floor was to be 10 feet 6 inches, the main living area 9 feet high, the second bedroom floor 8 feet high. There are detailed specifications for the timber to be used. The design to be followed was 'made and drawn in parchment', which would be a lasting record. The total price was £45, £10 to be paid 'in hand' – we would say 'upfront' – the rest 'in manner and form as the work is carried on' – stage payments.

Master carpenters were well paid, at 7 shillings a week. They were an essential part of Edward III's invasion fleet in 1346. He enlisted forty of them, ready to construct wooden towers and other engines of war for use in sieges, and to repair or build bridges that the enemy might destroy on his route across France, just as the Royal Engineers built Bailey bridges during the Allied invasion of France in the Second World War.

The Weaver

The London Weavers' Company could trace its ancestry back to 1155, making it the earliest craft guild in England. Weavers were mostly small master craftsmen, working at home on piecework rates, on yarn supplied by the customer. Their monopoly over the weaving trade was gradually eroded by the growth of other textile companies such as the Mercers, and the immigration from Flanders of Flemish weavers, relying on royal support. The London weavers' hostility to Flemings came to a hideous climax in the Peasants' Revolt of 1381, when 'the London mob beheaded all the Flemings they found, without judgement and without cause, even invading the sanctuary of a church where thirty-five Flemings had taken refuge, dragging them out and beheading them in the street'.[2]

The Dyer

Dyers could claim an ancestry that no other craft could compete with. There was a tradition that Jesus, in his boyhood before his ministry began, was apprenticed to a dyer. One day his master told him to dye three separate cloths in three different colours. His master then left him to it. When he came back he was furious to find that young Jesus had stuffed all three cloths into the same dye vat. But Jesus had used his supernatural powers: each of the cloths emerged from the vat coloured as planned. No doubt the London apprentices, prone to skiving off when their master wasn't looking, encouraged such tales.

For a more recent account of their origin, the Dyers' Company could trace their skills back to the ancient British liking for donning warpaint. 'The secret of dyeing wools and woollen goods was familiar to those who pursued that craft, as it was little more than an evolution from the British custom of staining the person with woad or some other pigment', according to a nineteenth-century history of the Dyers' Company. The present members of the company appear, regrettably, to have allowed the custom to lapse.

The most commonly used dyestuff was woad, which gave a good blue. It was imported from the English possessions around Bordeaux in Gascony, and increasingly grown as a field crop in England.

The process of manufacturing the dye was quite elaborate. The woad leaves were crushed to a pulp in a mill, and then moulded into balls, which were allowed to dry in the sun... until the pulp began to ferment. A crust formed over the balls, and care was taken to ensure that this did not split. When fermentation was complete the balls were pulped again in the mill and again formed into cakes. The whole cycle was repeated a third time before the fully-fermented balls were thoroughly dried and sent off to the dyer. It took a hundredweight of leaves to produce 10lb of the final dye, and the ammoniacal stench of the fermentation process was so disgusting that Elizabeth I issued a proclamation that woad production had to cease in any town through which she was passing.[3]

The Ancient Britons' secret weapon?
Woad could be mixed with yellow from the meadow plant weld, or from another native plant, dyer's greenweed (genista tinctoria; despite its English name it dyed yellow), to give the green that Robin Hood and his merry men famously wore. Red, another favourite medieval colour, could be obtained from the roots of another native plant, madder. Mixed with woad it produced a soft purple. A deeper purple came from a lichen, orchil, imported from Norway, or 'brasil', a wood imported from the East Indies and correspondingly expensive. The deepest purple came from kermes, derived from insects from the Mediterranean basin called by the Italians 'vermilium' ('little worms', hence vermilion) and by the English 'grains'. Its cost limited it to the most luxurious textiles. A good pink could be had from the resin of dragon's blood trees, although some medieval authorities traced it to the product of a battle between elephants and dragons in which both protagonists died.

Most of these dyestuffs needed a mordant to give some degree of light-fastness – usually alum, imported from Turkey and Greece.

The Tapicer

This trade received its ordinances from Edward III in 1331. Tapicers were primarily makers of tapestries, which had to be of regulation size – either 4 ells long by 2 ells wide, or 3 ells by one and a half ells, an ell being about 45 inches. They also produced 'bankers' – cushions to pad those hard medieval benches – and chalon, a thick fabric much used for blankets and coverlets. Tapicers, like weavers, were bound to use only 'good wool of England and of Spain', and never to blend the two together. There were less desirable admixtures: in 1342 some 'false blankets that had been vamped in foreign parts with the hair of oxen and cows' were publicly burned, by order of the mayor and aldermen.

The luxury market in tapestries was centred in Paris, where gigantic scenes from the Bible or legends were woven on looms 20 feet wide. But other cities such as Arras were developing a profitable industry. John of Gaunt bought Arras tapestries for his notoriously opulent Palace of the Savoy. It seems hard on Katherine Duchewoman – perhaps a native of Arras? – that she was penalized for having made a 'coster' (a piece of tapestry for the side of a bed) 'after the manner of Arras'. She had used 'linen thread beneath, but covered with wool above', that is with the warp threads of linen, which would give the piece strength, and the visible weft of wool; which seems a good idea, but not, it appears, if you were an English tapicer.

Fraternities

Full fresh and new hir geere apiked was [their clothes were
    adorned];
Their knives were chaped [mounted, trimmed] not with brass,
But all with silver, wrought full clean [handsomely] and well,
Their girdles and their pouches [purses] everydel [in every
    respect].[4]

All five men were clearly prosperous. They were dressed, not in the different liveries of each man's guild, but in 'one livery / Of a solemn and a great fraternity'.[5] This is more significant than it looks. Fraternities were religious societies and social clubs, concerned with their members' well-being, both spiritual and secular. They had their own rules, and their own livery by which their members could be known. Instead of being run by qualified Masters, their Wardens might include journeymen, the workforce of their trades, who had little say in the affairs of their company. Fraternities were often based on a parish church which needed funds to repair or enlarge its buildings, and invited membership, and donations, from any likely resident in the parish, regardless of what company he belonged to. But they were frowned on by the authorities because they could influence the election of aldermen, which was officially the sole privilege of the guilds; and their proceedings were held in private, where leading members could plan concerted drives to increase prices by threatening to withdraw their labour. Such 'combinations' – the early form of trade unions – were anathema to the authorities. Trade unions were not decriminalized until 1867. So Chaucer is blandly treading on a sore point here. His audience probably included several aldermen, whose views were unlikely to be in favour of fraternities unless they belonged to one themselves.

Aldermen

Each of the five Guildsmen 'was shaply [suited] for to have been an alderman, / for catel [moveable property] had they enough, and rent'. Aldermen had to be men of substance, a test that Chaucer's five Guildsmen passed easily. One advantage of their status was the lustre it reflected on their wives; Chaucer's Guildsmen were egged on to be aldermen by their wives, disregarding the often onerous tasks that their husbands would have to discharge, which included, for example, prompt attendance at all Council meetings, which began at 6 a.m. An alderman's wife would indeed be called 'Madame', or even 'My Lady', even if her husband died and she remarried someone who was not an alderman. She would take precedence on religious and social occasions.

> It is full fair to been called 'madame',
> And go to vigils [the night before an important religious
>   occasion] all before,
> And have a mantel royally ybore [carried like royalty].[6]

On the appearance of the king or any other member of a royal family, trains had to be lifted by their bearers and placed over the wearer's left arm. Although exalted, the wives of the Guildsmen were hardly likely to meet royalty. Chaucer's wife had long moved in royal circles, so he would have been well aware of the rule, but he was gently poking fun at these pretentious ladies.

The City of London had a sophisticated system of government, based on twenty-four wards (after 1394, twenty-five when Farringdon was divided into two). The wards were of different sizes, and contained different numbers of parishes. There was a tendency for men following the same trade to live near each other, so some wards drew their wealth from plutocratic residents, such as the goldsmiths or the mercers, while others were home to poor artisans such as the tallow chandlers. In earlier times the aldermen were elected by the guilds, but increasingly this changed, until by Chaucer's time election was by each ward.

The high status of aldermen is vividly illustrated by a case heard in 1387. The drama began one Monday night, when William Hughlot broke into John Elyngham's house and assaulted him with his dagger. John's wife saw an alderman, John Rote (JR) in the street outside and screamed to him for help. As an alderman he was 'bound to the utmost of his power to keep and maintain the peace', so in he went and told William to 'desist from his violent and evil conduct'. But William merely turned his attack, and his knife, on JR. JR managed to get William to put his knife away, but worse followed. William 'drew his sword upon the Alderman and would have slain him with it, had not the Alderman manfully defended himself'. Enter yet another person into this surely rather overcrowded room – a passing constable, John Wilman (JW), who, 'hearing the affray', tried to arrest William, but William got his dagger out again and wounded JW, 'as well in contempt of our

Lord the King as to the dishonour of the Mayor, the Aldermen and the sheriffs', let alone the physical injury to John.

The next thing we hear of William was his appearance in court. He was remanded in custody, to Newgate gaol, where he made the mistake of making rude remarks about the court, as 'the most false court in all England'. This was unwise. When he came up for trial he pleaded guilty. The court sentenced him to have his right hand amputated, 'with which he first drew the dagger and afterward drew his sword', and to show that the court meant what it said 'an axe was brought into court by an officer and the hand of the said [William] was laid upon the block there to be cut off. Whereupon JR and at the request of divers lords ... entreated for the said William that execution of the judgement aforesaid might be remitted', and it was. He got a year's imprisonment for the original contempt and assault, and in addition 'the disgraceful punishment of the pillory', and when he came out of prison he had to walk through the city from the prison through Chepeside and Fleet Street to the Church of St Dunstan, near the Old Bailey, carrying a heavy wax candle as a sign of his penitence. He did the candle walk straight away, found eight sureties for his good behaviour and was released from prison. The whole episode, from William's attack on John to his release after his penitential walk, took just eleven days.

The Common Councillors of London were elected annually by the aldermen. They had to be freemen of London, which excluded 'foreigners' – Englishmen who were not Londoners – and 'aliens' from overseas. Candidates had to be reputable, and fit both in morals and worldly goods for the office, so Chaucer's five Guildsmen would have easily passed that test. The mayor, who had huge powers and responsibilities, was elected by the aldermen from among their number.

The mayor's main duty was to preserve peace in the city, which was no easy task. He had almost a private army of officers, also elected, to help him, from the two sheriffs right down to the common huntsman. He presided over the Mayor's Court, with jurisdiction to hear cases between citizens and cases involving the Law Merchant. He enjoyed considerable prestige as he processed around the city, preceded by his sword-bearer. In the 1381 revolt, when the young King Richard faced the mob of rebellious peasants, he was accompanied by the then mayor, William Walworth, and his mayoral sword-bearer.

In 1355 Roger Torold, a vintner, 'shamefully reviled the Mayor'. The next day he was ordered to attend the Mayor's Court in the Guildhall, where he admitted that he had spoken as alleged. He was sent to prison for a week, during which he saw sense; when he came up before the mayor again, he offered '100 tuns of wine for the contempt and offence aforesaid, that he might be restored to his favour; which the said Mayor then forgave to the said Roger Torold'. But when John Constantine was about to cause a riot in 1384 he was seized by the mayor's officers, tried and summarily executed.

Chaucer must have had his reason for choosing this odd group. Perhaps he wanted to remind his audience, most of whom would have been prosperous and perhaps members of one of the Great Companies, that there was power inherent in the lower levels of London life.

IX THE COOK

The five Guildsmen had brought a cook with them. Some inn-keepers, such as Mine Host of the Tabard, provided meals. More humble landlords expected their guests to prepare their own, bringing in the raw ingredients and using the cooking facilities on the premises. This group wanted to be sure of being well fed on the journey, no matter where they had to stay overnight, so they had brought their own cook,

> To boil the chickens with the marrow-bones
> And poudre-marchaunt tart and galingale...
> He could roast and sethe [boil] and broille [grill] and fry,
> Make mortreux and well bake a pie.[1]

'Poudre-marchaunt' was a kind of flavouring. Galingale is a root that looks like ginger but tastes more like mint; it has only recently returned to English kitchens from Thailand, via 'fusion' cookery recipes. It's surprising that Chaucer chose to give it this prominence, when ginger would have been far more widely used. Perhaps he just needed a trisyllable, to fit into his metre.

Chaucer doesn't seem to have been very interested in the Cook. He rates only nine lines in the General Prologue, he never managed to finish his Tale,[2] and he was bawled out by Mine Host:

> For many a pastee hast thou laten blood,
> And many a Jack of Dover hast thou sold,
> That hath been twice hot and twice cold.

Of [from] many a pilgrim hast thou Christ's curse,
For of thy parsley yet they fare the worse,
That they have eaten with thy stubble goose;
For in thy shop is many a fly loose[.][3]

Mine Host was accusing Chaucer's Cook of prolonging the 'sell-by'
life of his pies by draining off the gravy, like letting blood from a
human, then pouring it back when he put the pie on sale again.
'Pastees', or pies, were the fast food of the day, sold on the streets,
popular with people who had no cooking facilities at home, which
would be the mass of Londoners and other town dwellers. At the
very beginning of Piers Plowman's visions he evokes an assembly of
every trade and profession. Inevitably the cooks are there, marketing 'Hot pies, hot! / Good geese and grys [pork]! Go we dine, go
we!'[4]

A Jack of Dover seems to have been some sort of pie which the
Cook reheated twice – just the sort of treatment any pre-cooked
food purveyor warns us about nowadays, for fear of salmonella.
A 'stubble goose' was a goose that had fed on the aftermath of
the corn field, so it should be fat and tender. But without any
means of refrigeration, it too might 'go off'. The bad taste might be
disguised with a large handful of parsley, perhaps using the roots,
which have a stronger taste than the leaves. Nor was the Cook's
image helped much by the inflamed sore, or 'mormal', on his shin,
nor the flies in his shop. So all in all, Mine Host did not think
much of his fellow-caterer's trading standards. Chaucer's statement
that the Cook 'could well bake a pie' looks like another of his
back-handed compliments.

Every proper London cook would belong to a professional body.
The Guild of Cooks had been formed in 1311, although it did not
get a charter until 1482. The Guildsmen's cook must have served the
usual seven years' apprenticeship, learning by example and practice.
He would certainly know how to 'roast and boil and broil and fry',
and much else besides.

Kitchens

In big fourteenth-century houses the kitchen was sometimes in a separate building, to lessen the risk of fire. Otherwise it might be next to the main dining hall, on the first floor. Its windows were unlikely to be glazed. The wooden shutters and louvres kept the worst of the winter weather out and let out some of the smoke, but hardly helped with the light level. When daylight faded, candlelight and firelight had to suffice. By Chaucer's time the cooking fire had usually moved from the centre of the ground-floor hall to the side wall of the kitchen, with a chimney and a flue. There might be a bracket let into the wall beside the fireplace with a horizontal arm, so that a cauldron could be swung over the fire. In front of the fire would be a rack holding one or more spits, probably of different sizes.

Ovens were separate structures from the cooking fires, although they might be built into the side of the chimney. The heat source was logs from the fire, put into the oven while burning and removed once the clay walls of the oven were hot right through, so that they retained the heat for bread-baking. Once the loaves were done the residual heat could be used for other things, such as pies and joints brought in for baking by paying customers. Where we wrap a joint in foil, to keep it tender and retain the juices, the medieval cook achieved the same result by enclosing the joint or bird in a 'chest' or 'coffin' of plain flour and water, which was not meant for eating. Judging from the number of times that the City authorities issued rules about the price bakers could charge for baking a joint in their oven, it seems to have been common practice to buy a joint or bird and take it along to the baker to be 'coffined' and baked, for which he was allowed to charge a fee.

Equipment

To a modern cook, the greatest omissions in a medieval kitchen, apart from a good light to see by, would be any way of controlling temperatures or setting exact times. Oven temperature can be judged by an experienced hand, as it was for centuries until the advent of modern stoves. Timing in minutes could be assessed fairly accurately by muttering the words of the Lord's Prayer – the Pater Noster – or the Ave Maria. (Try it yourself. The prayer to 'our Father', said slowly, takes just about thirty seconds; or you could use any poem you like.) For longer times, the local church bells might help.

Medieval recipe books rarely gave the quantities of the ingredients needed, leaving them to the cook's experience or common sense. In any case, brilliant cooks such as my daughter-in-law always vary a given recipe with their own 'little bit of this, and a splash of that' to produce their masterpieces, and no doubt good medieval cooks did the same. The modern cook would also badly miss a food processor, to liquidize or chop ingredients at the press of a finger. Its forerunner was a pestle and mortar. Mortars could vary from tree-trunk size, more like a miniature piledriver than a kitchen implement, to a hand-sized utensil used for grinding spices. Once something had been 'pounded' it might be necessary to sieve it, by putting it through a 'boulting cloth' of coarse linen. Skimmers were needed, to skim the scum that rises to the surface of boiling stock. Long knives and forks were used for carving, although table forks had not appeared yet. (It was rumoured that the pope used a fork to eat his meat with, but after all he was a foreigner.)

An inventory of the items in the kitchen of Richard Toky, a member of the prosperous Grocers' Company, in 1391 gives some idea of fourteenth-century kitchen equipment. It included:

for food preparation – two mortars and two pestles, two meat-hooks, two pairs of tongs, two axes and two hatchets, four 'tables' [abacuses: calculators], a 'dressing-knife', a skimmer, two ladles, and a kneading tub

for cooking – three brass pots, two little pans, two frying pans, one chafing pan [used over a charcoal fire for small, delicate dishes], two kettles, four copper pans, three iron spits and a rack, two grid-irons for grilling, two tripods, a grate, a bellows, and some wood and coal

for laundry – a water-tankard [the kind of big hod used to deliver water to the household by the tankard-bearer], two washing tubs and a barrel.

In a separate 'pantry and buttery' there were:

> two cupboards, two candlesticks, miscellaneous table linen, two
> iron funnels, a pair of table knives [for carving], two 'chargers' [big
> serving dishes], ten 'dishes', eleven saucers [small dishes for sauces,
> to be put between diners at table], nine 'trenchers', two half-gallon
> pots each holding four pints, three quart pots each holding two
> pints, and one pint pot, salt-cellars, a holy water stoup, two shal-
> low pewter bowls, a bottle [probably made of leather, certainly
> not glass], a hamper, a box, three round basins, one jar for ale, an
> earthenware pot, and various broken bits.

In a storehouse there were four 'balances' and weights to weigh
heavy items, and two 'small brass weighing-balances'; perhaps they
really belonged in the kitchen.

Recipes

Curye on Inglische (*Cookery in English*) draws on *The Forme of
Curie* (*The Proper Method of Cookery*), said to have been in use
in Richard II's household, as well as other sources, was probably
current long before Richard came to the throne in 1377. The editors
chose their selection, from which I have made my own selection,
so the following recipes may not be typical of the time, but they
are sometimes amusing and sometimes amazing, and, I hope,
interesting. I have tried to keep the feeling of the language, but
used modern English when the original is too obscure. Medieval
English used the word 'him' for he, she, it and them. The recurrent
command to 'smite him in gobbets' is so much more vivid than
'cut it into bite-sized pieces' that I've let it stand. Also, medieval
English used the verb 'do' where we use 'put'. I've left 'do' but think
of it as 'put'. Every recipe that follows, except the first, comes from
Curye on Inglische. You may like to try some of them at home. But
if you're not totally hooked on cooking, or obsessed by yet another
television show where competitors frantically try to out-do each
other in producing improbable dishes in television studios, you
may well decide to skip the next bit and home in again at FEASTS.

SOUPS

The first one comes from an unexpected source, a collection of prayers by a devout soldier, who wrote a book of 'Holy Medicines',[5] including what almost amounts to pressure-cooking.

Invalid soup: 'to reinvigorate a weakened patient, one places a small capon in a small earthenware pot which is closed tightly and placed inside another vessel filled with water; this vessel is placed on a fire, and the capon thus thoroughly cooked, and the liquid which exudes makes a very beneficial broth'. He goes on: 'Oh Lord I am in great need of such a remedy: the capon is your human nature, the small pot is the fear of torments ... the larger pot is the world filled with tribulations, and the fire is the fire of Hell', but for this chapter his way of making broth is all we need.

Onion soup: 'make good almond milk and make oil of almonds and slice onions and fry them in the almond oil and float onion rings on top, and when you have arranged them, strew sugar on them'.

Chaucer wrote that the Cook knew how to boil the chickens with marrow bones, 'poudre-marchaunt' and galingale. I haven't been able to find a recipe for this; perhaps because it was such an obvious thing to do that it didn't need a recipe. Medieval chickens were on the tough side, and boiling would produce a good stock. If bone marrow and spices were added, the stock would taste that much better. So many recipes refer to 'good broth' that one is perhaps justified in imagining chickens and marrow bones, in a stock pot, simmering on the fire, ready whenever 'good broth' was needed.

MEAT DISHES

Mounchlet: 'take veal or mutton and smite it to gobbetts. Seeth [boil] it in good broth; cast thereto a good quantity of herbs, and a quantity of minced onions, powdour fort [a prepared mixture of spices] and saffron, and thicken it with eggs and verjuice [soured grape juice, like vinegar], but let it not boil thereafter.'

Mawmenee: 'take a pottle [half a gallon] of Greek wine and two pounds of sugar. Take and clarify the sugar with a quantity of wine and draw it through a strainer into an earthenware pot. Take rice flour and mix with some of the wine ... Take pine[nuts] with dates and fry them a little in grese [fat] or oil and cast them together [add them]. Take cloves and flour of cinnamon [probably cassia bark] and cast thereto. Take powdered ginger, cinnamon and cloves. Colour it with sanders [a wood used for colouring red] a little if it be needed. Cast salt thereto, and let it boil warily [carefully] with a slow fire and not too thick. Take brawn [flesh] of capon or pheasants teysed small [shredded] and cast thereto.'

Froys: 'take veal and seeth it well and hack it small, and grind bread, pepper and saffron and do thereto and fry it, and press it well upon a board, and dress it forth'.

Mortrews (the dish Chaucer credited the Cook with knowing how to make): 'take hens and pork and boil them together. Take [the] flesh of [the] hens and of the pork and hewe it small, and grind it all to dust. Take grated bread ... and temper [mix] it with the same broth, and thicken it with yolks of eggs, and cast thereon powder fort [a strong prepared mixture of spices]. Boil it and do therein powder of ginger, sugar, saffron and salt, and look [check] that it be stonding [thick]. And flour it with powdered ginger.' There are many variants of this recipe, using different meats and poultry, and sometimes fish.

Coneys (rabbits) in gravy: 'take coneys; smite them to pieces; parboil them and draw [blend] them with a good broth [and] with almonds, blanched and brayed [pounded in a mortar]. Do therein sugar, and powdered ginger, and boil it and the flesh therewith. Flour it with sugar and with powdered ginger and serve forth.'

Meat jelly: 'take swines' feet and snouts and ears, capons, rabbits, calves' feet ...'

Hirchones (urchins, hedgehogs: Old French *herichon*): 'take the mawe [belly] of the great swine, and five or six pigs' mawes. Fill them full of the same farce [the usual stuffing?] and sew them [up] fast [tight]. Parboil them; take them up, and make small pricks [prickles] of good paste [pastry], and fry them. Take these fried pricks and set them thick in the maws, made after [like] an urchin [hedgehog] without legs. Put them on a spit and roast them, and colour them with saffron, and mess [serve] them forth.'

Bruce: 'take the white of leeks, slit them and shred them small. Take numbles [entrails: sometimes 'umbles' but never 'humble' as in 'humble pie'] of swine and parboil them in broth and wine. Take them up and dress them, and do the leek in the broth; seeth and do the numbles thereto. The self wise [in the same way] make of porpoises.'

For to keep venison from resting [going bad] take venison when it is new [just killed] and cover it hastely [carefully] with fern [so] that no wind may come hereto, and when thou hast covered it well lead [carry] it home and do it in a soler [in this context, a store room] that neither sun nor wind may come thereto, and dismember it and do it in a clean water and leave it there half a day, and after do it upon hurdles for to dry, and when it is dry take salt, and do after thy venison axit [put as much salt as the venison will take] and do it [to] boil in water that be so salt as water of the sea and much more, and after that let the water be cold, let it be thin [let the sediment sink to the bottom] and then leave thy venison in the water and let it be therein three days and three nights; and after take it out of the water and salt it with dry salt right well in a barrel, and when the barrel is full cover it hastely [so] that sun nor wind come thereto.

If, despite all that, you've lost the battle, do not despair: 'For to do away resting of venison, take the venison that is rest [rotting] and do it in cold water and after make a hole in the earth and let it be therein three days and three nights; and after take it up and frot [rub] it with great salt of poite [saltpetre] there where the rotting is and after that let it hang in rainwater all night or more.' It still doesn't sound very appetizing, but venison was expensive and a status symbol, not to be lightly thrown away.

POULTRY DISHES

To dress a swan: 'take him and undo him and wash him and do [him] on a spit and enarme [bard] him fair and roast him well and dismember him in the best manner and make a fair chyne [a chain: a decorative pattern?]'.

Cranes and herons should be 'enarmed with lardons of swine and roasted and eaten with ginger'.

Peacocks and partridges should be 'yperboiled [parboiled] and larded and roasted and eaten with ginger'.

Another recipe begins with cranes: 'The crane shall be [cooked] on a spit, the same as a woodcock. The sauce is ginger. And botores [another kind of marsh bird] and curlews [should be treated the same]. Cormorants should be scalded and parboiled and larded and roasted. The sauce is ginger. Plovers, mallards, teals, larks, finches, buntings: all these shall be roasted and served with friture [fritters] and braun [the breast meat]; the sauce shall be ginger'.

Cokagris (sometimes called a 'cockatrice' but this version makes more sense because it combines a cock with a pig, 'gris'): 'Take and make the same fars [the usual stuffing?] but do thereto pine nuts and sugar. Take a whole roast cock, pluck him and skin him altogether save for the legs. Take a pig and skin him from the middle downward. Fill him full of the fars, and sew them [the cock and the half-pig] fast together. Put them in a pan and boil them well, and when they are well boiled put them on a spit and roast it well. Colour it with yolks of eggs and saffron. Lay thereto foyles [thin pieces] of gold and silver and serve it forth'.

FISH

Lampreys (eel-like fishes) in galyntyne (jelly): 'Take lampreys and slay them with vinegar [how do you do that?] or with white wine and salt. Scald them in water. Slit them a little at the navel, and rest a little at the navel. Take out the guts at the end. Keep well the blood. Put the lamprey on a spit; roast him and keep well the grease [the fat that drips off it]. Grind raisins of Corinth [currants]; draw [cut] them up with vinegar, wine, and crusts of bread. Do thereto powder of ginger, of galingale, flour of canel powder [powdered cinnamon], cloves; and do thereto whole raisins of Corinth, with the blood and the grease. Seeth it and salt it; boil it not to thicken [stop before it thickens]. Take up the lamprey; do him in a charger and lay the sauce onoward [on top] and serve him forth.'

Chewets on fish day (when eating meat was forbidden): 'Take turbot, haddock, codling and hake, and boil them. Grind it small and do thereto ground dates, raisins, pine [kernels], good powders [spices?] and salt. Make a coffin as to a small pie; close [the mixture] therein and fry it in oil, or stew it in sugar and wine, or bake it, and serve forth.'

Sturgeon: 'for to make a storchoun he shall be in leses [slices] and steeped overnight, and soaked as long as flesh [meat] and he shall be eaten in vinegar'.

Oysters: 'for to make oysters in broth, they shall be shelled and soaked in clean water. Grind pepper, saffron, bread and ale and temper [mix] it with broth. Do the oysters therein and boil it and salt it and serve it forth.'

Lobster: 'for to make a lopister, he shall be roasted in his scales in an oven or by the fire under a pan [a pan with a lid] and eaten with vinegar'.

Chysanne: 'take roaches [a kind of fish], whole tenches [another kind of fish], and plaice, and smite them to gobbets. Fry them in oil. Blanch almonds; fry them and cast thereto raisins of Corinth. Make a lyour [thickening] of crusts of bread, of red wine and of vinegar, [each] the third part; therewith drawn [cut up] figs and do thereto powder fort [a strong prepared mixture of spices] and salt; boil it. Lay the fish in an earthen[ware] pan and cast the sauce thereto. Do minced onions and cast therein. Keep it and eat it cold.'

Blomanger of fish: 'take a pound of rice. Sieve it well and wash, till they [the grains of rice] burst and let them cool. Do thereto milk of two pounds of almonds. Take the perch or the lopuster and boil it, and cast sugar and salt thereto and serve it forth.'

Conger (eel) in sauce: 'take the conger and scald him and smite him in pieces and boil him. Take parsley, mint, peletory, rosemary and a little sage, bread and salt, and a little garlic, a little cloves. Take and grind it well. Strain it [the sauce] with vinegar through a cloth. Cast the fish in a vessel and do the sauce on top, and serve it forth cold.'

PASTA
Ravioles: 'take wete [white, hard] cheese and grind it small, and mix it with eggs and saffron and a good quantity of butter. Make a thin foil [sheet] of dough and close it [the cheese mixture] therein as tartlets, and cast them in boiling water, and boil them therein. Take hot melted butter and grated cheese, and lay the ravioles in dishes; and lay the hot butter with grated cheese beneath and above, and cast thereon powder douce [a mild mixture of ground spices].'

Makerouns (not macaroons, more like macaroni): 'take and make a thin foil of dough, and kerve [cut] it in pieces, and cast them in boiling water and [bring it to the boil]. Take cheese and grate it, and melted butter, cast beneath and above as losyns [linguini] and serve forth.'

VEGETABLES
Salat: 'take parsley, sage, green garlic, chibolles [spring onions] onions, leek, borage, mints, porrettes [?], fennel, and town cresses [not watercress; our 'American' or ground cress would do], rue, rosemary and purslane; lave [clean?] and wash them clean. Pick them [over]. Pluck them small with thine hand and mix them with raw oil; lay on vinegar and salt and serve it forth.'

Funges (mushrooms): 'take funges and pare them clean, and dyce them; take leek and shred it small, and do him to seeth in good broth. Colour it with saffron, and do therein powder fort.'

Fritour (fritters) of pasternakes, of skirwittes (both these could be
either carrots or something like parsnips) and of apples: 'take [all
of them] and parboil them. Make a batter of flour and eggs. Cast
thereto ale and yeast, saffron and salt. Wet them in the batter and
fry them in oil or grease [fat]. Do thereto almond milk and serve it
forth.'

Compost (compote of mixed vegetables with pears): 'take roots of
parsley, of pasternake, of rafens [radishes], scrape them and wash
them clean. Take rapes [turnips] and caboches [cabbages] pared and
cored. Take an earthen[ware] pan with clean water and set it on
the fire; cast all these therein. When they have boiled cast thereto
pears, and boil them well. Take all these things up and lay them kele
[carefully] on a fair cloth. Do thereto salt. When it is cold, do it in
a vessel; take vinegar and powder and saffron and do thereto, and
let all these things lie therein all night, or all day. Take Greek wine
and honey, clarified together; take Lumbard mustard and raisins of
Corinth, all whole, and grind powder of cinnamon, powder douce,
and whole anise, and fennel seed. Take all these things and cast
together in an earth[enware] pot and take thereof when thou wilt
and serve it forth.'

Spinach fried: 'take spinach, parboil it in boiling water. Take it up
and press out the water and hew [cut] it in two. Fry them in oil and
put thereto powder douce, and serve forth.'

PUDDINGS
Spine: 'take the flowers of the hawthorn clene [freshly] gathered
and bray [pulverize] them all to dust, and temper [mix] them with
almond milk and thicken it with amydoun [wheat starch] and with
eggs, well thick, and boil it and messe [serve] it forth, with flowers
and leaves above [on top].'

There are similar recipes using roses, strawberries – the woodland
kind, not the cultivated ones of our time – violets, primroses and
elderflowers.

Fruit rissoles: 'take figs and raisins; pyke them [pick them over?] and wash them in wine. Grind them with apples and pears, pared and pyked clean. Do thereto good powders and whole spices; make balls thereof, fry in oil, and serve them forth.'

Daryols: 'take cream of cow's milk, or of almands, do thereto eggs with sugar, saffron and salt. Mix it fere [thoroughly]. Do it in a coffin of two inches deep; bake it well and serve it forth.'

Lete (milk) lards: 'take parsley, and grind with a little cows milk; mix it with eggs and diced lard [fat]. Take milk after that thou hast done it, and make thereof various colours. If thou wilt have yellow, do thereto saffron and not parsley [... for white, omit saffron and parsley, add wheat flour; for red, use sanders; for purple, use tournesole, another herb; for black use blood]. Set on the fire in as many vessels as thou hast colours thereto, and seeth it well, and lay these colours in a cloth, first one and then another on top of it, and then the third, and the fourth, and press it hard till it be all out clene. When it is all cold, slice it thinly, put it in a pan and fry it well, and serve it forth.'

FRUIT

The recipes mention apples, pears, quinces, cherries and grapes, all of which could be grown in the England of the time. Dates, figs and dried fruit such as currants and sultanas were imported.

SAUCES AND STUFFINGS

Lombard mustard: 'take mustard seed and wash it, and dry it in an oven. Grind it dry. Sieve it through a sieve. Clarify honey with wine and vinegar, and stir it well together and make it thick enough, and when thou wilt spend [use] thereof make it thin with wine.'

Sauce madame for a goose (stuffing): 'take sage, parsley, hyssop and savory, quinces and pears, garlic and grapes, and fill the goose therewith, and sew the hole [so] that no grece [fat] comes out, and roast him well, and keep the grease that falleth thereof. Take galantine and grease and do in a possynet [a small pan]. When the goose has roasted enough, take him off and smite him in pieces, and take that that is within and do it in a possynet and put therein wine, if it be too thick; do thereto powder of galingale, powder douce, and salt, and boil the sauce, and dress the goose in dishes and lay the sauce onoward [on top].'

Sauce blanche for boiled capons: 'take blanched almonds and grind them all to dust; temper it with verjuice and powdered ginger, and messe it forth'.

Sauce noire for roast capons: 'take the liver of capons and roast it well. Take anise and grains of paris, ginger, cinnamon and a little crust of bread, and grind it small, and grind it up with verjuice and the fat of the capon. Boil it and serve it forth.'

There are recipes for green sauce – parsley, mint, garlic, a little serpell (wild thyme) and sage, with cinnamon, ginger, pepper, salt, saffron, bread, vinegar and wine – and for 'camelyn' (light brown) sauce – currants and nuts (unspecified) and bread.

SUBTLETIES

These were creations of crystallized sugar that could reach astonishing elaboration. In 1396 Lord Spencer entertained King Richard II to dinner. They were served: nine roast dishes, including boar's head and swans; while they were digesting those, two 'sotelteys'; eleven dishes including roast pig, venison, peacock and curlews, and then one 'sotelte'; fourteen dishes including 'dates in compost', violets, peacocks roasted 'endort' (gilded) and roast larks, followed by two 'sotelteys'.

But we don't know what they looked like. There is a recipe 'to make images in sugar'; 'if you will make any images or any other thing in sugar that is cast in moulds, seeth them in the same manner as the plate is'. Making 'plate' sugar was a complicated procedure involving caramelizing 'fair clarified sugar' until it turns yellow, then 'sett[ing] it on the fire again the maintenance of an Ave Maria', and pouring it onto a marble stone . . . I doubt whether the Cook would have been called on to make an 'image in sugar'.

Drink

The general drink was ale. Most households of any size made their own, every few days. The advantage of adding hops was that it produced a longer-lasting brew, but that was still in the future. Just as the City of London was almost neurotic in its quality control of the wine trade, it also supervised ale offered for sale, insisting that the cheap, thin ale selling at the controlled price of a halfpenny a gallon should be kept separate from thicker, more expensive ale selling at twice that price. This embargo may not have been strictly observed. The medieval mists swirling round Piers Plowman's visions occasionally part to disclose a pin-sharp scene of ordinary life; such was the alehouse described on pages 69–70 above. And here is the alehouse-keeper:

> 'Ye? Baw!' quoth a brewer, 'I will not be ruled,
> By Jesu! for all your jangling [arguing] with *Spiritus Iusticie*
>   [the Spirit of Justice],
> Nor after Conscience, by Christ! while I can sell
> Both dregs and draff [ale-leavings], and draw it at one hole –
> Thick ale and thin ale; for that is my kind,
> And not hakke after [grub about for] holiness – hold thy
>   tongue, Conscience!⁶

Back to *Curye on Inglische*; ale and wine for home consumption were often spiced.

For bragott (spiced ale): take eight gallons of good stale ale to one gallon of purified clean honey, and boil three gallons of ale with the honey. Before it begins to boil, do in the spicery [given in a previous recipe, but the amount blank in the recipe] cinnamon and galingale, grains of paris, and a little pepper, and make [a] powder, set it from the fire and stir it soft and let it cool, and strain it through a wide boulting cloth. Do it in a clean vessel and do good barm [yeast] above, and hang in a cloth the spicery in the ale and cover it well, and when it is fourteen nights old, drink thereof. Amen.'⁷ Perhaps the drinkers needed this blessing.

Clarrey (spiced wine, not to be confused with claret, the red wine from Bordeaux): the same spices and method as for bragott, but the amount of wine isn't stated.

Mede: 'take honey combis and put them into a great vessel and lay thereon grete sticks, and lay a weight thereon till it be run out as much as it will; and this is called live honey. And then take the aforesaid combs and seeth them in clean water, and boil them well. After press out thereto as much as you may and cast it into another vessel into hot water, and seeth it well and strain it well, and do thereto a quart of live honey, and then let it stand a few days well stoppered, and this is good drink.'[8]

Hippocras: 'take a half pound of dried cinnamon, a half pound of dried ginger, three ounces of 'grains' [probably cardamon], three ounces of long pepper, two ounces of cloves, two and a half ounces of nutmegs, two ounces of caraway [seeds], half an ounce of spikenard, two ounces of galingale, two pounds of sugar. Si deficiat [if is lacking] sugar, take a pottle of honey.'[9] This very highly spiced concoction doesn't state the amount of wine that is to be added. Perhaps it was a professional secret.

The word 'hippocras' is said to come from the hanging sleeves of someone called Hypocras. His sleeves lengthened to a long point, making a kind of bag if cut off at the wrist. The cook would hang a series of such bags in a row, each with a particular spice in it, so that the wine poured into the bag would take the flavour of that spice. If the cook misjudged the amount of cinnamon, for example, and put in too little, he could run the wine through it again; too much, and he could run the wine through all the other spices again and miss out the cinnamon. The valuable spices could be reused until their flavour had quite gone.

Bread

Bread was the staple of a medieval diet. In lordly English households a standard daily food ration for every individual was between two and three pounds of wheat bread, and about a gallon of ale. The monks of Westminster Abbey ate less bread, but still a startling amount to our eyes: each would consume a loaf weighing about two pounds, and worth three farthings, every day. Bread was normally made commercially. The bakers had been organized into a company as early as 1155. Each baker had to have his own seal, impressed on every loaf he sold. As well as the bakers' professional supervision, the City of London kept a watchful eye on the quality of the bread being sold. Every autumn, 'four discreet men' were chosen by the City to make the 'assize', or 'assay', of bread. The price was fixed for the coming year by a formula taking in the price they had paid for the wheat and other grains, a reasonable charge for labour and profit, and the weight of the loaves they had baked, presented 'while hot' to the mayor and aldermen at the Guildhall. Delicious though new bread is, they didn't have to eat them, just weigh them.

There were four categories. First there was 'wastel' bread, a biscuity loaf made from sieved flour, baked in a very hot oven. This was the kind Chaucer's Prioress fed, scandalously, to her pet dogs. 'French' bread, known as 'pouf', was in the same category. Then came 'white' or 'light' wheaten bread; and 'brown' bread, very coarse bread baked as horse food.

In 1381 London bakers were obliged to express their prices in farthings. To counter any plea that they 'had no change', the mayor had £80 worth of farthings specially minted.

In affluent households, a place setting for the main meal, at noon or later, was a cup for wine or ale, a spoon and a round of four-day-old 'trencher' bread, with sometimes a plate under it. The food, carved into bite-sized pieces according to elaborate rules, arrived on the diner's trencher, so that he need only pick it up with his fingers or the point of his own knife. A certain amount of gravy and sauce would soak into the trencher bread, which was given to the poor after the meal.

Feasts

Chaucer's Cook may not have had much experience of the great royal feasts with their elaborate ceremonies, although Chaucer himself, as a page and later an esquire in royal households, must have seen many. On 12 May 1366, for example, Edward III entertained the great officers of his Council to breakfast. The ceremonies would have begun with hand-washing. A page would present to each guest a bowl of warm water scented with rose petals or some other sweet-smelling perfume. With considerable dexterity he would pour the water over the diner's hands, catching it in the bowl below them. Then the diner could dry his hands on the towel slung over the page's shoulder, and take his proper place at table. The total cost of this particular feast, including the 'boat carriage by John the Cook', was £9 4s 1d. Six shillings were spent on bread. Two calves cost 9 shillings, two sheep 8 shillings, a lamb cost 1s 4d, other poultry included ten bitterns 33s 4d. The fish course included a conger eel, costing 3s 4d, and a turbot, 3 shillings. Smoked salmon came in at 3 shillings. 'Various sauces' cost 8 pence, but 'various spices' much more, 4 shillings. They got through 30 gallons of good ale (tuppence per gallon), but wine doesn't feature in the detailed account, presumably because there was enough in the royal cellars without spending money on more. We don't know how many guests were catered for at that feast, unfortunately. It must have been quite a meal.

But the costs of Edward III's feast were modest compared to the meals enjoyed by some of the great guilds of London. The Goldsmiths' Company spent more than twice as much as their king three years later, in 1369, for their annual dinner to celebrate their patron saint, St Dunstan. The cost had somehow escalated from £4 in 1357 to over £21. The Goldsmiths were doing well then – perhaps better than the king. Another guild, the Salters', enjoyed a Christmas Pie in 1394:

Take pheasant, hare and chicken or capon, of each, one, with two partridges, two pigeons and two coneys and [bone them] and do them into a foyle [pastry case] with the livers and hearts, two sheep's kidneys, forced-meat, eggs. Add pepper, salt, strong vinegar and pickled mushrooms. [Make a broth of the bones, add it to the foyle and] close it up fast, and bake it well, and so serve it forth, with the head of one of the birds stuck at one end of the foyle and a great tail at the other, and divers of his long feathers cunningly [skilfully] all about him.

'The present [1834] cook of the Company tried out the recipe and found it excellent.'[10]

Even grander feasts might include peacocks still wearing their gorgeous plumage. The effect was achieved by skinning the bird carefully and roasting the carcase, then dressing it again in its feathered skin, spreading out its magnificent tail feathers. Just as well that the peacock was thought to be 'self-preserving': even if the surface flesh was mouldy, the meat under it was still edible. Swans could have similar treatment. A modern cookery writer noted that swan tasted 'very fishy, rather stringy and reminiscent of moorhen'.[11] Perhaps she was unlucky – the Monk of the *Canterbury Tales* loved 'a fat swan . . . best of any roast'.

Food Colourants

The medieval eye was pleased by colours. Saffron has a distinctive taste, and produces a deep yellow if enough is used – it is very expensive for its weight, consisting of the pollen on the stamens of a special type of crocus. It grew in the Abruzzi Mountains near Aquila, so its journey through Europe to London was comparatively simple. Saffron Walden, in Essex, may have been growing saffron as early as 1400, but some historians date its introduction to England later. Blue could be made from powdered lapis lazuli in very plutocratic kitchens, or woad or indigo – both vegetable sources – in more normal ones. Woad needs a lot of leaves to make a good blue. One wonders what effect a bunch of woad leaves had on the taste buds; but it could be bought from Amiens as cakes of dried leaves and crumbled into the mix. Red came from the roots of madder, a vegetable dye, or sanders. Green was easy – parsley or sorrel leaves. The pallid flesh of pounded chicken could be transformed by colours.

Spices

Spices were an important part of medieval cookery. We take them for granted, and often taste them ready-mixed in our commercially produced food. The Middle Ages saw them as mysterious and precious. Herodotus, writing in about 450 BC, gave a useful account of cassia and its close relative cinnamon:

> [The Arabians] wrap their whole bodies and faces, except for their eyes, in ox-hide and other leathers, and then go out after cassia. The cassia grows in a shallow lake in and around which roost winged creatures which most closely resemble bats. These creatures emit a dreadful shriek and are very aggressive. The Arabians have to guard their eyes against them while they gather the cassia.
>
> The way they gather cinnamon is even more extraordinary... they say that the sticks which the Phoenicians... call cinnamon are carried by large birds to their nests which are built of mud plastered onto crags on sheer mountains where no man may climb... [the Arabians] cut up the bodies of dead yoke-animals... into very large pieces... and dump the pieces near the nests and withdraw... The birds fly down and carry the pieces of meat back to their nests, but the pieces are too heavy for the nests [and] the nests break and fall to the ground, where the Arabians come and get what they came for... from there it is sent all over the world.

In more enlightened times cassia was known to be found only in the nests of phoenixes. But more modern, medieval sources attributed cinnamon, with cloves, to the 'Spice Islands' of the Far East, making their complicated journey to English kitchens via Arab and Gujarati traders to Beirut and Alexandria, and thence in Venetian galleys, often hired by merchants from the Italian city-state of Lucca.

The principal spice of the Middle Ages was certainly pepper. It had the merit of being light for its value, and easily packed in camel bags and seagoing vessels – an ideal stuff to smuggle, well known to those Luccese merchants. It always found a ready market, since as well as adding a tang to otherwise bland food, it offset the salt which was so widely used to preserve foodstuffs. It had been imported from India to the west for 4,000 years. The Egyptian embalmers used peppercorns to shape the royal nose of Rameses II in 1213 BC. The Romans used it as a panacea for all ills, even impotence.

By the time a spice arrived in a London kitchen it might have lost much of its potency, from being harvested or packed carelessly in its country of origin and having suffered during the long journey by sea and land, through various hands. Again, the experienced cook would rely on his nose. As well as the spices for making hippocras, the cook would keep at least a day's supply of spices for frequently cooked recipes, ready pounded or powdered, in small leather pouches within easy reach.[12] The stock of a London grocer in 1399 included 159½ pounds of pepper – an inconceivable amount, considering how light pepper is – at 10½ pence a pound, 24 pounds of ginger and 100 pounds of almonds.

Ingredients

There were more wild birds on the market – although who would want to eat a thrush, let alone a bittern, or a bustard, or a cormorant, or a spoonbill? Wild boar and deer roamed the forests, under royal protection. The traditional boar's head on the Christmas table, and the venison enjoyed by royal guests, must have been given by the monarch, or legally marketed by royal foresters. They would provide a splendid feast. Even the entrails – 'umbles' – were used in pies (the 'h' of 'eating humble pie' is an incorrect Victorian usage). But you might search in vain, in your plateful of umble pie, for a stag's testicle: they were reserved for the noble hunter who had brought the animal down. Farmed animals were about the same as ours, but smaller. Cows tended to be dual purpose, giving both milk and meat. Offal and giblets were never discarded; every part of the animal was used, except – according to the hoary old joke – the pig's whistle.

'Strong' vinegar used up wine that had 'gone off'. Verjuice was similar.

Cow's milk was tricky to cook with, since it soured quickly

pia iunta remanert in dentium
quno fcipit· s· e· ueineus·
diffe
tur

Before she was rudely interrupted, this spinster was busy with her spinning wheel, turning it with one hand while drawing the thread with the other. Note the man's purse slung from his belt, before built-in pockets were invented.

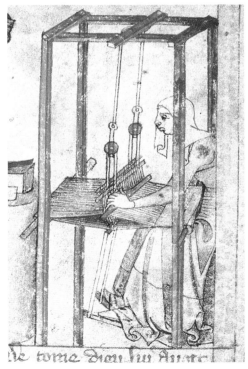

Her sister is operating a treadle-powered loom, a design that lasted for centuries until the advent of steam power and factories in the Industrial Revolution.

It takes two men to plough, one to guide the plough and the other
to control the pulling animals. Oxen are giving way to horses.

The farm bailiff supervises the harvesters. He can call attention to his
orders, by the horn at his side. The stubble left by the reapers is valuable
food for the farm livestock.

Once the corn has been dried and threshed, it is loaded onto a farm cart pulled by horses, to be taken to the mill and ground into flour. Note the iron cogs on the cart wheels, giving a better grip on slippery ground.

Traditional mills use water power to turn the mill stones. The water pressure could be increased by compressing the millstream into a narrow leet, or channel. Here, there are fish nets and eel traps in the pool after the water has turned the wheel.

On a hill, the power of wind could be used to drive the machinery. The ladle in the miller's belt may signify a false measure, for which millers were notorious. He loads a sack of flour onto a woman's back, while a more fortunate man rides towards the mill with his flour sack ready.

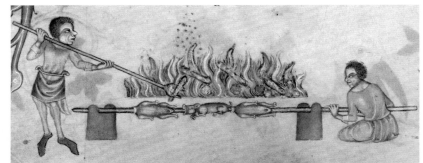

Cooking. Meat and poultry could be roasted on a spit in front of an open fire, or boiled in a cauldron. Ingredients were often 'pounded' (pulverized) by using a pestle and mortar. The artist has let his imagination run away with him here; this pestle looks more like a pile-driver than a kitchen implement.

A rich household at dinner. The table is a board resting on trestles, so that it could be folded away after the meal. The kneeling boy is the page who will have washed the diners' hands for them, and dried them on the cloth seen over his shoulder. Even in an affluent household, the tableware is simple.

There were several variants
of the modern violin, played in
different ways. See also the figure
in the margin of Plate 4.

A winetasting.
A vintner and his customer try
a wine, while a serving man taps
another barrel in the cellar.

This organ is powered by two hand-held bellows.

Medicine relied on astrology. Here, a physician consults the moon and stars, and is in touch with a demon. Every part of the body had its own zodiacal sign. Surgeons, however, were more down-to-earth. They had developed advanced techniques and instruments to perform at least some operations.

Dentists could do little other than extractions. This practitioner is applying silver forceps. (The silver has discoloured over time.) The necklace of previous patients' teeth advertises his skill.

Blood-letting was a favourite therapy.

No medicine could cure the Black Death of 1348. Here, mourners bring coffins faster than the sextons can bury them.

Two serjeants-at-law argue a case before two judges. The white coifs (close-fitting bonnets) they wear are the distinctive uniform of these high-ranking barristers. Their affluence can be judged from the fur linings of their robes. That pattern of white and blue represents the most expensive fur, miniver.

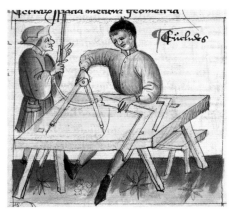

A carpenter at work. Most buildings were built on timber frames that could be assembled off-site, taken apart for transport and reassembled on-site. The carpenter was the most important craftsman, often acting as project manager.

Dyers at work. There was a tradition that Jesus was apprenticed to a dyer when he was a lad.

and, more importantly, it couldn't be used used in cooking on the numerous fasting days when animal products were forbidden. Almonds and walnuts made a liquid 'milk' which was much more amenable than cow's milk, and could be ingested by even the most rigorous faster. Almonds were imported from southern Europe in vast quantities. They were shelled, blanched and skinned, then ground up with wine, water or light stock. Three ounces of blanched almonds would make a pint of almond milk.

Figs were imported from Malta, dates and raisins from Damascus. Sugar from Sicily was preferable to honey as a sweetener in aristocratic kitchens, since it could be confected into those impressive 'subtleties'.

Anything grown in England was sold only in its natural season. Green peas were eaten raw and delicious – no one thought of cooking them. Other vegetables were being grown in a garden in Stepney by Henry Daniel, a contemporary of Chaucer. He recommended turnips, borage, mallows and orach for pottage, the kind of food the ordinary man depended on. Chestnuts could be roasted, and parsnip, that 'wholesome food', could be both baked and fried.

'Greek' wine may have come from Italy. Petrarch, the Italian poet who was almost exactly Chaucer's contemporary, wrote a *Guide to the Holy Land* in about 1357. It takes the form of a letter to a Milanese friend who had suggested that they should go on pilgrimage to the Holy Land together. Petrarch demurred – he hated sea travel as he was always seasick. But he gave his friend a detailed itinerary of the coast of Italy going south from Genoa, which he obviously knew well, dealing with the rest of the journey so fast that his friend would barely have had time to draw breath, let alone to worship at the holy places. After 'the hill of Falernus, worthy of note for its beautiful vineyard', his imaginary traveller reaches Naples and Mount Etna, which 'is marvellously abundant with wine', which is called 'Greek' because this part of Italy was possessed by the Greeks and was once called Magna Graecia. It seems plausible, and comes from an unimpeachable source.

Chaucer described the Doctor of Physic as knowing all about humours.[13] This complicated theory applied to diet as well as to medicine. *The Forme of Curye* was 'compiled by assent and avyssment of masters of physic and of philosophy', philosophy then meaning what we would call science. Thus beef, a 'dry' meat, should always be boiled, never roasted, whereas pork, being 'moist', should be roasted, and fish, being 'cool' and 'moist', should be fried. This knowledge constituted a large part of the cook's profession,[14] although one wonders whether it was universally followed in all its rigour; dietary rules do tend to slip, sometimes.

The Poor

Chaucer's Cook would not have had much sympathy with the very poor, who subsisted on bread made of bean flour and bran, or the kind of coarse bread made for horses, varied perhaps by the leftovers from rich men's tables thrown out by the servants, or – if they had some means of cooking – some stale fish from the fishmongers that would be unsaleable the next day. They probably drank the water flowing from the Great Conduit in Cheapside, or even the muddy water of the Thames.

X THE DOCTOR OF PHYSIC

With us there was a doctor of physic.
In all this world ne was ther noon him lik [there was no one
    like him]
To speak of physic and of surgery,
For he was grounded in astronomy.[1]

We are not told what he looked like, nor what he rode. He was
dressed in 'sangwin and ... pers ... lined with taffeta and with
sendal'. Sanguine was an expensive cloth dyed blood-red – a delicate echo of the medical fondness for blood-letting, perhaps. Pers
was another costly cloth, dyed either dark blue or a purplish blue.
Taffeta and sendal were silk fabrics of different weights. So you
could tell just by looking at him that he was prosperous.

More than eighty medical practitioners, both physicians and
surgeons, have been identified as practising in London during
Chaucer's lifetime, between 1340 and 1400. Fifteen of them held
appointments in royal households. Chaucer must have seen them
going on their rounds. Sir John Mandeville, whose book of *Travels*
was a medieval bestseller, was commemorated on his tombstone
as 'the gentle Sir John de Mandeville, knight ... born in England,
practitioner of medicine'. Some qualified physicians were monks in
the Abbey of Westminster. Others were employed by the City of
London, either full-time or ad hoc.

Astronomy

It is the invariable habit of anyone meeting a doctor of medicine socially to ask for advice – free, of course – about the twinge he had, definitely, last Thursday – or was it Friday? Chaucer's pilgrims were bound to be tempted, as they rode along, but perhaps the Doctor's aspect was sufficiently forbidding to deter them. In any case they were unlikely to have with them that essential prerequisite for diagnosis – their horoscope, giving the position of the stars and planets at the exact time of their birth. A medieval physician needed the patient's astronomical details, just as a modern GP would check his or her blood pressure.

'The exact time' sounds simple, with second hands on our watches and time measured electronically, but how did Chaucer's contemporaries manage? Curfew was rung from various churches. There were large striking clocks in the Palace of Westminster and in other royal palaces. Most religious buildings had clocks which alerted a monk or nun to strike a bell to signal the proper time for a religious observance. It would be unlikely that their chimes were synchronized; more probably the ear would be assaulted, in London at least, by a constant jangle of bells. Adding to the confusion, there were two different ways of measuring an hour. You could either use the solar time-keeping, with long summer days and long winter nights, or you could divide the hours equally throughout the twenty-four hours, which would mean that seven o'clock in the morning would be the same, summer and winter, light or dark. There was no general agreement.

If a midwife decided to rely on the clock striking the hour at the Palace of Westminster, she should still ascertain the minute, even the second, when the baby she had delivered was born; this in the middle of all the fuss and commotion attending a birth. Minutes could be measured by reciting the Lord's Prayer in English, or more probably in Latin, the Pater Noster (see p. 103). The Pater Noster takes just about thirty seconds, so to measure several minutes there would be a constant mutter of prayer greeting the newborn, unless of course the midwife or some other person in the birthing chamber took a strong line and settled on a time that seemed auspicious. Then it only needed someone to make a record of this precious fact, and see that it was kept safely. The days of recording family births, deaths and marriages in the family Bible were far distant.

Once a physician knew the time of his patient's birth he knew where to start, by computing the position of the heavenly bodies at birth and at the onset of the ailment. He might have with him, slung from his belt (pockets hadn't yet been invented), a neat little ready reckoner of folded parchment, correlating the position of the sun and moon at the onset of the illness with the planet governing the part of the body affected. A headache should be referred to Aries. Taurus governed the neck, Gemini the chest, Cancer the lungs, Leo the stomach, Virgo the abdomen, Libra the lower abdomen, Scorpio the penis and testicles, Sagittarius the thighs, Capricorn the knees, Aquarius the calves and Pisces the ankles. The colour of the patient's urine could also be relevant – any physician worth his salt would carry a shade card to match against the patient's sample. Thus armed, the physician could make his diagnosis and advise on treatment, including the best day for blood-letting.

The Humours

As well as his knowledge of astronomy, Chaucer's Doctor

> . . . knew the cause of every malady,
> Were it of hot or cold or moist or dry,
> And where engendered and of what humour[.][2]

There were four 'humours', choler, sanguine, black bile and yellow bile, which in the ideal man were perfectly balanced. It was the task of the expert physician to adjust any imbalance. This may explain the fondness of medieval doctors, and their successors for generations to come, for blood-letting: ridding the body of an excess of blood could do nothing but good. 'Purging' by laxatives could be useful too, and drugs to induce vomiting.

The theory of humours had begun with Aristotle (384–322 BC), who postulated four elements in the cosmos. Long before Chaucer's time it had spawned a complicated set of rules. Chaucer reels off a list – a favourite device of medieval writers – of the ancient Greek scientists:

> Well knew he the old Esculapius,
> And Deiscorides, and eek Rufus,
> Old Ipocras, Haly, and Galien
> Serapion, Razis and Avicen,
> Averrois, Damascien and Constantin,
> Bernard, and Gatesden and Gilbertin.[3]

'Esculapius', or Asclepius, was the ancient Greek god of medicine. 'Old' here means ancient, less matey than 'old' nowadays. Dioscorides flourished in AD 50; he wrote various medical textbooks. Rufus of Ephesus lived in the second century. Hippocrates lived between 460 and 375 BC, and gave his name to the Hippocratic Oath which some medical graduates still swear. 'Haly' was probably a Persian physician, writing in Arabic, who died in AD 994.[4] 'Galien', or Galen, was the presiding genius of medieval and early modern medicine. Serapion was another Arabic writer. 'Razis' (Rhazes, c.AD 854–925) was the greatest clinician of Islam and the Middle Ages. 'Avicen' (Avicenna, AD 980–1037) wrote *Canon of Medicine* and *Book of Healing*; he was almost as influential on western philosophy as Aristotle. 'Averrois' (Averroes, AD 1126–98) was the link between Muslim philosophy and Christian thought. Johannes Damascenus, St John of Damascus, wrote in the eighth century. Constantine was another link between Islamic learning and Christian thought.

Chaucer added three Europeans, Bernard de Gordon, a Scot, who had taught medicine in Salerno, the leading medieval university, in 1300; Gilbertus Anglicus (1180–1250) and John of Gaddesden (1280–1361).

Fourteenth-Century Diagnostics

John of Gaddesden held priestly office in St Paul's Cathedral from 1342, so Chaucer may have known him. He wrote *Rosa Anglica*, purporting to be a compendium of all current medical knowledge.

Rosa Anglica is a curious work. In part it is a serious examination of the ancient Greeks' medical theories. Gaddesden was a scholar and then a teacher at Merton College, Oxford, at that time the only English centre of learning offering a medical qualification. He would have followed the normal seven-year course of trivium and quadrivium, just as any student at Oxford University did, for which see pages 211–13, the Clerk of Oxenford. He would have imbibed a thorough knowledge of Aristotle's teaching during that time. He would also have imbibed the mental habit of disputing – stating the view of each opposing party to a debate, and finding a means of reconciling them. When Gaddesden is at his best, he quotes Avicenna and Galen, who held different views on the technique of blood-letting, for example, and then finds a tidy way to blend the two.

But as a handbook of popular medicine his *Rosa Anglica* leaves much to be desired. From time to time he deserts the ancients and strikes out on his own, with remarkable results. He subscribed to the medieval policy of polypharmacy – chucking in some-times dozens of ingredients on the principle that some of them were bound to do you good, ignoring the possibility that some of them might be toxic. As well as 'fistfuls' and 'half-handfuls' of miscellaneous greenery, ivory shavings cropped up quite often, sometimes having been burned first. The genitals of a cockerel might come in useful, if you could find them. Breast milk should be drunk 'from the breast by sucking, and if this be loathsome to the patient [regardless of the feelings of the donor] let him take it as hot as possible'. Cat lovers would be horrified by Gaddesden's recommendation of an 'astringent bath: take young cats, cut their entrails out, and put their extremities [paws and tail?] with [various herbs], boil in water and bathe the sick man in it'. Another feline recipe: put 'the lard' of a black cat, and of a dog, into the belly of a previously eviscerated and flayed black cat, and roast it; collect the 'juice' and rub it on the sick limb. 'The comfort derived therefrom is marvellous.' A specific for nervous disease is the brain of a hare. If the hunting party kills a fox instead, they could boil it up and use the resulting broth for a massage.

Treatment for a paralysed tongue sounds more cheerful: rub it with what the translator called 'usquebaugh', i.e. whisky; 'it restores the speech, as has been proved on many people'. Animal and avian droppings found many uses, such as peacocks' droppings for a boil. A cowpat made a good poultice, with added herbs. For those who could afford them, gold and silver and pearls, both bored and unbored, were bound to increase the efficacy of the medicine. Gaddesden recommended his own electuary, using eighteen ingredients including burnt ivory and unbored pearls, with a pound of (very expensive) sugar; 'I have often proved its goodness myself.'

In a final flourish, he suggests putting the heart of a robin redbreast round the neck of a 'lethargic' patient, to keep him awake, or hanging the same heart, with an owl's heart, above an amnesiac patient; it will 'give [his memory] back to him'. Even better, the heart of a swallow cooked in honey 'compels him who eats it to tell all things that happened' in the past, and to predict the future.

And yet, before you dismiss Gaddesden as a charlatan or a lunatic, remember that he was entrusted by King Edward II with the care of his son when the boy caught smallpox, although the therapy seems surprising. 'I permitted only red things to be about his bed, by the which I cured him, without leaving a trace of the smallpox pustules on him.'[5]

Apothecaries

Chaucer's Doctor was well organized:

> Full ready had he his apothecaries
> To send him drugs, and his letuaries [potions],
> For each of them made [the] other for to win –
> His friendships nas nat [were not] new to begin.[6]

Chaucer did not suggest how the Doctor's friendly apothecaries dealt with the gold and silver sometimes required in Gaddesden's prescriptions, beyond noting that 'gold in physic is a cordial; / Therefore he loved gold in special'. It seems to have been a win-win situation between the two professions. Was there a veiled hint that the Doctor and his apothecaries operated a price-fixing ring? Perhaps; but the mutual reliance between physician and apothecary was normal. Geoffrey Galfridus, a physician who was retained by Westminster Abbey from 1393 to 1409, was notably exceptional in supplying his own medicines.

Any apothecary worth his salt would have in stock a supply of the standard mixtures. The *Antidotarium Nicholai* (Nicholaus's Compound Medicines) was composed in Salerno in the twelfth century, and reigned supreme on apothecaries' shelves for many centuries. The most well known was theriac, *Tyriaca magna Galeni*, sometimes misguidedly translated as treacle. It contained sixty-one ingredients, of varying price and rarity. Mummy, for example, came from Egypt, as the tattered remains of excavated mummies.[7] Theriac was 'made against the most serious diseases of the whole human body', including leprosy and snakebite, in various dosages. One version of it added one dram of *Esdra magna*, itself a compound containing over a hundred ingredients, invented by the prophet Esdra while he was a prisoner in Babylon. At this stage, if not before, the optimistic customer as he watched his bill soar surely began to doubt the efficacy of the potion he was seeking. But, undeterred, he might invest in *Unguentum album* or white ointment, 'good for salty phlegm', which was mostly various highly toxic forms of lead, or *Unguentem aureum*, 'especially good against kidney stones', a comparatively innocuous blend of over forty herbs, plus bear fat, fox fat, 'petroleum'(?) and 'oil and wax as needed'. A woman might be attracted to *Oleum rosaceum*, 'the best thing for head pains or from the heat of the sun', which used 'slightly crushed fresh roses'. In every case the exact amounts are set out, although whether each apothecary followed the directions meticulously would never be known to his customers.

Surgery

The Doctor was versed in surgery as well as 'physic'. An English surgeon, John of Arderne, wrote *Treatises of Fistula in Ano* in English in 1376. His view of a surgeon's life contains some very practical career advice to his fellow-practitioners, some of which could be useful to medical practitioners nowadays:

First, it behoves a surgeon who wishes to succeed in this craft always to put God first in all his doings... and sometimes to give of his earnings to the poor... The study of books is of great advantage to the surgeon, both by keeping him occupied and by making him wiser. Above all, it helps him much to be found always sober... If he does undertake a case, he should make a clear agreement about payment and take the money in advance... If he sees that the patient is eager for the cure then [he] must boldly adjust his fee to the man's status in life... beware of asking too little, for this is bad both for the market and the patient. Therefore for a case of fistula in ano, when it is curable, the surgeon may reasonably ask of a great man... £40, with robes, and fees to the value of 100 shillings each year for the rest of his life...

And if the patient or his friends ask how long the cure will take, the surgeon had better always say twice as long as he really thinks... for if the patient should ask later why the surgeon estimated so long for recovery when he was able to cure the patient in half the time, the surgeon should answer that it was because the patient had a strong heart and bore pain well, and that he was of good complexion [that is, having such a combination of the four humours as would speed recovery]... and he must think of other causes that would please the patient...

A surgeon should always be soberly dressed... rather after the manner of a cleric, for any discrete man clad in cleric's dress may sit at a gentleman's table. A surgeon must also have clean hands and well-shaped nails, free of dirt... It is also expedient for the surgeon to be able to tell good honest tales that may make the patient laugh.

£40 was a huge amount then, about the annual salary of a middle-ranking bureaucrat. 'Robes' suitable to the recipient's status were frequently included as part of remuneration. The insistence on cleanliness contrasts markedly with the nineteenth-century careless-ness about operating conditions, in which a coat stiff with blood and pus from previous operations was a prestigious badge of the surgeon's busy practice.

Another picture of the ideal surgeon was written by the Milanese surgeon Lanfranc in his *Science of Surgery*, which was available in London, in translation from Latin into Middle English, from at least 1380 or earlier. He argued that surgery was 'a medicinal sci-ence, which teaches us to work with [our] hands in [a] man's body, with cutting or opening the parts that are whole and in healing those that are broken'. After a lengthy exposition of the theory of humours, he recommended a 'temperate complexion' for a surgeon. 'A surgeon must have well-shaped, long, slender fingers.' His body should not be 'quaking'. He must be intelligent – 'of subtle wit . . . for everything that belongs to surgery may not be written with letters. He must study in all the parts of philosophy, and logic . . . grammar . . . art . . . rhetoric . . . He should not give advice unless asked . . . He should speak courteously to the sick man, and predict his recovery though he despairs of him. But tell his friends the case as it stands . . . he should help poor men . . . and from rich men he should ask a good reward.' He deplored the practice of leaving surgery 'to labourers and *to women* [my italics]. Galen and Rasis did it [i.e. operated] with their hands, as their books tell', the implica-tion being that manual dexterity would not exclude its owner from professional status. A clumsy surgeon would never get anywhere.

Lanfranc gave detailed instructions for all kinds of minor surgery. To remove cataracts, for example, 'First, make the sufferer sit on a stool in front of you, and you shall sit a little higher than him. Bandage his good eye tightly . . . Have in your mouth a few sprigs of fennel. Chew them a little and blow into his eye two or three breaths, so that the fume of the fennel is forced into his eye.' Then use a silver needle to drain the fluid in the eye... and so on; the description is not improved by passing through the hands of non-medically qualified translators. But the absence of any anaesthetic is striking, unless the surgeon's fennel-imbued breath was enough to dull sensation.

An effective anaesthetic was available. Dwale would 'make a man sleep while men operate on him. Take the gall of a boar, or, for a woman, a splayed sow, and three spoonfuls of the juice of hemlock', adding wild briony, lettuce, opium poppy, henbane and vinegar. Boil it all up and store it in a tightly stoppered glass vessel. When needed, 'add three spoonfuls of this mixture to a pottle of good wine or good ale... let the man who is to be operated on sit by a good fire and make him drink of the potion until he falls asleep. And then men may safely operate on him. And when he has been fully served and you want him to wake, take vinegar and salt and wash well his temples and cheeks and he shall wake at once.' One cannot help adding – 'if at all'.

London surgeons had long struggled to differentiate themselves from barbers, who took on blood-letting, dentistry and minor surgery as sidelines. They had had some success. The Guild of Surgeons in London was established in 1368. The next year John Donhed was admitted, with two colleagues, as Masters in the guild. They swore a formal oath before the mayor and aldermen of the city:

> that they would well and faithfully save [serve] the people, in
> undertaking their cures ['cure' then meant care, therapy, not heal-
> ing], would take reasonably for them [charge reasonable fees] and
> would faithfully follow their calling, and would present to the said
> Mayor and Aldermen the defaults of others undertaking cures,
> so often as should be necessary, and that they would be ready at
> all times where they should be warned, to attend the maimed or
> wounded, and other persons, and would give truthful information
> to such maimed, wounded and others, whether they be in peril
> of death or not, etc. And also faithfully to do all other things
> touching their calling.[8]

By 1390 the oath in an amended form provided for the 'faithful oversight of all others, both men *and women* [my italics], occupied in cures or using the art of surgery'.

The oath drafted by Hippocrates had had slightly different priorities. The trainee medic had to undertake to keep his professor and his professor's family for the rest of their lives after he qualified, and he should not interfere with slaves. But the general principle, professional responsibility, was the same. Professional status carried with it certain duties, such as giving expert evidence in trials. In a case alleging medical negligence in 1354, three surgeons were called to give evidence. Eleven years later three more 'sworn surgeons to the City' testified that 'Giles Pykeman... was not in danger of death', presumably in some criminal case which depended on the severity of an injury inflicted by the accused.

Even outside a court of law, it would be useful to the physician, if not to the patient, to know whether the patient was likely to survive. One way of telling, popular among the aristocracy for diagnosis as well as prognosis, was to put a caladrius bird (perhaps related to our little ringed plover, Charadrius dubius) on the patient's bed, facing the patient, and watch how it reacted. According to a thirteenth-century bestiary, 'if the man is destined to die, it turns its face away from him... if he is destined to live, it directs itself towards his face, and as though it would take all the illness of the man on itself it flies into the air towards the sun, burning up as it were his infirmity and so the sick man is cured'. In humbler circles, a lettuce tisane could be useful – if it made the patient vomit, he was marked for death. Or add the sick man's urine to a woman's breast milk. 'If the milk falls down he shall die and if it floats above he shall live.'

Mental Illness

Mental illness is never easy to diagnose or to treat. The Muslim therapy prescribed peace, quiet and the sound of running water, which seems enviable compared to the western technique. There is an unnerving picture in one of the windows in Canterbury Cathedral of a madman being brought there for the saint to cure him.

As he staggers along, his 'friends' are beating him energetically, in no doubt well-meaning efforts to rid him of his affliction. Alternatively the shock of having a freshly killed bird upended on his head might be salutary as the blood ran down the sufferer's face, but could have tipped him into further madness.[9]

Perhaps, if he had a choice, he would have preferred a stay in London's only dedicated mental hospital, out beyond Bishopsgate. It had been founded in 1247 as the Priory of St Mary of Bethlehem as a hostel for pious travellers, probably with a small infirmary for the sick. It was soon renamed by Londoners 'Bethlem', or 'Bedlam'. By 1377 its patients included 'distracted' people, who were receiving the standard medieval treatment for mental illness – shackles, whips and ducking, a regime which will surely have ended their miserable lives prematurely. By 1403 most of its inmates were mentally ill, but when the changeover occurred, from the original purpose of the foundation to the exclusive care of the mentally ill, is not possible to trace. The alternative to Bedlam, custody within the family circle, may not always have been a good idea. Sometime in 1340 Alice, the wife of Henry de Warewyk, 'who for the last half year had been non compos mentis ... opened the door and ran by herself in a wild state to the port [quay] of Dowgate and threw herself into the Thames and was drowned'.

The Monasteries

Monasteries generally maintained infirmaries for the sick, where their souls could be cared for as well as their bodies. The Abbey of Westminster had been founded in the late tenth century. The infirmarer, a learned monk, had oversight of the abbey's provision for the sick poor. In 1357 the infirmarer was assisted by a physician who was paid £2 13s 4d a year. He (sometimes 'she') would usually diagnose and prescribe treatment, but any necessary surgery would be carried out by a surgeon. The monks' own ailments included 'morbus in tibia', probably varicose vein ulcers brought on by prolonged standing during divine offices. The usual treatment for their ill heath was a special diet and blood-letting. The medicines prescribed were unlikely to have had any beneficial effect on the patient. More effective was probably a period of convalescence in one of the abbey's country properties in Hendon or Hampstead.

Two monastic hospitals still exist, after various changes. St Thomas's Hospital was founded in about 1106, probably as part of the Priory of St Mary Overie, Southwark. St Bartholomew's Hospital and Priory were founded by Rahere, an Augustinian monk, in 1123, just outside the city walls, where a master presided over three brothers (monks) and three sisters (nuns).

Charitable donors helped to make the conditions in monastic wards marginally more comfortable. In 1349 William de Elsing, a mercer, left property to maintain a hospital for the 'poor, blind and indigent of both sexes, under the direction of a Prior . . . and he wills that no one else whatsoever, ecclesiastics or secular, shall intermeddle with the said hospital' – an early reference to hospital mismanagement? William de Rothyng, a merchant, left money to St Thomas's Hospital 'for the maintenance of a lamp to burn by night among the weak and sickly there housed', which must have been a great comfort to a sick person during long sleepless nights.

Common Diseases

Leprosy was still ravaging Europe. The only treatment was to isolate the sufferers. They had been banished from London in 1346. At least they had a refuge, in the Hospital of St Giles (later known as St Giles in the Fields), just outside the city bounds. There was another 'lazar-house' in Hackney. But sufferers from this terrible disease didn't always stay away from their usual haunts. In 1372 John Mayn, a baker, was ordered by the mayor and aldermen to leave London 'and provide for himself some dwelling outside it [they don't say how] and avoid the common conversation of mankind, seeing that he was smitten with the blemish of leprosy'. The plight of lepers often attracted legacies by charitably minded testators, in the form of Masses for their souls or, more pragmatically, contributions to the 'almsboxes for lepers around London'.

There were the usual fevers, some probably malarial. Cancer was known and recognized, and incurable. Strokes, then called 'paralysis', were irreversible. Miscellaneous lumps and bumps caused by tumours and abscesses could sometimes be lanced, with a good chance of success. Lanfranc proudly related how he cured a woman who had an abscess in her throat when a pupil of his, whose patient she was, had given up on her. He lanced it and put a silver tube down her throat, which probably saved her life, and certainly added to his professional reputation.

There is an interesting remedy for the common cold: 'Take a red onion, cut it up small, boil it in a little clary [sweetened spiced wine] . . . add a little honey . . . add a spoonful of mustard and boil a long time. Lay the patient on his back, put a little of the mixture up his nose, and let him stand up and sneeze. Do this twice a day for three days and he will be well.'

Most home remedies relied on common herbs, with perhaps some alcohol, and faith. A scalded penis (how could this happen?) called for the ashes of burned cloth, on a linen bandage. For snakebite, 'take thine own piss and drink it and thou shalt drink thy venom'. Anyone bitten by a mad dog should drink powdered flax seed in holy water; perhaps one ought to have these to hand, in case of sudden need. Burned slugs could 'break' a boil. A good ointment for the gout begins: 'take an owl and pull off the feathers and take out all that is inside it'.

Toothache can be wretched. It can certainly feel as if there are worms in your teeth. To get rid of them, 'take the seed of henbane and the seed of leeks, and incense, and put these three things upon a hot glowing tilstoun [a stone that had been heated in the fire] and make a pipe that hath a wide end and hold it over the smoke [so] that it may rise through the pipe into thy teeth and it shall slay the worms and do away with the ache'. Another used different ingredients but the same technique of inhaling medicated vapour 'and you shall see the worms falling out of your teeth'. 'For yellow and stinking teeth' an ointment of sage and salt used as a mouthwash every morning 'shall make them white and sweet breathed'.

The Royal Touch

But if all else failed there remained one sovereign remedy: the royal Touch. It can be traced back to King Edward the Confessor, who ruled from 1042 to 1066, and died just before the Norman invasion. The title of 'Confessor' was conferred on him posthumously in 1161, when the pope confirmed his canonization. ('Confessor' meant one who openly avowed or 'confessed' his faith, not someone who admitted his sins.) The doctrine drew its inspiration from a passage in Mark 16:18, or in Wycliffe's Bible, which is not divided into verses, at the end of that chapter. After the death of Jesus, He appeared to the disciples and reproved them for their 'unbelief'. In Wycliffe's version:

> He said unto them, Go ye into the world and preach the gospel to each creature. Who that believes and is baptized is safe. But he that believes not shall be damned. And these tokens shall sue [follow] them that believe. In my name they shall cast out fiends. They shall speak with new tongues. They shall do [put] away serpents. And if they drink any venom, it shall not noy [hurt] them. They shall set their hands on sick men, and they shall wax whole.

To a cynical unbeliever this seems a flimsy foundation for a doctrine that assisted both the English monarchy and the French monarchy for centuries. It reached its apogee with Charles II, who relied on it to demonstrate the legality of his newly restored kingship. He Touched 4,500 annually. He may even have believed in it. His predecessor St Edward the Confessor is said to have Touched over 1,700 subjects annually, whenever his absence on military service overseas permitted. In 1340, when Edward III claimed to be the rightful king of France, he challenged the incumbent, Philip VI, to 'stand the test of braving ravenous lions, who do not touch a true king, or perform the miracle of touching for the king's evil, as true kings are accustomed to do'. Not surprisingly, Philip declined.

Exactly what 'the 'king's evil' was seems to have varied. Medieval medicine was not so specific in its pathology as a modern clinician would expect. 'The king's evil' originally seems to have covered rheumatism, goitre, blindness and convulsions, as well as scrofula, a tuberculous infection of the lymph glands at the neck which can cause open sores if left untreated. This last is the meaning that persisted until the doctrine died a natural death under the Hanoverians. Whether the celebrant actually touched the sufferer or merely waved his/her hand nearby is equally unclear; I imagine that it would depend on the circumstances of each case. When St Francis of Assisi began his ministry, he did 'cleanse the lepers' with his own hands; whether a monarch felt equally obliged to make skin-to-skin contact, I doubt, and there is no contemporary account of the procedure. Three of the physicians listed by Chaucer referred to it, in slightly different terms. Gilbertus Anglicus said that it was called the king's evil because the king could cure it, but he didn't say how. Bernard Gordon's advice was that 'recourse must be had to the surgeon; or if not, we must approach the king'. John of Gaddesden had it the other way round – first try the king, and if that failed, go to a surgeon. Whether any of them was right is hard to tell.

The Great Pestilence

In 1348 a pandemic swept the known world. The Victorians, ever handy with a snappy caption, called it the Black Death. At the time, the English knew it as the 'Great Pestilence'. A contemporary chronicler, Henry Knighton, wrote that 'there was a general mortality of men throughout the world. It first began in India, then spread to Tarsis [Persia] thence to the Saracens [Muslims], and at last to the Christians and Jews.' It was the more terrifying because God was clearly angry, but with Christians as much as with infidels. No one, or everyone, was to blame. There was no remedy. Death came quickly, horribly and agonizingly.

The Ebola virus that ravaged West Africa in 2015 echoed some of the horror of the Great Pestilence 670 years ago. The medieval Pestilence left perhaps half the population alive when it had spent its extreme virulence. Ebola spared hardly a single sufferer. But at least it was more or less limited, or containable, in geographical extent, while the Pestilence spread its shadow over continents. There is one common, tragic factor. Before Ebola, it was the practice of African communities to mourn their dead with customary ceremonies and rites, washing the body with loving care and consigning it gently to the grave. During the epidemic, for good medical reasons, the infected body was abruptly removed by bearers in nightmarish bodysuits, to be wrapped in plastic and bundled into the ground as quickly as possible, away from the grieving community. For a medieval family, it would be unthinkable to omit the ceremonies of a 'good death'. The sick person must make a full confession of all his sins to an ordained priest, and express his repentance. Only then would the priest absolve him and solemnize the rites that would allow the dying man's soul to pass into purgatory and thence to heaven. Unshriven, the soul would be destined for everlasting hell. But priests themselves were victims of the Pestilence. God gave them no immunity. There were too few of them to attend every deathbed. The pope, recognizing this, allowed confession to be made to a lay person, even to a woman, if no ordained priest was available – a slight concession, but since no one but an ordained priest could celebrate the last rites, it cannot have been of much comfort to the dying or their family. Sometimes there was not even a gravedigger left alive to dig a grave. Bodies lay unburied in the fields till animals and birds picked the bones clean.

The Pestilence recurred at intervals throughout the fourteenth century, in 1361, 1369, 1375 and 1390, at times when the country was already under the stress of the French War. Cities were emptied of population, the countryside was desolate. Life did not begin to return to normal until about the time of Chaucer's death in 1400.

Women's Medicine

In 1200 Salerno, just south of Naples, had been the most respected school of medicine in Europe, but as Petrarch remarked in the following century, 'Salerno was the source of the study of medicine, but there is nothing that does not run dry over time.' In its heyday, it produced *The Trotula*. Trotula may have been a real-life female professor of obstetrics and gynaecology or a mythical figure, but in either case this collection of remedies loosely entitled 'Women's Medicine' circulated throughout Europe, including England, for the next three centuries.[10] It has gone through many shape changes, from Arabic to Latin to Middle English and many other medieval vernaculars, to modern English in Professor Monica H. Green's elegant translation. It comprised three works. *De Ornatu Mulierum* (*On Women's Cosmetics*) and *De Curis Mulierum* (*On Treatments for Women*) may not have been written by Trotula herself, they were just added to her work as time passed. The major part, *De Sinthomatibus Mulierum* (*On the Conditions of Women*) was written by Trotula. Most of the prescriptions in all three used herbs that grew freely in the Salernitan climate. Some of them would have been available in England, but only in summer, if at all. Copies of these manuscripts were unlikely to reach the hands of their ultimate customers, women; but perhaps women benefited indirectly from a quick reading of a copy by an infirmerar monk in his monastery. Of course, the monk may not have been all that interested in hair conditioners, let alone childbirth, but yet the manuscripts did survive in monastic libraries.

When I was transcribing the authentic cookery recipes in Chapter IX, I suggested that you might like to try some of the recipes yourself. I feel obliged to say here, of the medieval medical prescriptions in Trotula and elsewhere, *do not try any of them for anything at all* – they might seriously damage your health.

The Cosmetics book is the simplest. There are seventy numbered paragraphs. It begins: 'In order that a woman might become very soft and smooth and without hairs from her head down, first of all let her go to the baths, and if she is not accustomed to do so, let there be made for her a steambath in this manner.' So our saunas or Turkish baths would have been familiar to the Italian ladies.

When the woman has emerged from her steambath, the next step is a depilatory, of which there are six, scattered through the book. They deal with all body hair, including the pubic area. Next, hair conditioners (four) and dyes (thirteen). Six are to get a good black, including one which was 'a proven Saracen [Arab]' preparation. Another recommends: 'Take a green lizard and having removed its head and tail, cook it in common oil. Anoint the head with this oil. It makes the hair long and black.' Five are for 'golden' hair. One for 'whitening' the hair – very pale blonde? – is brief: 'Catch as many bees as possible in a new pot and set it to burn, and grind with oil, and then anoint the head.'

Next, the complexion. There are remedies for spots and sunburn, itchy places and 'worms of the face'. There are recipes for making the face white, or red (pink?), and four varieties of a soothing lip-stick. There are three remedies for bad breath, including a 'Saracen' one. There's a general face cream, and a herbal skin-peel. There are two recipes for 'whitening the teeth', including 'let her chew each day fennel or lovage or parsley which... cleans good gums and makes the teeth very white'. There are no recipes for deodorants – perhaps regular 'steambaths' were enough.

So far, so good, you may think – no more than might be found in any general advice on beauty care nowadays. But you are unlikely to find in a modern magazine three recipes 'so that a woman who has been corrupted [raped? trafficked?] might be thought to be a virgin'. She needed Armenian bole, a kind of clay which was com-monly available, and dragon's blood, which was not. But just the bole and oak apples might be enough to constrict the vagina and restore the semblance of virginity. The book then returns blandly to three complexion washes, and a pious prayer: 'Here ends Trotula. But thou, O Lord, have mercy upon us.'

De Curis Mulierum, at 110 paragraphs, is longer than *De Ornatu* but has the same discursive, chatty style. It begins rousingly:

In order that we may make a concise summary of the treatment of women, it ought to be noted that certain women are hot, while some are cold. In order to determine which, one should perform this test. We anoint a piece of lint with oil of pennyroyal or laurel or another hot oil, and we insert a piece of it the size of the little finger into the vagina at night when she goes to bed, and it should be tied round the thighs with a strong string. And if it is drawn inside, this is an indication to us that she labors from frigidity. If however it is expelled, we know that she labours from heat.

An appropriate 'fumigation' can be prescribed, in either case. Frigidity is 'better', since after the fumigation and a herbal pessary have 'cleaned out' the 'excessive abundance of humours, she is ready for conceiving'.

As she sat in her perforated chair being fumigated, the medieval woman must surely have wondered how her fellow-women managed to conceive and bear children, without all this carry-on; but they did not have the benefit of the latest medical advice, as she had, so she settled back into the aromatic steam and contemplated with mixed feelings the pleasures and pains of pregnancy and childbirth.

One prescription is metaphorically hair-raising; it is for the 'treatment of scabies in humans', thus including men. It was mostly mercury. 'Note that if anyone should anoint himself or herself with this ointment, let him/her keep cold water in his/her mouth, lest the teeth be damaged by the mercury, which flows around every which way.' It was certainly the case that mercury was used to treat skin lesions for many centuries, culminating in the 'mercury treatment' for syphilis in the eighteenth century, which may have alleviated the symptoms of the disease but loosened and blackened the teeth and had other dire effects. It is interesting to find a warning about it six centuries ago, though how one could stop mercury or mercurial vapour from attacking the teeth by holding a mouthful of cold water is hard to imagine.

The core of Trotula was *De Sinthomatibus Mulierum* (*On the Conditions of Women*). It opens with the big guns of medical theory – God, Galen and Hippocrates. God, the creator of the universe, made men hot and dry. The man is 'the stronger and more worthy person', therefore he should rule the woman, who is weaker, cold and humid. The man can balance his humours by hard physical work – we might say, 'working up a muck sweat'. Nocturnal emissions are also helpful. The woman has no such resources, so she has to be purged by menstruation. It is vital to her health to keep this cycle regular, interrupted only by pregnancy and ended only by the menopause. If the 'menses' are stopped for any other cause, or are excessive or insufficient, she risks serious illness, even death.

De Sinthomatibus, too, recommends a perforated chair, to deliver medicated smoke or steam to the womb via the vagina by 'suffu-migation'. Galen suggests a reed to conduct the steam directly into the vagina. Various herbs are prescribed to be burned or steamed under the unfortunate woman, depending on whether she is suf-fering from insufficient or excessive menses. She can look forward to vaginal pessaries and herbal drinks as well, after she has been fumigated. If her trouble is insufficient menses, and she has no fever, she should eat garlic and 'drink strong wine'. Sexual inter-course, and 'scarification' (abrasion drawing blood – but where?) 'also work well'. If she suffers from 'excessive flux', a recipe to be taken after meals caught my eye – its twelve ingredients included dragon's blood and burned elephant bones. Another recommends drinking sea water, and then: 'make a plaster of the dung of birds or of a cat . . . let it be placed on the belly and loins'.

'Sometimes the womb is suffocated.' This can cause an alarming trauma. 'Sometimes the woman is contracted so that the head is joined to the knees, and she lacks vision, and she loses the func-tion of the voice, the nose is distorted, the lips are contracted and she grits her teeth and the chest is elevated upward beyond what is normal.' Galen diagnosed the cause as a 'corrupt semen [that] abounds in [such women] excessively, and it is converted into a poisonous nature'. Treat by rubbing the hands and feet, and apply foul-smelling things to the nose and sweet-smelling things to the vagina; the womb always avoids foul smells and is attracted to sweet smells, so it will return to its proper place.

The womb may take to wandering. It could leave the vagina al-together, in extreme cases. Short of that, it might rise up to the vocal chords, or turn left or right within the body, causing miscellaneous aches and pains. (Perhaps we might recognize some of the pains as due to a grumbling appendix, which wasn't diagnosed until many centuries later. The medieval people made do with what knowledge they could get.)

If the womb would stay still long enough, and not suffocate, the next step was pregnancy. Here it's surprising to find that in cases of sterility it might be the 'fault' of either the man or the woman. The Victorians tended always to blame the woman; after all, she was the weaker sex. But to determine which medieval partner was at fault, take two pots and in each place wheat bran and put some of the man's urine in one and the woman's urine in the other. Leave for nine or ten days. [If it's the woman's fault] there will be many worms in her pot and the bran will stink... [and vice versa for the man]. If in neither, then there is no fault in either, and they can be helped to conceive by the benefit of medicine.

What that medicine might be may not seem attractive. Either partner should take the liver and testicles of a baby pig, dry them, pulverize them and drink the powder in a potion. If they want a son, 'let her take the womb and the vagina of a hare, or its testicles', dry and pulverize them and drink the powder in wine. Or the woman could similarly use the testicles of a male pig or a wild boar, taken with wine, and 'after the purgation of the menses let her cohabit with her husband and she will conceive'.

But perhaps she didn't want to become pregnant. A further recourse to the animal kingdom: 'Take a male weasel and let its testicles be removed and let it be released alive. Let the woman carry these testicles with her in her bosom... and she will not conceive.'

During the early stage of pregnancy, 'care ought to be taken that nothing is named in front to her which she is not able to have, because if she sets her mind on it and it is not given to her this occasions miscarriage. If she desires clay or chalk or coal, let beans cooked with sugar be given to her.'

So her pregnancy wears on. 'By the fourth month the fetus begins to move and the woman is nauseated [morning sickness?]. In the fifth month the fetus takes on the likeness of its father or mother.' In the last three months she should have a light diet, and 'let her avoid open-air baths and steam baths', just bathe often in sweet water. 'In the seventh month, Nature moves and the infant is made complete in the blessing of all its parts... In the ninth, it proceeds from the darkness into the light.' In a case of breech presentation, the midwife should gently move the fetus back to the womb and put it in its correct position. To expel a dead fetus there are several recipes, including two of which Galen would not have approved – spells written on butter, to be eaten.

Midwives had their own recipes for a safe delivery. A magnet held in the right hand should help, also a drink made from ivory shavings, or a coral amulet, or 'the white stuff that is found in the excrement of a hawk'. Midwives should prepare their patient, and themselves, 'with great care'.

Once the baby is born the umbilical cord should be tied 'three fingers from the [mother's] belly', which will determine the eventual size of a baby boy's penis. The baby's eyes should be covered to protect it from strong light. It should be 'bandaged', or swaddled. Curiously there's no mention of nappies or the need for them; perhaps an early copier got bored and omitted them by mistake? Nor does the writer mention that essential of birth, making the baby take its first breath. The writer then leaps several months, to weaning: 'let lozenges be made from sugar and similar things and milk, in the amount of an acorn, and let them be given to the infant so that it can hold them in its hand and suck on them and swallow a little bit of them ... [the baby] ought to be drawn away from the breast day by day in an orderly way'.

And then to early learning: 'There should be different kinds of pictures, cloths of divers colours, and pearls (surely threaded onto strings, not loose!) placed in front of the child, and one should use nursery songs and simple words ... one ought to talk in the child's presence frequently and easy words ought to be said.'

All this presupposes a certain degree of wealth, to employ wet nurses and midwives. How ordinary working women managed was probably much the same as it has always been.

XI THE SERGEANT OF THE LAW

A Sergeant of the Law, war [prudent] and wise...
There was also, full rich of excellence.
Discrete he was, and [deserving] of great reverence –
He seemed such, his words were so wise.[1]

Somehow one begins to suspect that Chaucer's tongue was already in his cheek, after such an encomium.

The pilgrims were indeed honoured by the presence of such a dignified personage. Yet he 'rode but hoomly [simply] in a medlee [striped] coat, / Girt with a ceint [belt] of silk, with barres smale [thin bars of metal]'.[2] His medley coat would have signified to the other pilgrims that he was not a cleric, as he would have been until recently, but a layman. Clerics would not be allowed to wear such a colourful garment. Missing from his portrait was the well-known coif, a close-fitting white linen bonnet, part of the distinctive dress of a senior lawyer until it was displaced by a horsehair wig in the eighteenth century. Perhaps Chaucer purposely omitted it, for some reason which we can no longer appreciate; but perhaps he simply forgot it. He does give some attention to the Sergeant's silk sash, or belt, decorated 'with barres smale'; perhaps this too had some significance which is lost to us now. Chaucer doesn't seem to have been very interested in the Sergeant of the Law, giving him only twenty-one lines, without the list of authorities with which he span out the Doctor of Physic, or the list of campaigns he used for the Knight. But he gave him many professional attributes which need expansion.

The Sergeant's Practice

The Sergeant had 'often been at the Parvis'. St Paul's Cathedral was not the orotund masterpiece we know, designed by Wren after the Great Fire. It was a vast Gothic building, much like its fellow cathedral which still exists upriver at Westminster. Its interior provided a handy space for all kinds of necessary activities, from prostitution to providing legal advice. There was a particular area where lawyers would make themselves available for consultation. This area was known as the Parvis.

Serjeants-at-law were the most senior of all the barristers who had been called within the Bar.[3] The next step would be onto the full-time judges' bench, and Chaucer's Sergeant was not far from it. He had unlimited authority, both monetary and territorial, to hear civil cases in the assizes, which sat at regular intervals, presided over by justices – judges – appointed by royal commission.

By 1320 more than half the judges of the King's Bench were serjeants-at-law, replacing the older system of appointing from the clergy. This meant that they could no longer be rewarded with ecclesiastical benefices, so their salaries had to be set at a rate that would make bribery unattractive: 60 marks a year for high court judges, 40 marks for lesser posts, but both could be supplemented by various perquisites.

> For his science [knowledge], and for his high renown,
> Of fees and robes had he many [a] one.[4]

'Fees' could be annual retainers, as well as payment for a specific case. The Doctor of Physic, too, was paid some of his fees in robes, which could be costly garments. In *The Vision of Piers Plowman* Langland inveighed against serjeants-at-law. In the Plowman's dream

> Hundreds in silk hoods [another word for coifs] hovered
>   about me
> They seemed to be Serjeants who served in the court rooms,
> Took pounds for pence, and pled for justice,

Nor for the love of our Lord unlocked their lips ever.
Better measure the mist on Malvern hillsides
Than hear a mumble from their lips till money is promised.[5]

Which seems a bit unfair, but Langland was very anti-establishment. There was no legal aid in Chaucer's time, but it has always been the tradition that a barrister would sometimes take on a poor defendant's case without charging a fee. So surely sergeants were entitled to a reasonable reward for their professional work? The legal profession was discouraged from overcharging by an ordinance of 1356 that 'pleaders shall take reasonable fees from their clients and not more than 40 pence'. As usual, one has doubts as to the extent this well-meant law was enforced.

The Courts

Justice he was full often in assize,
By patent and by plein [full] commission.[6]

The assize courts had been functioning since the beginning of the century. If authorized by royal patent, as Chaucer's Sergeant was, they had jurisdiction to try all the prisoners in the county gaols awaiting criminal trial ('gaol delivery'), and to hear any civil cases which had not been transferred to the central courts in Westminster (*nisi prius*, Latin for 'unless before' they had already gone up to Westminster). There were six circuits, on which the assize commissioners and their staff rode, twice a year, during the long summer vacation when London could become unbearable.

The Court of Common Pleas heard actions between subject and subject, which did not concern the king. Magna Carta had laid down that this court should have a permanent location. It never moved from Westminster Hall.

There were other courts dealing with specific areas of dispute. The 'forest law' covered huge tracts of the country. There were the Courts of Admiralty, originating in about 1340, to deal with cases on the high seas such as piracy, and to settle commercial cases involving international maritime law and other conventions upon which the western European trading area depended. They had two advantages over the ordinary civil courts. They could rely on infallible timing – evidence of one alleged offence timed it exactly at 'the first hour and at the first tide on the 28th day of March in the 14th year of the reign of King Richard the Second'; and they were presided over by admirals with years of experience of the sea. But this brought its own disadvantage: if the admiral was called to his ship for some naval emergency, the hearing had to be adjourned until, and if, he returned. The civil courts, especially the Court of the Mayor of London, complained bitterly that the Admiralty Courts were exceeding their proper jurisdiction and meddling in cases that properly fell to the local civil court to decide – and pocketing the relevant fees. In 1391, after years of pressure from the Commons in Parliament, the jurisdiction of the Admiralty Courts was specifically limited to arresting ships needed for the royal service.

Then there were the Courts of Chivalry, held by the Constable and the Marshal of England. The Constable of England heard the long-running dispute, begun in 1386, between the two ancient families of Scrope and Grosvenor about the right to bear a particular blazon of arms, in which Geoffrey Chaucer gave evidence, as well as John of Gaunt and a hundred other witnesses. These courts had special jurisdiction over disputes between captains and their men about the ransoming of prisoners of war, since such disputes concerned events outside the realm. They also heard cases where one of the parties was an 'alien' or foreigner. From 1285 a foreign merchant suing or being sued in an English court could insist on a 'jury of the moiety' (half) being merchants from that foreign jurisdiction. Where foreign law was relevant the English court would ask for evidence of that law from the foreign court.

Court Procedure

CIVIL CASES

Civil litigation had developed an elaborate and rigid system of 'pleadings', statements of a party's case and his arguments, which it would certainly take someone of the Sergeant's erudition to manipulate. The trouble was that no sooner had a legal formula appropriate to one set of facts been perfected, than another set of facts emerged which called for a different formula. The parties argued like a ping-pong match, using terminology that I record in case it may ever come in useful for you. The plaintiff led off with a 'count' or 'declaration'. The defendant came back with a 'plea' or 'bar'. Then came a 'replication', a 'rejoinder', a 'surrejoinder', a 'rebutter' and a 'surrebutter'. Long before that, as the costs mounted, most parties had decided to settle out of court.

But at least, after a law passed in 1362, proceedings in court were in English, doing away with the 'great mischiefs which have happened to many people [because] the laws, customs and statutes of this realm are not commonly known in the realm, because they are pleaded, shown and judged in the French language, which is too unknown in the realm'. The unfortunate court clerks writing down the day's proceedings still had to translate the language they heard – English – into the 'language of record' – Anglo-Norman French, which cannot always have been easy. The persistence of tradition in English law is shown by a case reported as late as 1629. Sea coal, so called because it was imported to London by sea from the north-country mines, caused acrid smoke which the plaintiff, a bishop's registrar, alleged had spoiled his papers. The record reads, in part, 'si home est cy tender-nosed que ne poit endurer seacoal il doit lesser son mease'; if he couldn't stand the smoke he had to get out of the kitchen or, in this case, move house.

CRIMINAL CASES

The first step was to ask the defendant whether he pleaded guilty or not guilty. If he refused to say, he couldn't be tried. So he was given the *peine forte et dure* – the Anglo-Norman for 'strong and hard pain' – until either he did plead, or he died. In its most rigorous form, he was tied up so that he couldn't move, and stretched on a stone floor; then stones were piled on him – sometimes under him too, so that his spine broke. He was given, on alternate days, dry bread and stale water. It could take him several days to die, in agony. A criminal who loved his family might choose this terrible death because his property, whatever it was, went to his family instead of to the Crown, as it would if he were tried and found guilty. This dreadful penalty persisted for generations, but it was based on a misreading of a word in the Statute of Westminster 1275. Someone, somewhere had read 'prison', as the Act clearly says, as 'peine'. Nowadays, sufferers from injustice have sometimes succeeded in actions against the Crown decades after the event. One wonders whether the descendants of those who died after *peine forte et dure* might have a promising right of action against the Crown.

If the defendant pleaded 'not guilty', his trial would depend on whether the alleged offence was treason or misdemeanour. The elements of an offence within the Statute of Treason were so clear, and the alleged offence so heinous, that God himself would decide whether the defendant was guilty. No amount of argument was relevant, no plea in mitigation could avail him, so the defendant did not need, and was not entitled to, a lawyer. But in lesser matters the issues might not be so clear-cut, and the defendant might employ a lawyer if he could afford to.

Once the defendant's plea had been entered, he was asked how he wanted to be tried. There was still a small chance of his choosing trial by combat, in which he or a 'champion' retained by him engaged with the prosecutor or his champion, in armed combat. In 1380 a 'judicial battle' was fought in the court at Westminster, and the crowd was said to have been greater than that at Richard II's coronation there three years earlier. But the usual answer to the clerk's question was 'by God and the country' – he opted for jury trial.

Trial by jury has been described as the 'palladium of English law', despite doubts sometimes expressed nowadays about its suitability for every case. For example, in a complicated and lengthy trial involving financial fraud, some jurors may be present only because they couldn't find an acceptable excuse for non-attendance, and may be functionally illiterate and/or innumerate. Medieval life was simpler, but the procedure of trial by jury was still laborious. It was preceded by the sheriff's efforts to collect a sufficient pool of potential jurymen to cope with the defendant's right to 'challenge' up to thirty-five men without giving any reason, and even more if he had good reason. Perhaps he recognized one of them as a supporter of a hostile lord, or suspected him of some personal spite. But at last twelve 'good men and true' were selected and sworn.

Trial procedure was flexible. Hearsay evidence by the prosecution witnesses was freely admitted, and since the defendant had no right to challenge it his chances of acquittal were slim. Medieval trials were brief. The same panel of jurors might have to hear all that day's cases. They had to reach a unanimous verdict in all of them, which they had to remember until the end of the day.

One striking feature of medieval punishments was that they rarely involved much expense to the state. Nowadays criminals are housed in prisons for years at the taxpayers' expense, costing as much as to keep a child at a fee-paying boarding school. In any event, an offender sentenced to imprisonment was unlikely to survive long in an overcrowded, insanitary and inhumane medieval gaol. The gaoler had no duty to feed his inmates, let alone to provide bedding or medical care. Gaol fever – typhus – was endemic.

A usual sentence was for a few days, a cooling-off period in cases of affray. But if the mayor of London or his aldermen were injured, either physically or by reputation, things got serious. In 1340 an argument between a member of the Fishmongers' Guild and a member of the Skinners' Guild escalated into a general fight. The mayor seems to have relied on his majestic presence to quell the riot, but one miscreant 'took the Mayor by the throat' and another 'wounded the Mayor's Sergeant with a stick so that his life is now despaired of'. At their trial in the Mayor's Court, they pleaded guilty. They were sentenced to death and immediately beheaded. In 1355 a vintner had 'used opproprious words against the Mayor'. He pleaded guilty but was released when he gave the mayor 100 tuns of wine. But in 1364 it was still wise to watch your tongue. Beatrice Langbourne was committed to prison for calling an alderman 'a false thief and a broken-down old yokel' when he quite properly arrested her for throwing filth into the street. A few weeks later William Lytherpool, a goldsmith, was committed to prison for saying in open court that the mayor and aldermen 'would not listen to him and do him justice'. No messing with the mayor.

A policy which we would recognize as 'naming and shaming' saved the cost of prison. Remember that it was normal for a man to wear some sort of head-covering, such as a hood or a hat or cap. Two men who had got into an argument were both sentenced to 'stand *uncapped*' (my italics) on the stool in Guildhall by way of penance. To be bareheaded in public was mortifying. Other minor offences, such as selling false pardons or rotten fish, could be punished by time in the pillory, which cost the government nothing, but inflicted public humiliation on the criminal, especially if his stinking fish were hung round his neck.

The death sentence for treason was elaborately and publicly hideous. The penalty for women was to be burned alive. For men the sentence was to be hung, drawn and quartered. Because the 'drop' from a gibbet hadn't yet been invented, the death was by strangulation, not a broken neck. It was not instantaneous. A well-organized criminal just might escape death if his friends managed to get him down in time to resuscitate him. For most, the next step was to cut his abdomen open while he was still alive and remove his heart, which was thrown onto the fire kept burning on the scaffold. Then the body was cut into four pieces, or sometimes more, and decapitated. In cases of treason the traitor's head would be impaled on a pole and put up above one of the gates of the city as a warning to everyone contemplating a similar offence.

Land Law

The Sergeant knew the 'termes' or correct legal language, which can blind any layman by its complexity. An interesting survival is the word 'mortgage', which combines the French words for 'dead' and 'pledge'. Mortgages are commonplace nowadays. A somewhat similar arrangement existed in Chaucer's time, but with vital differences. Imagine that John wanted to go on pilgrimage, for which he needed some ready money. He owned an apple orchard. He asked Henry to lend him the cash he needed, giving the apple orchard as security. Off he went to Santiago. He was away several years. Meanwhile Henry moved into the orchard. There were several bumper harvests. Henry made a good profit from selling the apples. John, back from his pilgrimage, turned up to pay off his debt to Henry. If Henry asked him for the original amount, making no allowance for the apple sales, that would be a 'mortgage', a dead pledge. It would be a form of usury, just as wicked as if Henry had exacted interest from John. If he did the proper thing, and deducted the apple profits from the amount John owed him, that would be a 'vifgage', a live pledge, which was perfectly acceptable. If John was away long enough, and the apple market continued to boom, John might end up not owing Henry anything. Which all goes to show how familiar words don't always mean the same now as they did five hundred years ago, and some words have simply disappeared.

(Another survival from the French: even today, the sovereign's assent is necessary before a Bill in Parliament becomes law. She signifies her assent in the words 'La Reine le veult', nowadays said by the Speaker on her behalf. The Speaker may or may not say 'Le Roi le veult', when in due course her Majesty is succeeded by her son.)

Chaucer's Sergeant was unbeatable as a conveyancer:

> So great a purchasour [conveyancer] was nowhere none;
> All was fee simple [unrestricted ownership] to him in effect.
> His purchasing ne might not be infecte [his conveyancing
>   couldn't be questioned].[7]

English land law has always been notoriously abstruse, despite periodic attempts to tidy it up with legislation. I don't guarantee to make it comprehensible here; it certainly wasn't tidy in Chaucer's day, and I managed to be called to the Bar with only a hazy idea of it.

When William the Bastard and his Norman friends conquered England, in 1066, William, who had only been a duke in Normandy, could as the king of England reward his friends with grants of land. He kept much of his new realm for himself, to indulge his favourite sport of hunting. Who knew what beasts this new hunting field might provide – and Normandy was poor hunting territory by now. But the rest was available to reward his followers, in the form of 'fiefs'. They had to swear allegiance to him, promising to provide men and war materiel when needed. These nobles were his 'tenants in chief'; they in turn could sub-contract their liabilities to others, who in turn... and so on. William could rely on a network of loyal supporters with obligations to the Crown. Subject to those obligations, they were the masters of their land. Their power depended on possession. Since you can't take up your land and hug it to your chest as you could a valuable piece of armour, you took 'seisin' of it, by a notional act of possession, usually by cutting a turf. A man wrongly evicted from his land was said to have been 'disseized', which Magna Carta disapproved of. The 'fee simple' was the totality of ownership out of which all lesser estates were carved, as perpetual and indestructible as the land itself.

Inevitably this tolerably clear position gathered complications as the years rolled on. Strange creations such as remaindermen and reversioners crept in. At every event affecting the land or the landholder, such as the succession of a son or the marriage of a daughter, fees had to be paid to the Crown, and they could be heavy. Tax avoidance is not a new concept. Surely, thought some medieval lawyer (certain, at that time, to have been a churchman), there must be a way of avoiding these fees? Who or what does not die or have marriageable daughters? The Church, of course. So thus was born the law of Trusts, or 'Uses' in medieval terminology. A landholder would give the title to his land to the Church, on the understanding that the Church would not only look after his immortal soul but also care for his temporal interests. He could train his son up to inherit, and marry off his daughter, without worrying about tax. A win-win situation for almost all concerned, especially for the Church, which accumulated vast landholdings in this way; but not for the Crown. It tried unsuccessfully to stop this diversion of income into the 'dead hand' ('mortmain') of the Church, which was ruled from Rome and was outside royal power. The Crown eventually had to settle for charging fees for a 'licence in mortmain'. By Chaucer's time someone who had the law of real property – for so the law relating to land was called – at his fingertips was indeed a skilful conveyancer.

The Common Law

As well as sitting as assize judge, and appearing in court to represent litigants, the Sergeant was a skilful legal draftsman:

> ... he could indite and make a thing,
> That could no wight [man] pinche at [find fault with] his writing[.][8]

He knew all the decided cases and judgements 'from the time of King William' – 1066 – onwards, in other words, the 'common law'. This is a bit of Chaucerian hyperbole. No one could remember all of the cases. Although there were of course no printed Law Reports or Digests to consult, a prosperous barrister would be expected to know at least the most important ones. Many Continental countries had adopted the code of civil law published in the reign of Justinian, who ruled the Byzantine Empire between 527 and 565. By Roman law, which in an amended form still applies in some countries, it should be possible to find a written rule that applies to any case. The system tends to be rigid, but has the merit of certainty, whereas under the common law similar cases decided in the past must be examined, and the principle guiding them must be extracted and applied. The rule, which still applies, is known as *stare decisis* – Latin for 'relying on decisions'. It is flexible, allowing for development, but it may be difficult to predict the outcome of any case which looks back to the past. Conditions that were relevant in the days of the Conquest might have changed out of all recognition. Would the decision about a horse with a cough really be helpful in assessing whether someone who had bought a sports car was justified in complaining about a knock in its engine?

Magna Carta

The Sergeant also knew by heart every statute. This looks slightly more possible. The first to come to any lawyer's mind must have been Magna Carta, the Great Charter of 1215, enshrining the freedom of the Church in England and the liberty of Englishmen. It is now revered all over the world, regardless of the facts that it applied only to free men, leaving women and serfs to live as best they could, and that it was designed to safeguard the interests of the barons who forced King John to sign it, after years of friction between them and the monarch. It was reissued in an amended form in 1225, and at frequent intervals thereafter, but ever since it has been regarded as the bastion of English liberty and the rule of law.

The first twelve sections dealt with domestic family law. Then section 13 ringingly declares that 'the City of London ... and all other cities, boroughs, towns and ports shall have their liberties and free customs'. Sections 17, 18 and 19 provide for the highest civil court of the land, the Court of Common Pleas, to be static instead of following the king around the country as it used to do, with all its officers and the litigants and their witnesses, which had been highly inconvenient for everyone. Sections 18 and 19 dealt with the quarterly assizes to be held in each county. Sections 20 to 32 contain miscellaneous provisions of legal machinery.

Section 33 suddenly diverged from the general law: 'all fish-weirs will be completely removed from the Thames and the Medway and throughout the whole of England, except on the sea-coast'. Fish-weirs – nets anchored in a river – in the Thames were still the subject of contention centuries later, so this section doesn't seem to have worked. Section 35 usefully imposed uniform measures of wine, ale, corn and cloth. Then back to legal machinery, until sections 39 and 40, which deserve to be written in gold:

39: No free man is to be arrested, or imprisoned, or disseized [evicted] or outlawed, or exiled, or in any other way ruined, nor will we go or send against him, except by the legal judgment of his peers or by the law of the land.

40: To no one will we sell, to no one will we deny or delay, right or justice.

'The legal judgment of his peers' developed into the present-day jury system. 'The law of the land' was as passed in Parliament, or which had been adopted from immemorial custom. Justice can be unbearably delayed nowadays, when suspect persons can remain on police bail for years. But Magna Carta is still revered as an aspiration.

Returning to more everyday matters, section 41 clarifies the legal position of foreign merchants. In wartime, merchants from an enemy country are to be 'detained' – we would say 'interned' – 'until it is clear to us ... how the merchants of our land are treated in the enemy country; and if ours are safe there, the others shall be safe in our land' – a more sophisticated and tolerant view than we displayed in the twentieth century.

More machinery sections follow, including one that applied to future sergeants hoping for promotion to the Bench. '45: We will not appoint justices ... other than those who know the law of the land and intend to keep it well', a test that Chaucer's Sergeant would surely pass with flying colours. The effect of the forest law was clarified, limiting the king's powers over the huge part of his realm declared to be forests.

Then, at last, King John's capitulation in section 51: 'Immediately after the restoration of peace we will remove from the realm all foreign knights, crossbowmen, serjeants [*sic*: this time, not lawyers but military officers] and mercenaries, who have come with horses and arms to the detriment of the kingdom.' There is a quick look at Welshmen who had been unlawfully deprived of their lands, and another at the position of the king of Scots (sections 56–9). Finally, twenty-five barons were to be chosen to oversee all these provisions, with power to demand that the king must rectify any transgression immediately – a fond hope, one would think. The royal rage that had contributed to the stand-off with the barons was curbed; the king was even made to say he forgave 'all ill-will, indignation and rancour that has arisen between us and our men, clergy and laity, during the time of discord'. The barons had won, for the time being at least. But they must have known it couldn't last. John went straight to the pope, who ruled that Magna Carta was null and void, so the barons began the war all over again, this time backed by a French invasion. John died in 1216, to be succeeded by his son Henry, who was nine years old and not interested in war.

Other Statutes

There were other statutes that any serjeant must have had in his armoury. Forest law had been codified in 1217, mercantile law in 1285. At about the same time various statutes were passed broadly limiting the power of the Church, which ruled from Rome, over life and death in England. Copies of them were sent to every monastery, county court and parish church.

The Treasons Act of 1351, parts of which are still in force, codified the common law on treason. Before then no one quite knew what treason was. Were highway robberies treason, as some judges had found? Or riots? In the 1340s, when the king was often abroad, local disorders had become a problem of alarming proportions. Were they treason? But the Commons took the view that men should know where they stood in law, and be protected against ill-fettered royal power. 'High treason' was defined in the Act as an offence against the monarch, whose status had an almost divine authority during the Middle Ages. As we have seen, it carried the appalling penalty of hanging, drawing and quartering, and the offender's property was 'escheated to' (taken by) the Crown. To plot the death of the monarch or his heir, or to violate the king's immediate female family, was high treason. Levying war against the king in his realm, or 'giving aid or comfort to his enemies in his realm or elsewhere', was high treason. This provision was used against Roger Casement in the First World War, in 1916, and William Joyce in the Second World War, in 1945. The working of the royal administration was protected. Counterfeiting the royal currency, and forging the Great Seal and the Privy Seal, were acts of high treason. Killing the high officials of the state – the chancellor, and judges while they were performing their offices – was high treason. The same concept of breaking a fundamental rule, although at a lower level, applied to acts by inferiors against their superiors. A servant who killed his master, a wife who killed her husband, a clergyman who killed his prelate were all guilty of 'petty treason', for which the penalty was death but without the gruesome quartering.

In Chaucer's time, the 1361 Statute of Westminster gave the local gentry wide powers by appointing them justices of the peace. As such they became responsible for enforcing the hated Statute of Labourers, after the 1381 rebellion. One of the aims of the rebels was to revive what they saw as the ancient, and proper, Law of Winchester, which gave power to the people, not to their superiors. This seems to have been a hallucinatory vision of the golden days of old, when monarchs behaved fairly and men were happy. No record of such a law has been found.

Canon Law

The principal competitor to English law was the system of 'canon' or 'civil' law operated by the Church, and overseen from Rome. This was the course taught at Oxford University, to which aspirant priests and monks came from all over Europe. The Church exercised a monopoly over spiritual matters, from baptism at or soon after birth, to ceremonies to ensure a good death and the mundane concerns preceding it, such as the distribution of property by a will or by the rules of intestacy. It asserted its right to solemnize matrimony, which properly came within the common law. Although a marriage once contracted could not be dissolved by divorce, it might in some circumstances be annulled by the Church, if the parties were found to be related to each other by increasingly complex rules, so unhappily married spouses who wished to be free of their matrimonial vows applied – if they could afford it – to an ecclesiastical court for a decree of annulment, alleging 'consanguinity'.

There were several irritants in the relations between Church and state. One was the 'benefit of clergy'. The Church looked after its own, in the face of Crown authority. If an accused person could show that he belonged, in any way, to the Church, his case would be transferred to the jurisdiction of the Church, which was forbidden to shed blood. He might be punished by other means, but not by death. A criminal hoping to establish a fraudulent claim to clerical status needed a certain amount of preparation. In earlier days it might be enough to dress in the long robes of a cleric, with your hair tonsured in a shaven circle at the crown – bad luck if you were bald anyway. So far, so good. But the secular authorities grew more suspicious and imposed a further test, that of literacy. The courtroom is hot and stuffy, the assize judge and his colleagues want to dispose of the list of cases and get back to their London practices or their country mansions. The only person in the room who can actually read is likely to be the clerk, who is trying to keep up with translating the oral evidence given in English into the Anglo-Norman French still used for written court records. He gives you a copy of the Bible. It will be the Vulgate version, in Latin, of course. Check that you're holding it the right way up, which you can usually do by finding a decorated initial somewhere: it will be in red, standing out from the black text, and the decoration on it drips downwards from the top, or shows a picture of a king or suchlike; get him the right way up. So, orient yourself, open the book about halfway through and take a deep breath.

In my own copy of the Bible, published in 1811, the psalms have been tidily divided into verses and renumbered, so that the medieval Psalm 50 is now Psalm 51. It begins well: 'Have mercy on me, O God, according to thy lovingkindness: according unto the multitude of thy tender mercies blot out my transgressions.' The last of the nineteen verses reads: 'Then shalt thou be pleased with the sacrifice of righteousness, with burnt offering and whole burnt offering: then shall they offer bullocks upon thy altar.' Perhaps a certain amount has been lost in translation. Reading the English version aloud took me just over two and a half minutes, which would be a feat of memory for the modern age, but not impossible when there were no means of consulting written texts, and vocal memory was far more retentive than now. Perhaps you would not have to go through the whole psalm; the first verse, known as the 'neck verse', was usually enough.[9] There are no statistics available for the number of non-clerical, intelligent criminals who took care to keep a tonsure clearly visible and knew the 'neck verse' by heart.

The next test was that a claimant had to be vouched for by his 'ordinary', the bishop of the diocese or his representative; but perhaps, given the state of corruption that William Langland and Chaucer complained of, this would not be too difficult to obtain. A prudent wrongdoer would have wisely provided himself with a confederate, who might even be a real cleric persuaded by a small donation to perjure himself. He would assure the court that you were indeed a member of the church in his diocese.

In an actual record, translated from the Latin, of a trial for robbery in 1323 before literacy was added to the tests for benefit of clergy, one Henry Lampard, 'having been asked as to how he wishes to acquit himself of the aforesaid robberies and felonies... says in the English language that he is a clerk [i.e. a member of the clergy, a clergyman] without making any other response. And he is asked whether he wishes or knows how to speak in the Latin or the French language. He says that he is English and born in England, and perfectly able to speak his mother tongue and unwilling to reply using any other language. And the archdeacon of Westminster, the ordinary of that place appointed to claim clerks, comes here and says that, *if the said Henry should be a clerk* [my italics], he would freely claim him as a clerk, otherwise he would not. And because the said Henry... has neither tonsure nor clerical dress... the penalty inflicted on those felons who reject the common law of the realm having been read out to him, it is put to the said Henry whether he wishes to say anything else instead of the reply he had given previously. He says definitely that he does not.' The unfortunate Henry was committed to prison and sentenced to *peine forte et dure*.[10]

Another irritating habit of the Church was to extend its protection to any offender against the secular law by giving him sanctuary. The general principle was that someone who had broken that law, and confessed, could find shelter within the bosom of the Church. Its scope extended from minor offences, such as breaking the Articles of Apprenticeship sworn by both apprentice and master, to serious crimes punishable in a secular court by the death penalty. There were more than a hundred parish churches within the bounds of the City of London, in any of which a criminal could find shelter. Outside the city were the Church of St Martin's le Grand, Westminster Abbey, St Bartholomew's Priory and St Katharine's Hospital beyond the Tower of London. The records of the City of London contain many complaints by apprentices that the masters who were supposed to be teaching them their trade had fallen into debt, or had committed some crime and had fled to sanctuary in a church, so that the apprentices were left high and dry. The boot could be on the other foot. In 1369 the mayor of London wrote to the abbot of Westminster: please could the abbey staff deliver up to his master a certain apprentice who had 'left his master and was living in the abbey so that his master was unable to recover possession of him, whereby a dangerous example is set for other apprentices'.

For serious offences, the criminal seeking sanctuary had first to confess his crime. Then he would be sentenced to 'abjure the realm' – leave the country – from a specified port, usually Dover but not always. There might be a group of exiled men walking along to Dover, carrying wooden crosses and guarded by royal officials to see that they were not rescued en route. One penitent was directed to Southampton, 'whence to cross the sea on the fourth day', having been allowed four days to walk there from London. If the weather was against him when he got to the specified port, he had to wade into the water up to his knees or deeper every day until he found an outward passage, just to show willing.

But the system was not watertight. In 1365 a man was prosecuted, when 'three malefactors had assaulted and wounded [the defendant's] servant... and had then taken sanctuary at Saint Antholin's church... [the defendant] went at midnight and released [them] and allowed the felons to escape'. Sometimes the irate populace refused to allow a miscreant to escape punishment by bolting into a church. In 1371 two men assaulted William de Hamenash in Holborn, and 'so illtreated him that his life is despaired of'. One of them escaped, the other took refuge in the nearby Church of St Andrew, 'whence he was taken by a large crowd of evildoers' – the record doesn't say what the 'evildoers' did to their quarry, but nothing good, for sure.

Here is a long and rambling story about two squires in the Black Prince's army, Robert Hanley and John Shakell, which touches on several aspects of medieval life including sanctuary. It begins with the prince's abortive campaign in Spain. At the Battle of Nájera in 1367, Robert and John captured a Spanish nobleman who, they thought, was good for a substantial ransom; they were in luck.

They released him to go home and raise his ransom – the normal practice – but kept his eldest son as a hostage, a safeguard that the ransom would eventually be paid. Years passed. Meanwhile the English and the Spanish courts were slowly negotiating peace terms. The King's Council demanded that Robert and John should give up their hostage, for use as a diplomatic bargaining counter. When Robert and John refused they were imprisoned in the Tower of London, without trial – so much for Magna Carta. In 1378, *eleven years* after they had captured the Spaniard who was going to make their fortune, they managed to escape from the Tower. They took sanctuary in Westminster Abbey, where, surely, they would be safe. But their ill luck followed them. Agents of the King's Council broke into the sanctuary and murdered John Shakell on the steps of the altar. They also killed a cleric who tried to defend him. The record doesn't say what happened to his partner, Robert Hanley, in the abbey, but he survived long enough to sell his rights in the ransom to a London fishmonger, John Horton. Between 1390 and 1432 Horton and, after his death, his executors sued John Shakell's executors in the Court of Chivalry, at first for his share in the promised ransom, and later for the letters of marque against Aragonese shipping which Shakell had obtained in default of the ransom, entitling him to well over 21,000 francs." And there the story ends. The moral was – do not trust wholly in the sanctity of sanctuary.

Pardons

The royal power to pardon may evoke a compassionate sovereign embracing his sinful subjects. The reality was rather different. Pardons could bring welcome additions to the sovereign's treasury. Following the example of the pope and his 'jubilee year' in 1300 (see p. 12), Edward III issued a general royal pardon in 1362, to mark his fiftieth birthday. He did it again in 1377, to mark the fiftieth year of his reign. It covered every offence except treason, murder and rape. It was well worth its going rate, 18s 4d for each pardon, which brought in a very useful sum of over £2,000.

General pardons also came in useful to bolster the royal

expeditionary army. An offender who was pardoned on condition that he enlisted in the army in France may well have arrived there, but many happy malefactors simply came straight home again and resumed their lives of crime. So blatant did this become that the Commons protested at the grants to 'well-known thieves and common murderers'.

After the Peasants' Revolt of 1381 there were huge numbers of pleas for pardons. If you had been spotted taking part, you were definitely wise to apply for one; but even if you had taken no part in the rebellion, some spiteful neighbour might bear false witness against you, so it was as well to be forearmed. John Creyk petitioned for pardon in 1383, because his name was on the list of those to be excluded from the general pardon. He said that he had been 'maliciously' indicted of involvement in the rebellion by his enemies. He duly got his pardon. As the rebellion died down, at least 3,500 people applied for a pardon. The going rate was between 20 and 30 shillings. Two people paid £40 each. The price steadied at 16s 4d, and by 1382, a year after the outbreak, the market had collapsed and pardons were given away free.

In 1385 John de Felsted, usher of the royal exchequer, petitioned for pardon through another man, Adam Ramsey, John being held in prison and unable to act for himself. His petition told how he had been instructed to guard the door of the exchequer against a certain chaplain who had gone mad and was wandering around Westminster Hall. When John stopped him, the chaplain 'beat John severely with a staff'. John drew his dagger to fend off the madman, in self-defence. John got his pardon. His case was unusual in that he relied on one individual, perhaps a friend, to forward it to the authorities. There were other cases where just one individual, of a humble status, forwarded a friend's petition. Alice Walleran, 'a poor woman', interceded for a friend in 1383. 'Roger, a soldier of Calais', interceded for a friend in 1386.

But if you could interest some powerful magnate, you stood a better chance. Henry of Grosmont, as earl of Derby (see Appendix A), gave his name to nearly a hundred applicants in the year 1345 alone, mostly as part of a general pardon to his troops. In 1347 Queen Philippa, Edward III's consort, famously implored his pardon for the burghers of Calais whom he was threatening to behead because their city had not surrendered as it should have done, necessitating the inconvenience of a long siege.

An odd quirk in the system was described as 'ancient custom'; if the monarch 'looked upon' a condemned man just as he was about to be executed, he would pardon that man. In 1397 William Walshman had been found guilty of stealing a silver locket, and sentenced to death. He was just going to be executed when Richard II happened to pass by and saw him waiting for death. The king ordered William to be released, and a pardon was later issued to him.

So at last we return to Chaucer's Sergeant of the Law, and a characteristic Chaucerian jibe. It was no wonder that

> Nowhere so busy a man as he there was,
> And yet he seemed busier than he was.[12]

XII THE SUMMONER

His Job

He was a minor cog in the machinery of an ecclesiastical court. These courts were normally presided over by the archdeacon of the diocese, who could impose punishments ranging from fines to excommunication. They dealt with immorality, offences against the canon law, whereas the royal courts dealt with illegality, offences against the common law or statutes. There is a list of the offences that might land people before an archdeacon in the Friar's Tale: fornication, witchcraft, pimping, defamation, adultery, robbing churches, oversight of wills and contracts, failure to receive the sacraments, usury, simony (selling church benefices) and lechery.[1]

The Summoner's function was to serve summonses or 'writs' to attend the court, on witnesses and offenders, and to act as usher while the court was in session.

His Appearance

Chaucer seems to have had a deep dislike of summoners. This one rated forty-five lines in the General Prologue, of which only two are at least half-heartedly positive:

> He was a gentil harlot [a noble rogue] and a kinde [pleasant
>   one];
> A better fellow should men not find.[2]

For the rest, his appearance is described in revolting detail, complete with his red face, his inflamed eyelids, his scurfy eyebrows and sparse beard and the pimples and boils on his cheeks. None of the standard remedies for such eruptions, such as quicksilver (mercury), litharge (lead monoxide), brimstone (sulphur), borax, ceruse (white lead) or oil of tartar (solution of potassium carbonate) had cured him. He was as 'lecherous as a sparrow', and 'well loved he garlic, onions and also leeks' – none of which would have helped his condition. He might have been diagnosed by a medieval physician as suffering from a type of leprosy.[3] No wonder 'Of his visage children were afeared'. But when they saw the ludicrously enormous garland the Summoner had put on his head, and the 'buckler' (shield) that he carried, made of cake, they must have laughed at him instead.

His Morals

His intellectual level was low. When he was mad drunk he 'spoke no word but Latin', quoting odd phrases from the language he heard all day in court, and that was as far as his intellectual capacity went.

His morality was equally low. He could be bribed with wine, by people whom it was his job to summon to the court where he worked.

> He would suffre [allow], for a quart of wine,
> A good fellow to have his concubine [mistress]
> A twelve-month [a year, until the next session of the court],
>   and excuse him at full [completely]

– presumably by losing the papers in the case, or otherwise delaying it. And if he found someone with similar morals, he would tell him not to be frightened by the most serious punishment the archdeacon could inflict, his 'curse' or excommunication. 'Purse is the Archdeacon's hell': the punishment might indeed hurt the offender's finances, but not his soul, so why worry?

Not content with all that, Chaucer makes the Summoner have a bad influence outside his work in the court.

In danger had he at his own guise
The young girls of the diocese,
And knew their counsel, and was all their reed.

'Girls' meant the young of both sexes. These three lines meant that he had them in his power, to do as he pleased with them. He knew all their private affairs, and was their exclusive adviser.[4] He sounds hideously like some of the child sex abusers who are crawling out of the woodwork in our days.

I have put his chapter next to the Sergeant of the Law, Chapter XI, because of their joint concern with the functioning of the law, although the Sergeant would have been deeply offended by any comparison with the Summoner, and he was at the top of the profession whereas the Summoner was on the lowest rank in every way. As pilgrims in Chaucer's imaginary cavalcade, the Summoner rode with the Pardoner (see Chapter XVII), whose moral standards were on a par with his own.

XIII THE MANCIPLE

'A gentle manciple was there of a Temple'.[1]

The Inns of Court

At about the same time as students were congregating in Oxford to study the laws of the Church, practitioners of the common law began to gather together in London, where the principal royal courts usually sat. Some young aristocrats aimed to acquire only a smattering of legal knowledge, and a useful network of friends, before returning to their family estates, equipped to check legal documents and preside over local courts. Years later, if they decided to come to one of Chaucer's readings, they might well have been reminded of the Manciple who had been part of their lives when they were young men, enjoying a not too onerous life in the Temple. Others settled in for a long course, aiming for a place in a royal household, the medieval version of the civil service.

There were, and are still, four Inns of Court, Gray's, Lincoln's and the Inner and Middle Temples. An 'Inn' in Chaucer's time could mean a hostelry such as the Tabard, but it had another meaning, apparent if you look at the map of London – a residence, including its grounds and outbuildings, all owned and occupied by the same family.

In 1287 a famous lawyer, Henry de Lacy, Earl of Lincoln, gathered round him a collection of pupils studying the common law under him. His Inn lay at the north end of what became Chancery Lane, but to accommodate his students he also used the adjacent buildings abandoned by the Black Friars, who had moved to new premises near the river. The friars had been great gardeners, and their grounds included a fertile garden and orchards. Henry de Lacy died in 1311. Despite one or two legal hiccups the property remained the property of the earls of Lincoln, and the law students remained there as lodgers or tenants.

In the early 1300s another lawyer, named de Grey, came down from Chester to settle in London, probably bringing with him his clerks and some fellow-lawyers. By 1330 his Inn, just north of Holborn, was home during the law terms to several law students. It included gardens, a 'dove-house' to provide food throughout the year, and a windmill. The spelling had changed from 'Grey' to 'Gray' by 1397 or earlier.

Some doubt, and friendly rivalry, exists as to which of the two, Gray's or Lincoln's, was the earlier legal training ground, but in the absence of any written proof on this crucial matter, neither side can win.

The two Temples pose a conundrum: were they originally one, which at some time split into two, or were they always separate entities? The Order of the Knights of the Temple of Solomon, the 'Knights Templar', had been founded in 1119, to protect pilgrims visiting the Holy Land. It flourished in the countries that had produced the crusading movement, particularly France. It became rich, through religious donations and by acting as bankers to traders and pilgrims to the Middle and Far East. In London, the order acquired a vast site between the river and Fleet Street. Their church still exists, though much battered by time, restorers and the Blitz. It is round, as the Templars' churches always were, echoing the layout of the holy sepulchre in Jerusalem. It was the heart of an extensive complex of buildings, including a hall which housed not only the Templars' religious life but their flourishing international banking business. There were numerous lay brothers and domestic staff, who used the unconsecrated buildings at the eastern end of the site, which included another hall.

But the Crusades failed to 'liberate' the Holy Land from the Saracens; the energy of the crusading movement lapsed, and the Templars lost their function. Their wealth attracted the rapacity of the monarchs wherever they were based. In 1307 the French king, who badly needed funds at the time, accused the order of religious and sexual misconduct, a pretext serving as an excuse to dissolve it. Its fate was sealed. Its wealth fell into the hands of the French monarchy. Other monarchs followed suit. In England the Crown dissolved the order in 1312. In a complicated deal between the pope and the Crown, the Templars' estates in England, including the Thames site, were given or sold to another order, the Knights Hospitaller of St John of Jerusalem, which had been founded to give medical care to pilgrims to the Holy Land. The Hospitallers were quite happy in their headquarters out at Clerkenwell, so they used the windfall of the Temple site to produce income by letting it to lawyers.

By 1339 more lawyers had moved into the former Templar buildings as rent-paying tenants, conveniently near the royal courts now settled permanently in Westminster. Meetings, moots (mock trials) and lectures were integral parts of legal training for which large halls were needed, and it seems likely that one group of lawyers settled round the Temple church, in the 'inner' part of the Temple, using the hall there, and another group used the hall in the eastern part of the site, which became known as the 'Middle Temple'. So there was probably never just one 'Temple' of lawyers, which split into two; but the jury is still out. An obvious question: was there ever an 'outer' Temple? It seems not.

There is some evidence – but very faint – that Chaucer may have been a student in the Inner Temple at some point between 1360 and 1368. It depends on several leapfrogs of time. In 1598 a respected Tudor scholar, Thomas Speght, was writing a life of Chaucer. He mentioned that William Buckley, a master of the Inner Temple and keeper of its records in the 1560s and 1570s, had 'not many years hence' seen a record of Geoffrey Chaucer having been fined 2 shillings by the Inner Temple for beating a Franciscan friar in Fleet Street. The records of 1360 would have been available to Buckley, though unfortunately lost to us. But this evidence would hardly stand up in a court of law.

One benefit of a legal education which, I fear, you may have noticed, is an ability to obfuscate any perfectly simple question. The exact rights of the lawyers to their chambers in the Temple

– surely a matter needing no clarification as between lawyers – were not defined until the Crown brought any discussion to an abrupt end by seizing the land, at the Reformation. But one tragic event was all too clear. In 1381 the rebellious peasants were convinced that lawyers and all their works had contributed to their woes, and should be exterminated. They erupted into the Temple and 'seized all the books, rolls and remembrances kept in the cupboards of the apprentices of the law within the Temple, carried them into the high road and burned them there'.[2] Anyone who even looked like a lawyer was killed. Someone must have known of the part the Hospitallers played as landlords to the lawyers in the Temple, since some of the rebels went out to the Hospitallers' Priory in Clerkenwell and burned down the master's house.

Legal Education

Just like any other apprentices, aspirant lawyers learned by following the masters of their trade or profession, and practising how they would work when they were qualified. For them this meant oral disputations, or 'moots'. But to get to that stage an 'apprentice of the Bench' would have spent two or three years in rigorous study of what written records and precedents there were, committing them to memory or to his own notes, and attending 'readings' or lectures given by men 'learned in the law' who had at least ten years' seniority. He would have learned Latin at school, although the Latin of the courts and of legal documents was not the elegant language of the classics. If he was not already familiar with the version of French spoken in royal or cultured circles, he would have to become so. (French was used for recording the formal arguments or 'pleadings' in court until 1731, though its use in the outside world had long disappeared.) He would need to be fluent in the English spoken by some of his clients. So with all this to master, as well as the common law, he would have little time, inclination or talent for the minutiae of daily living – what to eat, where to buy it, and so on. This was the function of the Manciple.

The Manciple's Job[3]

Chaucer's Manciple looked after more than thirty members of his Inn, which was either the Inner or the Middle Temple. Twelve members were particularly well qualified to act as stewards for any landowner. These will have been the young aristocrats mentioned above. They may have been particularly apt to criticize the Manciple's administration.[4] That leaves at least eighteen men who were there to study the whole body of common law. Each member may have had a servant to look after his daily needs, and the Inn's domestic arrangements will have employed at least as many men as there were members. So the Manciple was catering for a community of perhaps a hundred people. Chaucer describes him as 'wise in buying of vitaille' (food).[5] But:

> ...whether that he paid [in cash] or took by tally,
> Algate he waited so in his achaat [he always took such
>   precautions in his bargaining],
> That he was ay biforn and in good staat[6]

– or in modern English, he was always in a sound financial position. Transactions on credit were recorded on tally sticks: long narrow pieces of wood, rather like the pairs of chopsticks that we might use in a Chinese restaurant nowadays. The amount owing was 'scored' across the width of the stick, which was then parted into two, one part retained by the seller and the other by the buyer. It could be sealed with the parties' seals, which would prove the contract in a court of law as validly as if it had been recorded in a written deed.

Food-Shopping

Medieval London did not enjoy the proliferating rules about food safety of today, but it did its best to control the wholesale and retail merchandizing of food. Where each trade could set up its shops and stalls, how much it could charge and during what hours it could trade – all these were overseen by the guilds, which in turn were in the hands of the mayor and aldermen. Most food was sold in markets dealing in that kind of produce.

Bread formed a large part of any medieval diet. It was made by members of the Bakers' Company and strictly controlled in price and quality, so it would not give the Manciple much room for crafty bargaining.

Fish was landed every day at Billingsgate, at the riverside just below London Bridge. Due to the strict religious rules fish was eaten about as often as meat. Retail sales were tightly controlled. Fish from the Thames, such as salmon, lampreys, dace and eels which were caught upriver from London Bridge, could be sold in Cheapside, and fish caught downriver could be sold in Cornhill. Four overseers were appointed by the mayor and aldermen to supervise sales.

One easy way of catching fish was by a 'weir', a net stretched across part or all of the stream (see p. 157). The barons who had confronted King John in 1215 had made one of the conditions for their cooperation that 'in future, all fishweirs will be completely removed from the Thames and the Medway and throughout the whole of England, except on the seacoast'.

But clearly this did not happen. The mayor and aldermen of London, as the conservators of the river from upstream Teddington to the mouth of the estuary at Gravesend, were in constant dispute with the fishermen, the City complaining that the fishermen's nets were so fine that they caught too many young fish, which never had a chance to grow to full size. From the frequency of litigation on this it seems that the fishermen were incorrigible.

In 1386 the mayor and aldermen summoned twenty-four fishermen, twelve from upstream of London Bridge and twelve from the lower reaches, 'to inform them how and by whom the fish in the Thames were so destroyed that hardly a seasonable fish could be found in it'. The downstream fishermen explained that the fault lay not with them but with two religious houses whose lands bordered the Thames, the Abbey of Stratford and the Abbey of Barking. These holy monks and nuns craftily fixed weirs or nets at the mouths of 'breaches', inlets from the river, so that at half tide 'the fish usually entered at the breaches . . . in order to feed on the land there and to be more at ease and comfortable than in the current of the Thames, and there they stayed until the tide ebbed and they could not pass back to the river but betook themselves to the ditches which remained full of water, which ditches the Abbot and Abbess hired out to people who put weirs and other machines in them ... whereby all fish, great and small, were destroyed, and thus the Abbot and Abbess were the principal maintainers of the destruction of fish'. Ingenious, and a lesson for comfort-seeking fishes. The hearing resulted in rules being made about close seasons for varieties of fish, but whether they were observed remains doubtful. There was even a 'fishery' under London Bridge, which was let by the bridge owners for 20 shillings a year.

There were originally two powerful city companies concerned with dried fish, the Saltfish-mongers and the Stockfish-mongers. They were amalgamated in 1536. William Walworth, the mayor of London who made his name when he faced the rebellious peasants in 1381, was a Stockfish-monger. No doubt the Manciple took care to have a stock of salted, dried or pickled fish, in case his supply of fresh fish ran out.

Meat was sold in the Stocks market (on the site of the present Mansion House), built in 1283, and named after a pair of stocks there. The considerable revenue from it was used to maintain London Bridge. Butchers were allowed to use the market on meat days, but the fishmongers took over on fish days. There were more meat markets in St Nicholas Shambles and East Cheap. The maximum price for standard joints was agreed by their guild – 2 shillings for the best sheep carcase, a loin of beef 5 pence, a loin of pork 4 pence.

We have no record of the kinds of meat available to these hard-working students, but we can use the diet of the monks of Westminster, a form of upper-class diet, as some guide. 'Meat', according to their rules, didn't include such things as offal, or chopped or pre-cooked meat, so a devoted carnivore could still satisfy his appetite for meat even if cuts from the joint were not on the menu. Another monastic source comes from the thirty-seven ladies of Barking Abbey. When they weren't enjoying those luckless fishes, they subsisted on beef from their own estates three times a week, rather less pork, including cheek, ears and trotters, but very little mutton. Sheep were reared for wool, and made poor eating.

Poultry: here is William Walworth, six years before his starring role in Smithfield, but already mayor of London:

> When he was walking among the poulterers at St Nicholas Shambles to see at what price poultry was being sold, he came to John Andrew, a poulterer, and asked him the price of a goose. The poulterer told him... 8 or 7 pence, and the Mayor told him to charge no more than 6 pence, to which he answered that he would not bring any geese to the city for forty days. He was committed to prison. Three days later [and prisons were very nasty places then] he was brought before the Mayor and Aldermen and made to swear that he would not buy, sell or bring any poultry within the liberties of the city for... seven weeks, on pain of the pillory.[7]

It had been unwise to answer back to William Walworth.

Vegetables and fruit: the Gardeners' Company had existed since before 1345, when they successfully petitioned to be allowed to sell their produce publicly. (In this context, 'gardeners' were not the gentle horticulturalists later to appear regularly on television screens, but commercial entrepreneurs more like our market gardeners.) They had to move their stalls from beside St Paul's Cathedral, because the noise they made was a nuisance to the clerics and laymen attending the church. It looks as if other 'gardeners' could sell the produce of their gardens. In his annual accounts Adam Vynour, 'gardener to the Lord Bishop of Ely in the manor of Holborn', accounted to the bishop for onions and garlic, sold for 16 shillings, and 'herbs, leeks, parsley and herbage' for another 9 shillings.

Apart from these major items, the Manciple needed small quantities of high-priced spices and condiments. These were controlled by the Guild of Grocers (originally 'Pepperers', until 1373 when their name changed to 'Grossers', i.e. dealers in bulk or 'gros', and later to 'Grocers'). The Pepperers had a valuable niche market, and prospered accordingly. In 1345 the guild's twenty-two members, mostly Italians, enjoyed an annual 'mangerie' or feast costing 12 pence a head. By 1348 each member was welcome to bring his wife or a 'compagnon demoiselle', if he liked, but the price had gone up to 20 pence each. The guild was booming, judging by the annual increase in its funds, from £7 in 1346, to £14 in 1347, £22 in 1348 and £32 by 1349, the funds of the last three years being held wholly in gold. It was powerful enough to insist that all goods within its remit must be sold openly, through authorized brokers, who charged a fixed brokerage fee. Pepper, almonds, rice, dates, liquorice, cinnamon, nutmegs, cloves, mace and saffron were all available in apothecaries' shops, which must have smelled wonderful. Sugar, which was treated as a spice, was imported from Egypt, Cyprus and the other Muslim-controlled lands bordering the Mediterranean and was funnelled through Venice, where it was refined into conical 'loaves'. Some salt was mined in England, in Droitwich, but most of it came from salt pans on the Atlantic coast of France.

Shops were good income-producing investments by those with capital to spare. The Priory of St Bartholomew could count on over £44 a year from the rents of various shops. Only freemen of London could own them; outsiders were forbidden to trade, although it looks as if some shopkeepers managed to evade the rules 'and take great profit therefrom, and bear no charge within the city'. They were mostly narrow-fronted properties, with store rooms behind in a yard where a horse could be stabled. Shops selling the same commodity would be grouped along the same street, which accounts for street names such as Bread Street, Wood Lane and so on. There were also 'selds', lines of shops along both sides of a narrow alley, giving off a main street – rather like our shopping malls, but much smaller. And, of course, no advertising, and no artificial lighting: only the voices of the young apprentices standing outside the shop door, inviting passers-by to buy their master's goods, and daylight and the light of candles. Shopping hours would cease in any event at curfew, which meant that everyone had to be off the streets until the next day.

Butchers bought their animals live, at the fair in west Smithfield, and drove them through the streets to their premises. This could be a frightening experience both for the beasts and for any onlookers not spry enough to get out of the way, in those narrow cluttered streets. Some people thought that a bull's meat was more wholesome if the animal had been 'baited' – driven hard, and frightened – before meeting its death in the butcher's yard. This provided good sport for the butcher's young apprentices. Butchers had a bad habit of carrying 'the offal of beasts and other filthy and putrid matter from the slaughtering of beasts through the streets' so that 'some of the offal fell from the vessels in which it was carried', and throwing it into the Thames, 'making the water foul'; and the blood from the Shambles 'found its way down the streets and lanes to the Thames, making a foul corruption and abominable sight and nuisance to all dwelling near or using those streets and lanes . . . it would be more decent that the butchers should slaughter their cattle outside the City'. Regulations were made to that effect, but despite all these complaints from high levels the problem remained until proper slaughterhouses were made compulsory, centuries later.

A comparable stink must have arisen round the fishmongers' stalls. At the end of the trading day they threw out any unsold fish. This was fine for a poor person, if he could find a way of cooking it, and for the daytime customer who could be sure the fish he bought was fresh, but it must have made the surrounding area both slippery and smelly.

His Accounts

So the young future barristers, back from a hard day in court or weary from study, could rely on a square meal in their Inn. The usual main mealtime was around noon, but surely if the courts sat all day, or the 'readings' took up most of the daylight hours, the students would eat in the evening, and the Manciple would have to arrange accordingly.

Considerable sums went through the Manciple's hands. His accounts were always immaculate. Yet – and here's the Chaucerian sting –

Now is not that of God a full fair grace,
That such a lewed [ignorant] man's wit shall pace [surpass]
The wisdom of a heap of learned men? . . .
And yet this manciple sette hir aller cappe [made fools of
    them all].[8]

THE RELIGIOUS LIFE

XIV THE MONK

A manly man, to [have] been an abbot able ...
... his sleeves purfiled [trimmed] at the hand [wrist]
With gris [a kind of fur] ...
And to fasten his hood under his chin
He had of gold ywroght [made] a curious pin;
A love-knot at the greater end there was.
His head was bald, that shone as any glass,
And also his face, as [if] he had been anointed;
He was a lord full fat and in good point [in good condition].
His eyes stepe [prominent] and rolling in his head ...
Now certainly he was a fair prelate[.][1]

An abbot ruled over an abbey, which could be a considerable establishment with property scattered over the country, as well as its
core church and outbuildings. A prior could be an official serving
under an abbot, or the head of a separate community usually, but
not always, smaller than an abbey. His female counterpart was a
prioress. 'Convent' applied to both male and female communities,
although now we use it for female ones only. Monks lived enclosed
lives within their cloistered buildings, but some contact with the
outer world was necessary, varying from community to community.

The Monastic Orders

St Augustine (sometimes abbreviated to Austin) was bishop of
Hippo, on the north coast of Africa in modern Algeria, from 395
until his death in 430. As the son of a Christian mother, leading a

hedonistic life in an affluent Berber family, he had famously prayed, 'Grant me chastity and obedience – but not yet.' He was converted to Christianity in 386, and began a life of austerity and prayer. He wrote several theological studies for which he became revered as one of the founding fathers of the early Church. Physical work was part of his regime, to counteract the listlessness and depression that could infect a monastic life.

In 530, in Monte Cassino in Italy, St Benedict formulated his Rule for the monastic life, devoted to the love of God, and demonstrated by poverty, obedience and chastity. He adopted St Augustine's emphasis on the value of physical work. The Rule covered every aspect life in a community of men, to prevent disharmony. Rule 33 was especially stringent about personal property, which was forbidden: 'this vice ought to be utterly rooted out of the monastery... let no one presume to... have anything of his own, anything whatever, whether book or tablets or pen or whatever it might be; for monks should not have even their bodies and wills at their own disposal'. For a scholar, imagine the pain of not even owning your favourite pen, or, worse still, seeing it in the hand of a clumsy scribe. Rule 34 invoked Acts 4:34–5. After a great meeting of the converted, 'as many as were possessors of lands or houses sold them, and brought the prices of the things that were sold and laid them down at the apostles' feet: and distribution was made to every man according as he had need'. Not an equal distribution, but one much more subtle and difficult to administer. According to the Rule, 'he that needeth less, let him thank God and not be discontented; he that needeth more, let him be humbled for his infirmity and not made proud by the mercy shown to him; so will all the members be at peace. Above all, let not the vice of murmuring [complaining] show itself in any word or sign.'

The food and drink of the monks was carefully regulated, as were their clothes and even their footwear and underwear. Monks were told how to conduct themselves if they were sent on a journey, always travelling in pairs so that one might help and encourage the other. Admission to the order was made difficult, so as to discourage the faint-hearted. Any chronic illness or disability would disqualify the hopeful candidate. During the first eight months of novitiate, a postulant could still leave. Before he was accepted he had to give all his property to the poor or make a formal donation of it to the monastery. His vow was then irrevocable.

The unchanging routine of the Offices punctuated the day and night. Vespers began at 6 p.m., then compline, after which the monks retired to sleep, only to rise at midnight for matins, then lauds, prime, terce, sext at noon, and nones soon after 3 p.m. These tidy three-hourly intervals varied, depending on latitude and season, but that was the general idea. In the hours of darkness, when the abbey or priory would be dimly lit and very cold, the monks walked sleepily to their places in the church with their cowls over their heads. Sometimes there were floor tiles marked to show the way, easily followed by downcast eyes. Sometimes the chill of the stone floors was alleviated by a layer of rushes.

The first monastic movement to reach England had come from the Benedictine monastery of Cluny, in France. In 1089 four monks arrived to found a monastery in Bermondsey, in London, intending to live according to St Benedict's Rule in all its original simplicity. Next arrived the Cistercians, in 1122. They built their monasteries where pure water and pasture for sheep-rearing were available, since wool and its derivatives provided their wealth. By 1300 they had established 694 houses, including Kinloss on the remote north-east coast of Scotland, Rievaulx and Fountains in Yorkshire, Tintern and Waverley in the south of England. They owed their secular success to their efficient organization. They enlisted the religious enthusiasm of 'illiterate' (unable to read Latin) lay brothers, whose skills achieved technological advances in sheep-rearing, textile production, black-smithing and, above all, the use of water-driven mills. Despite their insistence on personal austerity, the buildings they erected in their remote valleys were awe-inspiring in their towering magnificence.

The Carthusians came to England in 1178–9, at the invitation of Henry II, who had vowed to found several new monasteries in penance for his part in the death of Archbishop St Thomas Becket. They were never a numerous order. Only ten Charterhouses were founded in England. In 1348–9 Sir Walter de Manny, one of Edward III's bravest knights, had given land outside the walls of the City of London as a burial ground called the 'Pardon' graveyard, for the victims of the Black Death. In 1370 he founded a Carthusian monastery on the site. The buildings were planned by the royal architect, Henry Yevele. Each monk lived alone in a 'cell', a small two-storey house standing in its own little garden, with living space on the ground floor and a workroom upstairs. Their food was brought by lay brothers, except for Sundays and feast days when they ate together in a refectory, after which the silence rule was relaxed and they all went for a three-hour walk outside their monastery. This had to stop in 1405 because of the distractions of the nearby Bartholomew Fair. Charterhouse School is a survivor of Manny's endowment, after many twists and turns of fate.

What might be tolerable in the Italian climate would have caused pneumonia in the English weather. Warmer clothes were allowed, and shoes instead of sandals, and parts of the open cloisters of monastery courtyards were sometimes closed in to make cosy individual study rooms. One of the most startling changes from the founder's intentions was the custom of giving wages to monks, as pocket money for buying spices and other comforts. There were private rooms in their monasteries, and they could look forward to holidays with pay at one of their abbey's country houses.

The life of the monks of Westminster Abbey was certainly not too austere. A light supper was served in the evening, except on fast days. The main meal was at 11 a.m. or a little later. There would be three cooked main dishes – two rather dull, vegetarian offerings which would not have offended St Benedict, and a third more interesting 'pittance'. On feast days, which happened sixty or seventy times a year, pittances could include small birds and expensive fish dishes such as pike served with a cinnamon and ginger sauce, or salmon from the Thames nearby. On fast days the fish had been either preserved, by salting, smoking or pickling in brine, or bought fresh by the abbot's kitchener from the London fish market.

The monks observed the Benedictine prohibition of meat, but offal didn't count as meat, nor did pre-cooked, salted or minced meat. For a keenly carnivorous monk, there was another possibility. The east end of the refectory had been partitioned off to make three separate rooms called the misericord, and the monks took turns to eat there, five or six days a week, with meat dishes being served every day except for the fasting times of Advent and Lent. Moreover the abbot had a duty to entertain important guests, often as a fund-raising exercise, and he could hardly treat them to the meagre monastic diet. He had a separate kitchen to provide the elaborate meat dishes normal to the tables of the nobility. Some lucky monks would assist him in receiving his guests.

A Benedictine monk was still expected to spend some time each day in physical labour, as well as in solitary study, but somehow the labour was often spent working at a desk, copying or illuminating manuscripts, instead of out in the fresh air exercising his muscles and working off indigestion or a fit of bad temper or depression.

His Worldly Prospects

But Chaucer's Monk did not even spend time in studying.

> What [why] should he study, and make himself wood [mad],
> Upon a book in cloister always to pore,
> Or swinken [work] with his hands, and labour,
> As Austin bids? How shall the world be served?
> Let Austin have his swink to him reserved![2]

He was well able to 'serve the world'. He was an 'outrider', the businessman of his monastery, supervising the landed estates from which it drew its income. He may perhaps also have dabbled in commercial trading. One of the victorious English ships at the Battle of Sluys in 1340 belonged to the prior of Christchurch, Canterbury. It was based at Sandwich, and was probably one of the merchant fleet trading to Flanders with cargoes of wool or woollen textiles, and Cornish tin, and perhaps lead from the mines in Derbyshire.

Chaucer's Monk was, as well, the 'keeper [supervisor] of the cell', which was a dependency or offshoot of the monastery. This was a recognized step up the career ladder towards an abbacy. So Chaucer's Monk was a man on his way up, in this world at least. And in this world, he enjoyed life.

Full many a dainty horse had he in stable...
Of priking [tracking] and of hunting for the hare
Was all his lust [pleasure]; for no cost would he spare.

St Augustine would have been turning in his grave at the thought
of a monk owning horses and greyhounds. Perhaps the hunting
field was getting overcrowded with all these monks. In 1390 Richard II forbade hunting with hounds, ferrets or snares to anyone
with less than 'lands and tenements to the value of 40 shillings a
year, or any priest or clerk [cleric] if he has not preferment worth
£10'. Royal game such as deer were forbidden anyway, but a great
deal of fun could be had by the ruling classes from chasing a hare,
on horseback, with swift greyhounds.

The Monk wore a robe which showed a fur lining at the wrist.
It may have been fur-lined throughout, which certainly would
have been much more comfortable in the English climate than
the poor-quality robes of the original Benedictines. He fastened
his hood under his chin with a gold pin made in the shape of a
love-knot – again, hardly consistent with a vow of poverty.

So it was all very wrong, to lead such an enjoyable life when
he was supposed to embrace privation. One can't help liking him,
though, as Chaucer intended. His portrait is the most vivid of any
of the pilgrims.

What was he doing in a monastery at all? Chaucer does not
impute any religious feeling to him. He was a modern man with
modern views. Where else was he to find the opportunities for
advancement that the Church and the monastic system offered? The
business world of our day did not exist. Laymen such as Chaucer
himself were gradually infiltrating court circles as administrators,
but most jobs still went to churchmen. Provided his bishop was
satisfied with him, the Monk might well be promoted to be an
abbot, where he could exercise his talent for administration, and
still find time to hunt.

XV THE PRIORESS

There was also a nun, a Prioresse,
That of her smiling was full simple and coy...
And she was cleped [called] Madame Eglantine.[1]

She had another nun with her as chaperone and secretary, and three priests. At first sight it may seem surprising that the Prioress was accompanied by no less than three men. One priest was certainly needed, because the nuns must perform their religious duties while away from their convent, and only priests could celebrate Mass for them. Perhaps the other two priests were just out for a pleasant holiday. The Prioress and her staff provided an island of comparative calm in the cavalcade of pilgrims, away from the strident voice of the Wife of Bath and her admirers. But there was no sign that God directed their travel plans.

Her Character

Chaucer has drawn a delightful picture of a pretty woman on holiday from her everyday life. He describes her in terms that make one exclaim 'How sweet!' Madame Eglantine was so tender-hearted that she wept if she saw a mouse caught in a trap. She was very fond of dogs – she had brought her little dogs with her. She passed all the tests for contemporary beauty: a high forehead, a straight nose, shining grey eyes and red lips. She spoke French 'after the manner of Stratford atte Bowe', where a Benedictine nunnery had been founded in the twelfth century, and where, perhaps, she had been educated. Her 'French' accent was understandable, since the

version of French spoken by the upper classes in England had long
ago diverged from the original language brought over by William
from Normandy in 1066. She could sing the holy offices in the
approved style, intoning them down her nose. Her wimple was
elegantly pleated, and she wore a bracelet of coral and green beads
with a shining gold brooch on it, 'On which there was first written
a crowned A, / And after, "*Amor vincit omnia*" [Love conquers
all].'

Table Manners

Chaucer makes such a point of the Prioress's table manners that it
seems right to give them a separate section. She was so well trained
that

> She let no morsel from her lips fall,
> Ne wette [she didn't wet] her fingers in her sauce deep.
> Well could she carry a morsel and wel kepe [take care]
> That no drop ne fall [would fall] upon her breast...
> Her over-lippe [upper lip] wiped she so clean
> That in her cup there was no ferthing [particle] seen
> Of grease, when she had drunk her draught;
> Ful semely after her mete she raughte [she reached for her
>   food in a graceful way].[2]

Being so tidy at table can't always have been easy in those long,
voluminous robes. But it still seems odd to give such prominence
to her table manners. Perhaps it implied a reproof to those pilgrims
with whom Chaucer was travelling, whose manners fell far short
of the Prioress's.

The usual habit of eating, in polite circles, depended on the knife
that any man would have at his belt. The five Guildsmen each had
a silver-mounted one. It would be handy for spearing the 'gobbets'
(see Chapter IX) of food that landed on your trencher, or cutting
up the slices of meat and poultry served to you from the efforts of
the carver. A knife and a belt were an integral part of male costume;
but where did the Prioress stow hers? And, more to the point, why

did Chaucer make such a point of her agility in managing? I can only suggest that we are meant to see her at table and admire her, while wondering whether she showed an equal spiritual conformity in her religious life: devious, perhaps, but Chaucer knew what he was about, and often used such touches to show negatives as well as positives.

No one should come to the table with dirty hands. A page would be ready with a jug of water, no doubt warm and scented, and perhaps with a sliver of soap in it. The diner would hold out his cupped hands, the page would pour a little water from his jug on to them, with his right hand, catching the drips in a bowl held in his left hand. The diner could dry his nice clean hands on the towel slung over the page's shoulder.

Life in a Nunnery

But what was she doing on the road to Canterbury? She should have been in her priory, looking after her nuns and praying to God, not junketing off on pilgrimage. But she was much too fun-loving for that; it 'pained her to counterfeit [pretend] cheere of court [the behaviour of court], and to be stately in manner, and to be held worthy of reverence'.[3] The Rule of St Benedict enjoining poverty, obedience and chastity applied to her just as rigorously as to the Monk. The bishops who had overall supervision of convents made their displeasure as to pilgrimages plain. Yet, as so often, the nuns managed to circumvent their ecclesiastical masters and off they went, Madame Eglantine among them.

Her soft-heartedness to animals would have been better spent on her fellow-humans. The 'roasted flesh, or milk and wastel [sweet white] bread' that she fed to her dogs would have overjoyed a poor family, subsisting on hard, coarse bread if they were lucky. The high forehead that Chaucer asks us to admire should have been covered by her veil. And she certainly shouldn't have been wearing coral beads and that brooch proclaiming that 'Love conquers all'. If it had said something about the love of God she might have got away with it, but she should have known that it came from Virgil's earthy *Eclogues* – and if she didn't, Chaucer's audience certainly might. Even her name – Eglantine, or honeysuckle – was hardly canonical.

The minimum age for entry to the conventual life was twelve. There could be a sinister motive behind putting a girl into a nunnery. In law, nuns were 'dead to the world', so they could not inherit property, and their rights passed to the unscrupulous relatives who had sent them there. On the other hand, a nunnery could shelter girls born out of wedlock, or with physical or mental disabilities, who would have been lost in the outside world. As well as the nunnery at Stratford-at-Bow, there were Benedictine nunneries at Barking, founded in about 666, St Helen's Bishopsgate, founded in 1204, and another out at Clerkenwell. The Poor Clares or 'Minoresses', the sister order of the Franciscans, had a nunnery just outside the city walls, founded in 1293.

Most nuns were recruited from the upper classes. Where else could surplus daughters go? Girls born lower down the social scale could usually find employment – and husbands – in their fathers' circles, but a well-born girl would be expected to bring her husband a considerable dowry, which came expensive for the father of several girls. Even entering a convent cost the proud parent a sum down, plus the cost of furniture for her cell, but at least the girl was off her parents' hands. In 1393 William Wyght left £50 to each of his four daughters 'for their marriage or for entering a religious house'.[4] John of Gaunt paid more than £51 on the admission of Elizabeth Chaucy to Barking Abbey in 1381.[5] These were very considerable sums in those days. The Rule laid down by St Benedict forbade the payment of such 'dowers', but in practice they were always demanded, and could amount to £100 or more.

One disadvantage of life in a fashionable convent was the constant stream of visitors imposed on it by outside powers. The king or the local bishop could 'nominate' some rich woman to spend time in a nunnery, bringing with her a coterie of servants and dogs and monkeys and other pets, and her ultra-fashionable wardrobe. She would expect to be entertained, disrupting the nuns' peaceful routine, and making no contribution by way of dower. This could be a severe strain on the finances, as well as the nerves, of the community. Visitors might be charged for their keep, but they often simply stayed on without paying, and it might be impolitic for the prioress to object too loudly. The king treated the monastic houses of his realm as a vast rest home for worn-out royal servants, saving him the expense of pensioning them off. The nunnery most favoured by royalty was that of the Poor Clares. It owed its foundation to the earl of Lancaster, brother of King Edward I. Queen Isabella, the mother of Edward III, retired there towards the end of her life, and died there in 1358. Thomas, duke of Gloucester (1355–97), the youngest son of Edward III, placed his daughter Isabel there as a child. She grew up to be its abbess.

But it was not a bad existence, if you didn't miss male company. You could set your sights on being elected to be prioress, as long as you were over twenty-one and 'of good reputation', and that was a job for life. You could have your own establishment and entertain your inner circle of friends, and your relatives from the outside world, with better food from your own kitchen than in the convent refectory. Granted, it involved getting up in the middle of the night for matins and then lauds, and again at 6 a.m. or 7 a.m. for prime, and then stumbling back to the cold chapel at intervals during the day until compline at 7 p.m. in winter, an hour later in summer. Those little pet dogs made useful hand-warmers.

And if the lack of male company became intolerable, there were ways... In 1367 the bishop who 'visited' (inspected) St Sepulchres Convent in Canterbury found that 'Dame Johanna Chivynton, Prioress there, does not govern well the rule nor the religion of the house, because she permits the rector of Dover castle and other suspect persons to have too much access to sisters Margery Chyld and Juliana Aldeless, who have a room contrary to the injunction made by the Lord [Archbishop] and these suspect persons often spend the night there.' Chantry priests and vicars and chaplains, too, came and went – and sometimes stayed. Langland, with his usual acerbity, puts a vivid picture of conventual life into the mouth of a prioress's 'potager' or stew-maker:

> Dame Joan was a bastard,
> And Dame Clarice a knight's daughter – but a cuckold was
>   her father,
> And Dame Pernele was a priest's concubine – she will never
>   be a prioress,
> Because she had a child in cherry-time, all our Chapter
>   knew it![6]

A prioress was entitled to emerge into the world on proper occasions such as the wedding of a close relative. She might also inspect the farms and other property owned by her nunnery. One has to doubt whether she inspected everything they owned, such as the brothel known as the Rose on Bankside, next door to another called the Little Rose. This seems to have been a paying concern, assessed at over £4 due to the king, which Edward III 'forgave' in 1362 since the income was used by the nuns 'to find [fund] works of piety'.

What else did the nuns do all day, when they weren't praying? St Benedict's insistence on physical work had somehow been relaxed by Chaucer's time. The nuns were certainly not expected to share in the housework or cooking; for one thing, they had no idea how to do such things, not having learned those utilitarian matters in their parents' homes. Such work was done by lay sisters. In houses of any size, men oversaw the necessary brewing and malting processes, and the kitchens. The nuns might do a little light embroidery or fine spinning, and perhaps some gentle gardening. They would need to look after their little dogs and other pets. In 1387 the bishop of Winchester wrote to the prioress of Romsey in stern words: 'some of the nuns of your house bring with them to church birds, rabbits and such like frivolous things'. Madame Eglantine's little dogs getting in everyone's way were an example of the notorious fondness for lapdogs indulged by any fashionable woman.

They might run a small school for upper-class children, including boys, up to the age of nine or ten, when the boys went off to be taught manly things such as warfare, and the girls stayed on, quietly learning to repeat the holy offices in Latin. They would learn them by rote. A proper study of the Latin language would be unfeminine and unnecessary. They might be taught to read, which they would need if they were to follow the prayers in their books of hours, but they had no particular requirement to be able to write: a paid secretary would do this for them, in the outside world.

St Benedict's disapproval of personal property for monks applied just as strongly to nuns – and was just as widely ignored by Chaucer's time, as shown by the Prioress's coral beads and gold brooch. In 1349 Isabella de Leyre, the widow of a goldsmith 'of Cheap' (Cheapside), left the rent of certain properties to a nunnery, 'one moiety [half] to be distributed to every nun for clothing and other necessaries'. The basic nuns' robes would have been supplied by the nunnery, so Isabella's legacy enabled them to perk up their wardrobes.

In 1385 the nuns at Bishopsgate were scolded by their bishop for the number of little dogs kept by their prioress, for wearing ostentatious veils and for kissing secular persons. This was just a year before Chaucer began to write the *Tales*; had he somehow heard rumours that inspired his picture of the Prioress?

XVI THE FRIAR

A friar there was, a wantowne [jovial] and a merry...
In all the orders four is none that kan [knows]
So much of daliaunce [conversation] and fair language.[1]

The Four Orders

The Franciscans and the Dominicans were the best known of the 'orders four'. Their orders had both arisen in the early thirteenth century. By then the waves of religious emotion that had caused thousands of men all over Europe to forsake their lands and families and make for Palestine to free the Holy Places from the infidels had receded. The Fourth Crusade, launched in 1202 to conquer Jerusalem via an attack on Egypt, resulted in the shameful sacking of Constantinople by the Crusaders. No wonder that men inspired by religious faith sought another outlet.

What were they to do, when the Crusades had failed? They could retire into a monastery and live the secluded life of a monk, praying and praising God, or they could live their faith actively in the outside world.

The Franciscans

St Francis chose the latter course. He was born in 1181, the son of a prosperous silk merchant of Assisi. He led a varied life as a young man, including a year in a Perugian prison, before he felt the vocation to lead the strict religious life that was so alien to the home he had grown up in. When his father refused to approve his choice, Francis dramatically stripped off his rich clothes, handed them to his father and adopted a life of unremitting poverty. He took literally Jesus's bidding to his disciples in Matthew 10:6–10: 'But go rather to the lost sheep . . . And as you go, preach, saying "The Kingdom of Heaven is at hand." Heal the sick, cleanse the lepers, raise the dead, cast out devils: freely you have received, freely give. Provide neither gold, nor silver, nor brass in your purses, nor scrip for your journey, neither two coats, neither shoes, nor yet staves, for the workman is worthy of his meat.'[2]

Francis began by cleansing the lepers near where he lived: a revolting task from which he shrank, but he swallowed his disgust and persisted. He preached the Word of God to all who would hear him, and – according to legend – when there was none to hear, he preached to the birds. Far from marrying the suitable, well-endowed bride that his family had chosen for him, he espoused 'Holy Poverty'. Towards the end of his life his sanctity was evidenced by the stigmata, the signs on his body of the wounds suffered by Christ on the Cross. Many followers flocked to him, so that it became necessary to regularize his way of life. At that time, the pope did not look kindly on new rules, so Francis adopted the existing Rule of St Benedict. The pope gave his informal consent to the Franciscan order in 1210, which was formally ratified in 1223, three years before Francis died.

His followers came from every land in Europe, and from every class. They were expected to serve the poor and disadvantaged, setting them an example by living according to the Christian idea. In 1224 nine of them arrived in England. Five stayed in Canterbury and four came to London, where they were given land just within the city wall, where they built a monastery. Their simple life attracted many disciples and benefactors, including royalty. Their numbers had risen to eighty by 1243. By 1348, the time of the Great Pestilence, in which it is generally reckoned that about half the population died, a hundred Grey Friars perished, which supposes a pre-1348 number of perhaps two hundred.

The extreme austerity of their founder was slightly relaxed to suit the northern climate. In winter they were allowed to wear shoes instead of the sandals that had sufficed in Assisi, and in very cold weather they could even wear two habits, both of grey, undyed wool. They were known as the Grey Friars from the colour of their habits, or the Friars Minor, because St Francis had said, 'Let the brothers always be less [minores] than all others.' He also called them the Joculatores Dei, God's minstrels. He was an excellent singer himself, and he encouraged his followers to sing.

Since their mission was to preach to the ordinary people, Franciscan brothers or 'friars' had to learn the local vernacular wherever they went. Their sermons often used homely metaphors and even jokes to draw the crowds, who were more accustomed to listening to pedlars and jugglers than the Word of God.

The obvious conflict between the refusal of St Francis to own anything, and the possessions that flowed to his order from his followers, was resolved by a neat piece of papal juggling: 'No one is considered to own what he merely possesses so long as he does not in conscience consider himself as owner.' By Chaucer's time, their mere possessions had accumulated and were still growing. In 1340, for example, John de Oxenford, a vintner, left bequests of wine and money to 'the various orders of friars in London', including the Franciscans. They even took apprentices, who had no religious vocation. In 1360 a widow left to her apprentice 'the third best part of copies and instruments appertaining to the making of pictures, and one of her best chests to put them in; the said apprentice to be delivered over to the care and teaching of Friar Thomas... of the priory and convent of Bermondsey for a term of three years'.

Brother Bozon

By a series of fortunate chances, we have the very words of a Franciscan preaching to a crowd in 1320. Brother Bozon wrote a 'Little Book' of his notes for a sermon, which survived into our own age.[3] His Little Book was written in Anglo-Norman French, the language of the educated classes from which he came, but he will have preached, as his order required, in the local patois of his audience, which from internal evidence was probably somewhere in the north of England. His Little Book takes the form of 204 'metaphors', each with its moral. His technique was to take a theme, from Scripture or from classical authors such as Pliny or Aristotle – that favourite of medieval scholars – or from his own imagination, and embroider it with a crowd-pulling 'Tale'.

No doubt he held his audience spellbound, especially when he started on elephants. He told them how the elephant 'protects himself with his ears against gnats and flying flies'. God 'has given to the elephant such a nature that though he may be of such strength that he can carry many people, well armed . . . yet he fears a mouse'. And 'twice a year the elephant goes to wash at the river, and takes his son with him', which demonstrates the desirability of frequent confession. Elephants exemplify the power of cooperation, and love for our fellow-men. 'An elephant cannot sleep lying down. He provides himself with a tree where he can support himself and sleep standing. Then [someone] comes who knows his retreat . . . and saws the tree nearly through . . . and when the wretch [the poor creature] comes to his support as he is used to do, he is deceived and falls to the ground crying piteously. Then it is the nature of the elephant to aid him who is fallen, so they come and put their trunks under his back and raise him up by great strength and save their companion from danger.'

One of his metaphors concerns a hippopotamus, 'which is now fish, now beast'. Another suggests how to catch a tiger 'that delights to see and regard his likeness [in a mirror] that through craft is put in his way'. Coming nearer home, he describes a badger as 'a base and stinking animal . . . so burning in lechery that in their rutting time they will even attack a man'. Perhaps medieval badgers were fiercer than in our time. He doesn't confine himself to the animal kingdom. In the Red Sea one can find, of course, rubies. The cinnamon tree grows in the jungles of Ethiopia. He pauses to give several useful prescriptions. A general anaesthetic can be made from a mandrake root cooked in sweet wine, 'and when [the patient] shall have drunk . . . he can sleep so sound that one can do to him what one wants without his feeling hurt'. For snake bite, more commonly met with in the north of England than elephants and hippopotamuses, take rue and water and 'the kernel of nuts' – which nuts, he doesn't say. As he surveys his audience he is moved to give a prescription for baldness – the bark and leaves of a sweet chestnut tree, burned and pulverized and 'tempered' with sweet wine, 'so if you be young and wish to be seemly before God, haunt the chestnut, which means chastity'. If on the other hand you are excessively hirsute, try thistle juice.

The Dominicans

St Dominic's life differed radically from his near-contemporary St Francis. He was born in Castile in 1170. He was ordained and became a prior, with none of the struggles that beset Francis in his youth. He soon realized that the conversion of heretics required more than Francis's simple piety; it needed intellectual power. He founded the Order of Friars Preachers. His followers became known as Dominicans, in Latin *Domini Canes*, the hounds of God, which is why they are often symbolized as black dogs with white spots, the white habit of their order covered with the black travelling capes of Spanish priests. He set up schools to educate as well as proselytize. Unlike his friend St Francis, he was an able administrator.

The Dominicans came to England in 1221, the year of their founder's death. Like the Franciscans, they founded a monastery in London, known as Blackfriars, just within the city walls at the south-western end of the city. By 1250 their annual General Chapter was attended by more than four hundred friars. Their order became rich and powerful, always maintaining its emphasis on education. It was the first to dispense with the Benedictine rule requiring daily physical labour.

The Austin Friars and the Carmelites

The two other orders that made up Chaucer's four were the Augustinian or 'Austin' Friars, whose monastery was built in the city in 1253, and the Carmelites, so called because they had been driven from their monastery on Mount Carmel by the Saracens. They arrived in England in 1241, where they established a priory on the south side of Fleet Street. They were called 'White Friars', from the colour of their gowns.

Although this city is described as 'Constantinus nobilis' (Constantinople) the artist has drawn the only city he knew: London. There's St Paul's, topped by a weathercock, and an inn with its sign of a green bush, the stone walls and timbered houses, and even a group of dancers jigging their way out of town to the music of pipe and drum.

This picture shows two successive events in the Peasants' Revolt, 1381. On the left, the peasants' leader, Wat Tyler, is killed. On the right, the fourteen-year-old King Richard II turns to the angry mob and persuades it to disperse, by promises he subsequently breaks.

Jousting gave knights practice for real warfare. Here is a knight in full jousting armour. His battle armour would be much simpler.

In the English victory of Crécy, 1346, the English longbow archers fire steadily into the enemy ranks, putting to flight the enemy crossbowmen. As they flee, they block the advance of their own cavalry.

This map was drawn by Muhammad al-Idrisi, for King Roger II of Sicily, in 1154. It gave a remarkably accurate world view, and was consulted for centuries until the great Age of Exploration. The so-called *mappae mundi* were really didactic religious documents, showing Jerusalem as the centre of the world – not much use for travellers.

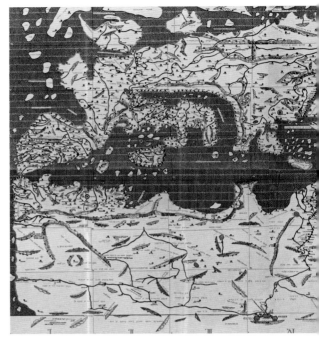

Naval warfare followed much the same tactics as land battles. Archers fire from raised platforms ('castles') and armed men swarm onto the enemy ship for hand-to-hand fighting. Running away is not an option; anyone who falls overboard will be drowned.

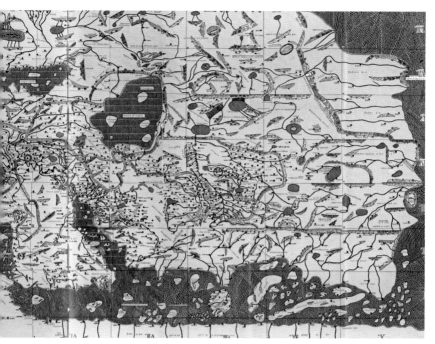

Marco Polo's book of *Travels* was a medieval bestseller, written in about 1299. There were several manuscripts of it, all differing, and it was translated into many languages including English. Here he is on his way home to Venice from India, calling at Hormuz in the Persian Gulf, with two laden camels and a laden elephant.

The Three Kings or Magi, following the star leading them to the birth of Jesus.

The three shepherds, also following the star. One of them is playing the bagpipes.

Legends grew up to fill the space left in the Gospels, about Jesus's early life. Here he is, nimbus and all, sliding down a sunbeam while his playmates break their legs below. He was also able to walk up water, leaving his playmates to drown, and he could mend broken pots.

This friar is preaching to a mixed collection of passers-by in the open air, from a mobile pulpit. The mendicant (begging) orders such as the Franciscans and the Dominicans were founded as a reaction to the pomp and riches of the established Church. The figure in black is a cook, holding a roasting spit. The man at the back with his purse is well off, in contrast.

Clerics should have been worshipping God in their monasteries, not hunting rabbits (then much-prized animals) with greyhounds and bows and arrows.

The closer a worshipper could get to a holy relic, the stronger its influence. The tomb of Saint Edward the Confessor was designed so that worshippers could even touch his coffin, bringing miraculous cures.

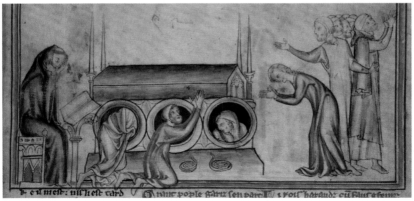

They made their way on horseback or on foot,
even limping with crutches.

There is a faint hint, not inconsistent with some modern cults, that friars, and monks too, were apt to entice young people to join their order when they were too young to make an informed choice. In a pseudo-Chaucerian poem, *The Court of Love*, the friars and monks complained: 'see how they cry and wring their hands, for they so soon went to religion'.[4] In 1392 a ten-year-old schoolboy was approached by some friars near his school. They asked if his Latin was good enough to translate a passage from English to Latin. It read: 'I oblige me to be a friar of the cross.' He proudly did so, upon which 'one of the friars kissed him and said that all the bishops in England could not absolve him from becoming a friar of their order, and so they took the boy away and dressed him in the habit of their order and withdrew him from the custody of [his guardian]'. The guardian promptly complained to the Warden of the City, who ordered the friars to return the boy to his guardian. Quite what would have happened to the boy if his guardian had not been so alert is all too clear.

All four orders were alike in answering direct to the pope through their administrative hierarchies, bypassing any local parochial organization. This did not endear them to parish priests.

Chaucer's Friar

Chaucer's Friar was called Huberd. We are not told which order he belonged to, but he sounds like a Franciscan. He was a 'limitour', which meant that he was authorized to beg on behalf of his convent, in a specific district assigned to him by his order. He was 'the best begger in his house'.[5]

Even better, he 'had power of confession':

> Full sweetly heard he confession,
> And pleasant was his absolution.
> He was an easy man to give penance...
> For unto a poor order for to give
> Is [a] sign that a man is wel yshrive   is well shriven [has
>   made a thorough confession][.][6]

The power to hear confession was a bitter bone of contention between parish priests and friars. Parish priests relied on the income from donations and bequests by their parishioners, in gratitude for, or to induce, absolution, so they resented friars trespassing on this profitable field. Huberd's astute selling point was that to make a handsome donation to the 'poor friars' – himself? – was a clearer indication of true repentance than any amount of weeping and prayers. His absolution was 'pleasant' and simple – a straightforward money transaction, painless to the sinner as long as he had enough funds. He could also promise complete discretion, whereas the penances imposed by the parish priest sometimes attracted the attention of the penitent's neighbours, even if the confidentiality veiling any confession was observed. The penitent would not have to face the man who had heard his confession in the daily life of the parish, since the friar to whom he had confessed his sins might be off to another parish the next day.

Hubert concentrated on the franklins, the local landowners, and the 'worthy women of the ton' (neighbourhood), where he could be sure of a good 'pittance' (payment). He also knew all the caterers and other rich men, the tavern-keepers and innkeepers and barmaids, better than he knew any leper or beggar. It wouldn't have been suitable for a man of his status to have anything to do with lepers and 'such poraille [poor people]'. Yet he wasn't above extorting a farthing from a woman so poor that she had no shoes. His gains 'on the side' were worth more than his regular income from donations.

Another sideline, and another fruitful field for bribes – he could preside, with the dignity of a university graduate or one of the several popes then reigning, over 'lovedays', when disputes were settled out of court.

He also acted as a marriage broker. He had 'made full many a marriage / of young women' at his own cost. Only Chaucer's audience would have appreciated exactly what the innuendo here was. And despite his imposing dignity he was not above currying favour with pretty women by distributing knives and pins – invaluable for medieval dress – that he carried in his hood. He must have been an asset to any party. He had a wide repertoire of songs and could play the zither. Sometimes he lisped slightly, to 'make his English sweet upon the tongue'. Far from the threadbare habit of an early Franciscan, or a monk or a poor scholar, he wore 'double worsted', an expensive and crease-resisting fabric that always looked as if it was newly ironed.

But if 'profit should arise, courteous he was, and lowly of service'. Holy poverty had got lost along the way.

XVII THE PARDONER

His Appearance

Although Chaucer promised to tell us the rank and even the dress of every pilgrim, we are sometimes left in the dark. But we have an unforgettable picture of the Pardoner.[1] He had popping eyes 'like a hare'. He sang love duets with the Summoner, on their way –'Was never trumpet of half so great a sound' – although the Pardoner's voice was 'as small as a goat's'. Instead of a hat or the more usual wrap-around headgear, he was bareheaded except for a cap with a pilgrim's badge, a vernicle. (A vernicle symbolized the cloth that St Veronica used to wipe the sweat from Jesus's face as he was carrying his cross to the execution site. It showed that the Pardoner had been to Rome.) His lank, blond hair lay in locks on his shoulders. 'He thought he rode all of the new jet' (the new fashion, which Chaucer is laughing at). 'No beard had he, nor never should have ... I think he was a gelding or a mare.'[2] In Wycliffe's version of the New Testament, in Matthew 19:12 Jesus is reported as saying: 'There are geldings which are thus born of the mother's womb, and there are geldings that are made of [by] men, and there are geldings that have gelded themselves for the kingdom of heavens.' The word in the King James Bible, in Matthew 19:12, is 'eunuchs'. Chaucer seems to be hinting, unkindly, that the Pardoner was homosexual, but he stopped short of a direct statement since the homosexual act of sodomy was a crime punishable by death.

Pardons

Two articles of faith would have been familiar to Chaucer's audience but have almost faded from our mental horizons now. One was the doctrine of pardons. The other was the importance of holy relics. Much ink and some blood have been shed on them.

The Pardoner had come straight from the papal headquarters in Rome, with the appropriate pilgrim's badge and a bag full of pardons. He was 'of Rouncival'. This could mean that his base was the Hospital of our Lady of Roncesvalles, on the pass through the Pyrenees on the main pilgrim route to Compostela; or, more probably, it could refer to the dependent house in London, St Mary Roncevall. Chaucer's reference to it would remind his audience of certain unsavoury rumours about that house, which specialized in selling pardons and had been formally accused of selling false pardons only a few years earlier, in 1379. Anyone found guilty of extortion by selling false pardons could be sentenced to stand in the pillory and be publicly exposed as a fraud.

The doctrine of pardons had been constructed, without any biblical foundation, by the papacy, which made a solid income from it. The unending virtue of Jesus and the saints had created a 'treasury of merit' in the care of the holy Church. Sincerely repentant Christians could draw on it in advance by buying remission from the everlasting punishment otherwise awaiting them in purgatory. But first they had to show their true repentance by giving alms to the Church. 'Pardoners' – sellers of pardons – spread out over Christendom like travelling salesmen selling snake oil, or estate agents taking deposits on non-existent flats. They transmitted their takings back to Rome, less, perhaps, a small service charge. But papal interference with English affairs was becoming more and more unpopular. In Chaucer's *House of Fame*, written in 1379–80, his antipathy to pardoners was already evident:

> O, many a thousand times twelve
> Saw I eke [also] these pardoners
> . . . With boxes crammed full of lies[.]

The money spent on pardons granted by Rome should stay in England, and save English souls, rather than swelling the pope's funds.

Relics

The objects surrounding, or used by, a particularly holy person, and any available body parts were believed to retain his or her influence after death. The doctrine developed from the understandable human desire to see, and touch, and even to possess some object still conserving the life force of the object of veneration. If the saint's physical body could be obtained, it was even better. It guaranteed a source of income from the huge crowds of pilgrims flocking to see it, and to buy mementos of their trip. Any monastery of any importance had to have at least one relic – the more the better.

The most blatant theft of a holy relic had taken place in 828. St Mark, the Evangelist, had become bishop of Alexandria. Travelling one day to Rome, on evangelical business no doubt, he stopped at Venice, where he met an angel who blessed him and said that his body would rest in that very place. This seemed unlikely, since when he died in AD 68 he was buried in Alexandria. Sixty years later, however, two Venetian merchants returned from Alexandria with a corpse which, they claimed, was that of St Mark. Its guardians had parted with it, according to the Venetians, in the praiseworthy hope of saving it from the Saracens. It seems more likely that bribery or actual theft played a part. The Venetians' story was to some extent confirmed by the strong odour of sanctity emanating from the body. But this sweet smell caught the attention of the local Muslim officials, who demanded to search the ship. Thinking quickly, the Venetians masked their precious freight in a layer of pork meat, which repelled the pious Muslims, and the ship set sail for Venice. All was not yet over: the ship would have been wrecked if St Mark himself had not alerted the sleeping captain. So his body was carried into Venice with acclamation, and St Mark became the powerful patron saint of Venice. It would not be easy to trump the possession of an evangelist.

But St James ran him a close second. After the death of Jesus, according to legend, James travelled abroad to spread the gospel, even as far as north-west Spain. But when he got back to Jerusalem the Roman authorities disapproved of him and beheaded him in AD 44. Somehow his body found its way, with angelic help, to the north-west coast of Spain, where it was secretly buried. In 813 the burial site was miraculously discovered. From then on, streams of pilgrims made their way to it. It became the premier medieval pilgrimage site, even surpassing Venice. One would have expected an evangelist to outrank a mere disciple. Perhaps Venice lost a certain amount of goodwill because of its mercenary attitude to the Crusaders. Perhaps Santiago had more efficient public relations people, and had a few years' start on St Mark. Yet another legend linked St James with the scallop shells to be found on the Spanish beach where the boat bearing his body had landed. They became the symbol worn by every pilgrim who had reached St James's holy site.

Sir John Mandeville's *Travels* were widely read in the late 1300s. In Constantinople he saw 'a piece of the cross that God was put on, and the sponge with the reed that they gave Christ to drink when he was on the cross. And there is one of the iron nails that Christ was nailed with ... A piece of the crown of thorns and one of the spear heads that Christ was tortured with ... are in France, in the King's chapel ... I myself have one of the thorns.' Another of these remarkably long-lasting thorns had been acquired by the bishop of Soissons in 1205, who helped himself to a piece of the Virgin Mary's robe as well, and the head of John the Baptist, which both ended up in his cathedral at Soissons.

Nearer home, Sir William de Langeford bequeathed, in 1346, 'a silver vessel containing the blood of Christ crucified'.

Chaucer's Pardoner

He carried with him a pillowcase that he said was part of the Virgin's veil, and a piece of the sail of St Peter's fishing boat (Matthew 4:18). He had a brass cross 'full of stones' – we can infer that it was set with imitation jewels – and a glass full of pigs' bones. With those relics he could get more money in one day than any poor country parson could in a year:

> And thus with feined flattery and japes [tricks]
> He made the parson and the people his apes.[3]

But he could act the part of a serious churchman when needed, especially when it came to the offertory, the donations from the congregation.

So there he is: a gay pilgrim, his long hair waving in the wind, riding beside the equally amoral Summoner on his way to Canterbury, ready to fool the ignorant into parting with the cash earned in this world by his false promises about the next.

XVIII THE CLERK OF OXENFORD

What a contrast to the Merchant, whom he followed in Chaucer's parade of pilgrims.[1] Both he and his horse were as lean as rakes and his short woollen jacket was threadbare. He was a teacher and scholar at the University of Oxford. 'Gladly would he learn, and gladly teach.'

Oxford University

Oxford University had begun in the twelfth century, without any fanfare of trumpets. The town had long been a favoured venue for Church courts, with convenient access by river to London. High-ranking ecclesiastical judges required suitable accommodation for themselves and their retinues. Students of canon law were drawn to the court hearings, and they in turn attracted teachers. In 1201 the title of 'Magister scholarum Oxoniae' (Master of Oxford schools, 'schools' being faculties in a university, not schools for children) had appeared for the first time in official correspondence. The two or three hundred students of that time could chose from the liberal arts, Roman and canon law, theology and, for a few, medicine. In 1209 the townspeople rounded on the scholars and hanged two or three of them on a trumped-up charge of rioting. This caused such outrage that the whole academic establishment upped sticks and went off to Cambridge, where they founded England's second university. After a few years they decided to go back to Oxford, leaving Cambridge University to flourish on its own.

In 1254 the status of Oxford University as an academic corporation was formally recognized by the pope, but this did not defuse

the tension between 'town' and 'gown'. In the very next year
there was another riot between the scholars and the townspeople,
in which nearly a hundred people died. But in 1355 Edward III
granted a 'Great Charter' to the university, recognizing its powerful status. In return he drew increasingly on the university for the
administration of his government – the medieval equivalent of the
civil service, and a 'think-tank' to advise the ruler on problems. The
university continued to attract scholars from all over Europe.

The Dominicans

By 1267 there were four monasteries in Oxford, housing friars who
found the facilities of the university useful for honing their preaching skills. The Dominicans had arrived in 1221, the Franciscans in
1224, the Carmelites in 1256 and the Austin Friars in 1266. According to the original Rule of the Dominican Friars approved by the
pope in 1217, friars under training for worldly preaching 'shall not
study the books of pagans or philosophers, except they may glance
over them for an hour. They shall not learn profane sciences nor
even the arts which are called liberal' without a time-limited special
permission. This sometimes led to bitter disputes with the nascent
university. By 1336, however, there had been a radical change.
Every district of the Dominican province of England was obliged
to contribute to the cost of sending a 'student-friar' to Oxford
University, where he would inevitably spend most of his waking
hours cheek by jowl with Aristotle, that archetypical 'pagan philosopher'. In 1343 the General Chapter of the order ordained that its
friars might practise medicine and surgery as long as they were duly
licensed by their Prior Provincial, so they must have been able to
study the growing corpus of medical texts. By 1376 there were 70
Dominicans, 103 Franciscans, 49 Augustinians and 57 Carmelite
friars studying in Oxford, some as members of the university and
others following courses in their monasteries. They had an advantage over their fellow-students, since their orders provided them
with books that they could keep for life. John of Gaunt employed a
friar, Brother William Appleton, as his personal physician. He had
surely read all the relevant books, and passed all appropriate tests.

The Life of an Undergraduate

Oxford was settling, not always peacefully, into its role as a university town. The rents charged by landlords for students' lodgings, and the prices charged to them for food, had been strictly controlled since 1214, and a fund had been set up to help poor students, to which the university contributed. One hundred poor scholars could look forward to a free dinner every 6 December, St Nicholas's day. But university life was not so exorbitantly expensive as it has now become. A prosperous peasant could probably afford the £2 or £3 a year it would cost him to keep a son at Oxford; certainly a father from the yeomanry or lesser gentry could find it feasible.

The students attracted to the university lived in lodging houses scattered through Oxford. Some were said to lead shockingly dissolute lives, with no one to administer discipline or see to their physical well-being. To remedy this, in 1264 Walter de Merton founded Merton College, endowing it with property sufficient to support a warden and priests who would, in the usual medieval way, pray for the souls of the founder and his family in the next world in return for his help in this world. The college was to support twenty students, or more when the funds allowed. There was also provision for the children of the founder and his kin.[2] The study of medicine and law was prohibited by the founding statutes, but neither prohibition seems to have had much effect. By 1350 Merton was renowned throughout Europe for its learning.

By then six more colleges had been founded in Oxford: Balliol and University College during the thirteenth century, Exeter, Oriel, Queen's and New College in the fourteenth. All were funded by private donors, as chantries, hoping in this way to ensure the salvation of their souls.

The daily life of a medieval undergraduate was hard. The usual age at entry was fifteen to sixteen. 'Ordinary' lectures, mostly on Aristotelian themes, lasted from 6 to 9 a.m., nearly every day. The rest of the day was spent in extra lectures and inter-student disputations, a vital part of medieval university education, sharpening the

wits of the contestants in oral argument. An entrant to the faculty
of arts, the largest faculty, began by paying a Master who would put
him on his class list ('matriculation'). As an arts student Chaucer's
Cleric will have studied the 'trivium' – grammar, logic and rhetoric
– before progressing to the 'quadrivium' – arithmetic, music, geometry and astronomy – plus the three philosophies, moral, natural
and metaphysical. 'Moral philosophy' included ethics, economics
and politics.

After four years of lectures and colleagiate disputations the
undergraduate was tested in a public disputation; if he passed, he
was a Bachelor of Arts. Then three more years of study and hard
work, and he would if successful become a Master of Arts, formally
mounting the steps (hence 'graduation', *gradus* being the Latin for
step) to a Master's chair. This seven-year course was analogous to a
normal apprenticeship to a Master of any craft, even including, in
some guilds, the step up to 'bachelor', short of full qualification.
The new Master was obliged to teach in his turn, as a 'Regent',
for two years before at last setting out to earn his living as best he
could, unless he decided to go on studying in one of the superior
faculties, theology or canon law.

Lectures were all in Latin, of course, and there were no convenient electronic devices for note-taking; a student might use wax
tablets to jot down reminders for himself, which could be erased
when he had made a fair copy of his lecture notes, or he might,
reprehensibly, use a blank space in a manuscript for his own notes.
There were three terms, dictated by the Church festivals and saints'
days: Lent term from 14 January to Palm Sunday, Easter term to
6 July, and Michaelmas term to 16 December. Lighting and heating
in the long winter months were minimal. In Merton's library the
only concession to human frailty was a layer of rushes on the floor,
keeping the readers' feet from freezing, and contributing a fresh
smell to that of unwashed humanity and old parchment. Otherwise, the reader's posterior met the flat oak board of the bench
without any cushioning other than his scholastic gown. Members
of the lower ranks of the clergy such as Chaucer's Cleric were supposed to wear the standard long gown of a cleric, but a 'courtepy'
such as he was wearing when he joined the Canterbury pilgrims

was not part of proper clerical dress. Perhaps the dress code was relaxed when he was outside university and college premises.

It was little wonder that Chaucer's Oxford Cleric

> was levere [would rather] have at his bed's head
> Twenty books, clad in black or red,
> Of Aristotle and his philosophy,
> Than robes rich, [a] fiddle, or gay sautrye [psaltery: a stringed
>   instrument like a zither].

Perhaps some of his contemporaries would have happily exchanged their Aristotles for expensive clothes and musical instruments. Modern undergraduates might recognize some of their medieval predecessors' tastes in music, or at least the means of recording and amplifying it. They might also recognize the philosophy of enjoying youth while it lasts, leaving Chaucer's Oxford scholar absorbed in his studies of Aristotle. According to the song which was familiar to every medieval student, and is still sung in some universities,

> *Gaudeamus igitur*
> *Iuvenes dum sumus.*
> *Post iucundam iuventutem*
> *Post molestam senectutem*
> *Nos habebit humus.*

(So let us rejoice while we're young, / After cheerful youth and troublesome old age, / The earth will have us.) And so on, for many verses, which go well with a tankard or a glass in the hand.

The Books He Read

Merton's library had glass in its windows, to deflect the cold wind and exclude some of the rain. The reading desks, each 7 feet 9 inches long, had double-sided sloping lecterns on which the books were both stored and read, at right angles to the central aisle, giving room for about seven books stored flat on each side, about 476 books in all, with their names written on the ends of the desks facing the aisle. No doubt Chaucer's Cleric knew just which place was best situated in the light, and out of the draught, and in front of the books he wanted to read. The books were attached to the desks by long brass or iron chains, so that they could be lifted onto the inclined surface of the desk but not be taken away. Apart from the chains, they were like a reference section in a modern library, open to all who had the right to be admitted. There was another collection of books, kept in chests and available only to Fellows, the senior members of the college, who could choose which ones they wanted to borrow and keep for almost as long as they wanted – more like a modern lending library. In 1372, for instance, 141 books of 'philosophy', mostly commentaries on Aristotle's scientific works, were distributed among twenty-three borrowers.

There is a heartfelt plea from the bishop of Durham, who died in 1345, in his *Philobiblon.* Determined to improve academic habits, he wrote that

books should never be unclasped in precipitate haste, nor ... be put away without being duly closed ... [on frosty days] a head-strong youth's nose drips on to it. He marks passages with his black nails. He distributes a multitude of straws, which he inserts to stick out in various places, so that the haulm [at the end of the straw] may remind him of what his memory cannot contain ... he does not fear to eat cheese or fruit over an open book ... [in spring, he] stuffs his volume with violets and primroses ... the handling of books is specially to be forbidden to those shameless youths who ... wherever they find an extra margin about the text, furnish it with monstrous alphabets ... [and he] tries the fitness of his pen ... and cuts out margins and pages at the end ... <u>Washing should invariably precede reading</u> [*my underlining*].

(And I thought I had seen everything, when I noticed that to the charmingly archaic rule of the Bodleian Library in Oxford, forbidding the import of 'fire', it had been necessary to add that chewing gum is equally prohibited.)

Chaucer may never have known about three surprising books in Merton's library: a copy, in Latin of course, of the *Travels of*

Marco Polo, and, even more remarkably, a copy, also translated into Latin, of the Koran, originally commissioned by Peter the Venerable, abbot of Cluny (d. 1156) from a team of scholars at Toledo. It was bound with a Prologue, no doubt helpful to those seeking to convert Muslims to Christianity as Peter the Venerable hoped, explaining the 'heresies' and the 'lying and ridiculous chronicles of the Saracens'. They were shelved next to a copy of that other medieval travelogue, Mandeville's *Travels*. (For both, see Chapter XXIII: The Shipman.)

The works of Aristotle, and commentaries on them by learned ecclesiastics such as St Augustine, formed the main content of the library in Chaucer's time. Aristotle inspired the Lyceum, a teaching school and library, in Athens in 335 BC. He wrote hundreds of books, categorizing every aspect of human existence including medicine, with zoology and geology as well. Some of them, inevitably, have been lost over time. But there remained, for study by medieval scholars, eight books on 'Physics' (natural science), four books on the heavens and four on meteorology. Then two books on generation and corruption, followed by three on the soul ('Anima'). Ten books on animals awaited them, with a few other 'short treatises' and some other works, possibly not by Aristotle, on plants. His work *On the Heavens* formed the foundation of astronomy for many centuries. In *On the Nature of Things* he adopted the theory of an earlier thinker, Empedocles, that the material world consisted of four elements – earth, air, fire and water. All four were different aspects of the same 'primary substance', which contained within it the potential to take on all four of the different forms; thus it might be possible to change the balance of the elements, so as to create a different material. This gave rise, indirectly, to the theory of alchemy. (A modern scientist might observe that the idea was not all that strange; it has brought us the hydrogen bomb, nuclear fission and fusion and the present studies into harnessing the power of the sun.)

The Great Translation Movement

The years between Aristotle and Chaucer's Canterbury pilgrims had not always been kind to the ancient Greeks. But the story that had begun so long ago in Greece shifts, providentially, to the great days of the Abbasid caliphate with its capital in Baghdad, and to its ruler Al Mamun (r. 813–33).³ As a boy Mamun had dreamed of talking with Aristotle. He became obsessed with collecting all the knowledge in the world, and translating every learned document into Arabic. By 950 or so, every available document had been translated, from Syriac, Persian and the Indian languages as well as Greek, and the Great Translation Movement began to lose impetus. The tide swept down the Mediterranean to Córdoba, at that time the largest and most cultured city in Europe. The Andalusian caliph, Al Hakam (r. 961–76), was as obsessed with collecting and translating ancient manuscripts as Mamun had been, but his task was easier since he could build on Mamun's library of translations.

In 1041 the Andalusian caliphate collapsed. By the mid-thirteenth century only the kingdom of Granada survived, of the once powerful Moorish Empire in the Iberian peninsula. But a French Benedictine monk, Gerbert d'Aurillac (c.945–1003), studying in Barcelona, had immersed himself in the Islamic culture and science being taught, in Arabic, nearby in Córdoba. When his order moved him to France he brought his studies to Europe, where he became famous as a writer and scientist. He was elected pope in 999, taking the name of Sylvester II. The great days of Córdoba University were over. But through Pope Sylvester's endorsement, the renown of Aristotle and other Greek savants such as Euclid, Ptolemy and Hippocrates was preserved, translated from Arabic and Greek into Latin and treasured in centres of learning throughout Europe.

In 1190 Alexander Neckam was lecturing in Oxford on Aristotle's scientific works, using the translations by the Persian scholar Ibn Sina, known to the west as Avicenna. By 1200 Edmund of Abingdon was lecturing on another of Aristotle's works, *Sophistici elenchi*. The ingenious mind of St Thomas Aquinas even managed to reconcile the doctrine of transubstantiation (that the Host becomes the real body and blood of Christ at the Eucharist) with Aristotle's theory of physics. By 1400 Merton's library contained more than fifty commentaries by various famous scholars on Aristotle's works, as well as several copies of those of his writings that were extant.

Parchment and Vellum

How were books made before the coming of the printing press? Paper was not yet commonly used in Europe, although the Chinese had invented it long ago, and the Islamic scholars had used it since the eighth century. Europe still used animal skins, of which there were plenty available.

The best vellum was made from the skin of a very young or stillborn calf. (The term 'vellum' should strictly refer to calf skin – think of veal – while the skins of other young animals such as lambs or kids produce 'parchment'; but the terms are sometimes used interchangeably, which can be confusing.) The process of converting a skin into a writing surface began by removing the animal's skin within a few minutes of its death, before the hide began to shrink and stiffen.[4] The next stage was to get rid of the hairs. The skin was immersed in a trench filled with urine and dog turds, and trampled by a man known as a 'walker' – hence the surname, from the age when surnames often denoted the occupation of the bearer. There it stayed for perhaps as long as six weeks, before the loosened hairs could be scraped away. For the next stage, bird droppings, dog dung and more urine were invaluable. One begins to see why a tannery was not a desirable neighbour. The great landowning monasteries collected their occupants' urine for use in the tanneries and cloth-making enterprises which they often ran. We are indeed a 'throw-away society'.

Once the skin had been de-haired, it was stretched on a frame to dry. It was ready to be cut into pages when it made the right sound, nowadays described as the right 'ping', such as a drum makes when tapped. The colour of the finished vellum could vary with the weather. After a fine summer the skin could be a lovely honey colour; otherwise it was a pale shade of ivory.

Parchment tends to be greasy, so chalk or powdered pumice

was rubbed over it to absorb the lanolin. Vellum too would be rubbed with pumice, to make a 'key' for the pen nib. Where it was destined for a work of art such as an illuminated psalter, the skin could be pared down to an even thinness, almost transparent, but sturdy enough to support solid pigments.[5] Normally, vellum was used to make the binding of a book, parchment for its pages. Rich lay patrons, and the Church, might order vellum for the pages, in which case the finished volume would be much thicker than one using parchment.

Parchment is almost indestructible. When the rebels raged through the Temple burning all the legal documents they could find in 1381, they may not have noticed that the bonfires they set failed to destroy the documents they so hated. The documents may have curled up slightly when released from their bindings, and the writing may have been blurred by the smoke from the fire; but destroyed? No.

Most medieval scribes used an ink made from crushed oak galls, with a piece of rusty iron, or vitriol. Where red ink was needed, vermilion, a synthetic mercury sulphide, could be used. Books for religious reading normally included lists of feast and fasting days, in which the most important dates were written in red ink – hence our 'red-letter days'– and the beginning and end of a book or treatise were signalled in red ink. It is unlikely that our Cleric could afford one of the sumptuously illuminated religious books of the time – Bibles, psalters, breviaries, books of hours – even if his friends contributed to the price. Such works glittered with gold and rich pigments, and since their pages have been protected from light, they are as brilliant now as when they were made. But in any case, the Cleric preferred Aristotle, in a modest colour scheme of black and red.

The scribe would use a pen (from the Latin for feather, *penna*) made from a goose or swan pinion feather, cut with a medium nib in the shape familiar to anyone who has used a fountain pen. The shape must have been efficient, since it lasted unchanged for centuries until modern ball-points superseded it. The stem or 'quill' of the feather was hollow for part of its length, which made a reservoir for the ink, drawn up by capillary action. The scribe would trim off the rest of the feather, leaving just enough to make it a convenient writing tool, unless he decided to leave a tuft of white on it to make it easier to find if he dropped it. When the nib wore down it could be reshaped, using the sharp little knife any scribe would keep by him, until he decided to make a new pen. If he made a small slip he could scrape it out with his penknife. He would hold a pointer, or ruler, in his left hand to keep the page flat as he wrote page after page of immaculate, even, black letters.

Book Production

But all was not always what it seemed. The immaculate-seeming pages of black letters sometimes contained serious shortcomings. Gray's Inn possesses a collection of medieval manuscripts varying in date between the twelfth and the fifteenth century.[6] In the meticulous catalogue of them compiled in 1869 by A. J. Horwood, one finds such comments as '[various page numbers] are accidentally omitted', and, dealing with a volume of 333 leaves, 'from a mistake of the scribe, the numeration goes to 347'. Sometimes the copyist interpolates a comment of his own. In one, a legal textbook, 'the scribe has evidently, by accident, passed over an entire quire [a bundle of pages] of what was given to him for copying' – not something any advocate would enjoy when he consults his text in court only to find the vital pages missing.

Even the definition of a 'book' has changed. It could apply to one work, such as no. 1 in Horwood's catalogue, a 'small folio MS of the 12th century, distinctly written on 98 leaves of parchment', which measures 9½ by 6 inches. It could equally apply to one part of a document, such as no. 2 in Horwood's catalogue, a 'Folio MS of the 14th century on 197 leaves of parchment', one of the largest in the collection, measuring 13 by 9 inches and containing eight separate 'books'. Two of them are, serendipitously, works by Aristotle – the *Problemata Aristotelia* on twenty-eight sides, and the *Ethics Aristotelis . . . secundum translationem Hermanni Alemaani ab Arabico in Latinum* (Aristotle's Ethics . . . according to the translation by Herman Alemaan from Arabic into Latin), on nine sides. Br Bozon's 'Little Book' that we looked at in Chapter XVI fills only thirty-two folios, out of the total of 286 in manuscript no. 12 in Gray's Inn's collection; the rest of the manuscript is taken up by various religious subjects. The first item in the catalogue of Merton's medieval manuscripts, the works of Augustine, has 370 leaves, containing fifty-seven separate works of Augustine and six others by other early Church Fathers.

There was rarely an index to the contents. So when you undid the straps and opened your manuscript there was no knowing what you might find, but at least Aristotle's 'books' were not so daunting as a modern reader might fear, imagining academic treatises of four hundred pages or more, packed with facts and figures, as published by Oxford University Press. They were more like extended essays. The medieval manuscript-maker may have made, or commissioned, a collection of particular writings that appealed to his particular taste. Or he may have been a commercial book producer, marketing a commercially viable item such as the Bible, both Old and New Testaments, bound in one 'book', written in Latin and known as the Vulgate.

Monks spent much of their time producing copies of religious books, as part of the labour enjoined by their Rule. Monasteries could be commissioned to produce specific books in the monastery scriptorium, but a practice was growing of outsourcing book production to professional scribes. In London they were centred around Paternoster Row, near St Paul's Cathedral. Another thriving market in books and manuscripts had grown up in Oxford. There was certainly a commercial second-hand market for books, or they would not have been stolen as often as they were. In 1337 a jury heard a charge of theft of a 'book written in English, called Legends of the Saints [a very popular book of the time] of the value of forty shillings'. It found the defendant guilty but assessed the value of the book at 30 shillings. Another report of criminal charges related to 'a book of romance of King Alexander in verse, well and curiously illuminated', valued at the huge sum of £10, a psalter valued at 6s 8d, and 'another large book containing several grammatical treatises' valued at 33s 4d.

Books were valuable enough to be left as specific bequests. In 1349 John Sprot, a chaplain, must have had a considerable library,

since he left to a fellow-chaplain 'his book called Pars Occuli Sac-
erdotis [a treatise on moral and religious duties] with all quires
[bundles of unbound pages] thereto annexed'; to another, a 'por-
tifory [small book] or book of Legends' (i.e. the legends of the
saints); and to a third, the sixth book of the Decretals (six books of
papal decrees, 1230–98, required reading for any student of canon
law). Another testator directed his wife to educate their son Thomas
as a cleric, and left him 'all his books, bound and unbound, on the
canon and civil law, literature, grammar, dialectic, theology, as well
as geometry and astrology'. One wonders just how old Thomas
was, and how pleased he was by this massive bequest.

On the lighter side, there were many 'romances' around. The
term does not mean the boy-meets-girl slush that it conveys to us;
it is more likely to denote a narrative of chivalric adventure written in a vernacular Romance-based language instead of Latin. Sir
Bartholomew Bacon, who died in 1389, left a 'Romaunc' to his wife
for life [my underlining], and then to be sold 'for his soul'. Imagine
her, turning the pages with the tips of her fingers, desperate to
see the end of the story without endangering her husband's soul.
Richard II spent £28 on a copy of that medieval money-spinner
the *Romance of the Rose*, and another romance, the *Romance de
Percival*. The £28 was not all for romances: it included a copy of
the Bible, in French. Chaucer himself had translated a large part
of the *Romance of the Rose* from French into English. France was a
rich source of romances and popular literature, disseminated by the
troubadors and brought back to England by travellers and fighting
men home from the French War.

But there was a growing corpus of English literature. One not-
able survivor is called the Auchinleck Manuscript, because it was
owned by Lord Auchinleck, who presented it to the Advocates'
Library in Edinburgh – it is not in any other way Scottish. It was
written in Middle English, and produced in London between 1331
and 1340. It contains eighteen stories about English and French
heroes such as King Alexander and Arthurian characters such as
King Arthur, Merlin and Sir Tristram, and some not very good
poems. The probable owner was a merchant, who perhaps read it
as he jogged along between markets.

Writing as a Profession

One aspect of writing as a profession is glaringly absent from medieval life: the complex network of literary agents, contracts with publishers, the agreed rate of royalties, how much to be paid in advance, world rights, hardback and paperback and other media, literary festivals, book-signings and intellectual property law – in short, how a writer makes a living. Chaucer had none of them. He lived on an income from his patron, John of Gaunt. He wrote for his own pleasure, and read his work aloud to groups of his friends. If they wanted a more lasting reminder of an enjoyable evening they would commission a copy of the manuscript he had used, from a professional copyist. I have not come across any indication that any payment was made to Chaucer himself, at that stage or any other. There was a Guild of Scriveners, with a charter dated 1373, but they were concerned with legal documents, so we're no further forwards.

Chaucer's Cleric

Coming, at last, to the Clerk's dream of twenty books 'of Aristotle and his philosophy', we stumble at the first hurdle. He was training to be a churchman, perhaps even to be ordained. How was he to acquire the proper knowledge of the Church Fathers, let alone the Scriptures, if he spent all his time on Aristotle? Aristotle was definitely not a Christian. Nor was Virgil, nor Seneca – much quoted in the Middle Ages. But perhaps they meant well, and after all they knew no better, so it would not be right to consign them to hell with other people who had been offered the chance of adopting the Christian faith but had refused it. The doctrine of 'limbo' had no biblical justification. Its main thrust was the plight of babies who had died without being christened; since they lacked that essential passport into heaven, what was to become of them? It was not their fault that they were unbaptized, they did not deserve hell, so limbo was invented. Under the benign aegis of Pope Sylvester II the doctrine extended, rather insecurely, to cover such worthy pagans as Aristotle, Socrates, Plato, Ptolemy, Julius Caesar, Virgil and even Saladin. They would never make it into the Christian heaven with the other saved souls, but they might inhabit a kind of Elysium, or limbo, where, according to Dante, they would find the afterlife not too uncomfortable. It does not seem to have worried those who set the syllabus for the two universities, so why should mere students worry?

So it was permissible for the Cleric to dream of possessing twenty books of Aristotle at the head of his bed. The twenty-first-century reader has to forget any idea of a neat row of paperbacks standing in line, spine outwards, along a shelf. Properly kept books lay flat, their vellum covers closed and sometimes clasped by ornate fastenings, or at least by tapes or straps to keep them flat. There was no uniform size; the scribe would use whatever size of page he could find. Short works were more easily accommodated on smaller pages of parchment, so they could be produced more cheaply than something that demanded a wide spread and a big piece of parchment, such as a calendar of saints' days throughout the year. Perhaps the Oxford Cleric's prized collection would consist of fewer than twenty manuscripts, since some contained more than one 'book', so that they could easily lie on a shelf at the head of his bed.

> But al be [despite] that he was a philosopher,
> Yet had he but little gold in [his] coffer.

Chaucer's Cleric may have hoped that Aristotelian alchemy would improve his finances, a hope that has been shared by many. The words 'alchemy' and 'chemistry' are both derived from the Arabic word *kimiya*, a transliteration of the Greek word *chymeia*, which was connected with smelting metals.[7] Alchemists taught that by subjecting lesser metals to prolonged, intricate – and above all secret – processes, it was possible to create the noblest of all metals, gold. An 'elixir of eternal life' and the 'philosopher's stone' would be by-products, or causes, of this miraculous transformation. But, inevitably, astute entrepreneurs marketed their promises to the credulous, while wrapping their alleged researches in impenetrable obfuscation. It is as difficult, now, to assess exactly what they were doing as it was for their contemporaries. Charlatans came in on the act, producing gold-coloured powders which were mere 'fool's gold'. Suffice it to say that alchemists never quite achieved their goal. The world would be a different place if they had.

The quiet halls of the University of Oxford seem a curious place for Chaucer's Cleric to pursue his research. But he had not processed as far as practical experiments. No doubt he ruminated on what help he could derive from Aristotle as he made his way along the road to Canterbury, blinking in the unaccustomed light and relishing the warm sun. But perhaps the journey reminded him of the travels of his youth. As usual with Chaucer, there's an unexpected facet to this pilgrim. If only the Cleric had known about them, he could have given his audience rousing excerpts from *Marco Polo*, or horrified them with a few 'fables' from the Koran. The Tale that he chose to tell was that dreary story of patient Griselda, who suffered cumulative abuses and tortures just to please her husband. Where had he heard it? In Padua, where he picked it up from Petrarch. So he had not always been immured in a college library.

Coda: The Canon and his Yeoman

Having set out such an elegant scheme for his Tales, and getting thoroughly into his stride in the General Prologue, Chaucer suddenly disrupted his scheme by introducing two new characters, a Canon (yet another fraudulent churchman) and his Yeoman (in this context, his personal servant). The Yeoman assured the Host that his employer could tell them a good story, but he oversold the Canon, who 'fled away, for very sorrow and shame',[8] leaving the Yeoman to tell a Tale of alchemy. Indeed he told two, but both are tedious. The first is a confused farrago of the technical terms of alchemy, the second a story about a fraudulent canon who deceives an innocent priest into parting with gold to enable the fraudster to harvest more gold from it, but of course it ends up in the fraudster's pocket. Chaucer spent nearly a thousand lines on this whole episode. Various erudite Chaucerian scholars have debated what drove Chaucer to interpolate this diatribe in his scheme of story-telling pilgrims. My own suggestion, for what it's worth, is that Chaucer had come across a particularly irritating case of alchemical fraud in his daily life as he wrote the *Tales*, and, lacking the marvellous facility of a modern computer to 'cut and paste', he let off steam in this clumsily added coda. Why did he not ventilate his anti-alchemy feelings in the Cleric of Oxford, as he had added pilgrimages to the Wife of Bath? Perhaps he had forgotten about the Oxford scholar, and missed the chance. He rewrote and amended his manuscript as he went along, as most writers do. Maybe if he had reread the whole work when it was finished the Canon and his Yeoman would have been jettisoned.

XIX THE POOR PARSON

He waited after [looked for] no pomp and reverence . . .
But Christ's loore [teaching], and his apostles twelve,
He taught, but first he followed it himself.[1]

So far, none of the religious establishment among Chaucer's pilgrims have evinced any religious feeling. They have all been worldly, or corrupt, or both. With relief, we turn to the Poor Parson.

The Ideal

Chaucer's Poor Parson was an ideal, contrasted with the corruption and worldliness of other members of the Church. Although he was poor in this world's goods, he was rich in holy thought and works. He was intelligent and educated. He visited all his parishioners on foot, in fair weather and foul, no matter how far away they lived in his widely scattered parish. He was patient in adversity. If a poor parishioner didn't pay his tithes he wouldn't excommunicate him, as he was entitled to do; instead he would give him something out of the church offerings, and even out of his own money, which was little enough.

He was not scornful of 'sinful men', but in his teaching 'discreet and benign':

To draw folk to heaven by fairness,
By good example – this was his business.

Chantries

He set not his benefice to hire,
And left his sheep encumbered in the mire,
And ran to London unto St Paul's
To seek him a chantry for souls,
Or with a brotherhood to be withholde [maintained] . . .
He was a shepherd, and not a mercenary.[2]

There was a brisk market in benefices. There were brokers in London who could arrange the exchange of a poor country living for a more profitable one. Rectors who did this were known as 'chop-churches'. But 'chantries for souls' could offer a much easier way of life than that of a parish priest.

After the Great Pestilence of 1348 'there was so great a scarcity of priests everywhere that many a parish was left destitute'.[3] At first, the pope promised a general remission of all sins up to the point of death. But his fiat may not have been generally known. And when this terrible death came, how could it be faced without the familiar rites of confession, repentance and priestly absolution? Purgatory and the jaws of hell gaped.

Perhaps it would help to implore God to be merciful. The priest was the conduit between man and God. When he elevated the Host during Mass, it became the very flesh and blood of God. If he brought your name to the attention of God while doing so, perhaps your time in purgatory might be shortened. So the custom grew of paying priests to offer a Mass for you. Gradually one Mass became dozens, hundreds, even thousands. In 1348 Geoffrey Fayrher directed that five trentals (a trental was thirty Masses) be performed 'immediately after his decease' and a chantry was to be maintained for five years, after which, he must have reckoned, God would let him off a measurable time in purgatory. In 1350 William de Thorneye required his executors to provide for 10,000 Masses. The next year a widow directed that '11,000 Paternosters and as many Aves' – the two principal prayers of the service – 'should be said in honour of the 11,000 virgins'. In 1388 William Courtenay, archbishop of Canterbury, whose example could surely be trusted, left money for 10,000 Masses. He also made a great nuisance of himself by directing that he should be buried in Exeter Cathedral, which meant shunting three deans further down the cathedral to accommodate him.

All these prayers and Masses would take some time to say, no matter how fast the celebrant gabbled them, if he was trying to combine them with his normal parochial work. So chantries were founded, endowed by testators and manned by priests employed to say, or chant, the necessary Masses. They sometimes had time on their hands for other things, such as running schools. It was generally held to be, in modern parlance, a cushy job. St Paul's Cathedral in London was a general recruiting ground for chantry priests, as it was for many other secular and clerical purposes.

The next of kin must have viewed these bequests with mixed feelings. A thousand Masses could cost £4 3s 4d. A modest three hundred Masses would set you back 25 shillings, but you might be able to find a priest prepared to oblige for as little as a penny per Mass. Some testators were so generous with their post-mortem wishes that there were not enough funds to perform them: King Richard II set aside the will of his grandfather, Edward III, on that ground.[4]

Sometimes a group of people decided to pray together, and hire a priest perhaps just once a year – far simpler and cheaper than the elaborate machinery of a chantry. These 'fraternities' or brotherhoods often wielded considerable influence in local politics. Appointment to one would not be onerous; perhaps an enterprising priest could gather a portfolio of them.

Wycliffe

Chaucer must have come across Wycliffe's teaching, as it percolated from Oxford, where Wycliffe lived and taught, to London. The two men would have had much in common. John Wycliffe was a radical theologian and teacher in the University of Oxford. In 1377, when he was asked to advise the court whether England was obliged to remit money to Rome to fund the pope's Italian wars, he wrote:

'Since therefore God does not give any creature power unless that power can be legitimately used, it follows that our realm can lawfully keep its treasure for its defence' – just what the king wanted to hear. But his views became increasingly anti-establishment of any kind, alienating his powerful supporters, who included John of Gaunt. In 1378 he published *On the Truth of Holy Writ*. His central tenet was that only the Bible, not the established Church, had any authority to lead a Christian to God. The next year he went even further and denied Christ's real presence, the doctrine that Christ was present in the bread and wine of the Eucharist, in his *On the Eucharist*. In a remarkable exercise of religious tolerance, he was encouraged to retire from his Oxford University teaching post and go and live quietly in the country, where he spent his remaining years still writing until he died of a stroke in 1384.

The book known as Wycliffe's Bible was not written by him but by a group of his followers, who became known as Lollards. A version of the Old and New Testaments had been translated into Latin from the Greek sources, in the days when Latin was known to most educated people, hence it could accurately be called the Vulgate (i.e. in the vulgar or generally known tongue). But those days were passing, and the ordinary Englishman needed to read this precious book in his own language if he were to follow Wycliffe's teaching. The scholars in Wycliffe's circle set about the translation of the whole of the Vulgate into current English. Their second edition, known as the Later Version, appeared in 1388 and was widely disseminated among adherents to Wycliffe's teaching. It was seen as so anti-establishment that by 1401 possession of a copy was made punishable by death.[5]

We never hear of Chaucer's own religious affiliation. It would perhaps have been impolitic or unwise to speak freely in those times to his probable audience. There is just a hint of Chaucer's views when Mine Host asks the Parish Priest, our 'Poor Parson', to tell a Tale, 'for God's Bones' and 'by God's dignity'. The Parson answers, 'Benedicite! / What aileth the man, so sinfully to swear?' Mine Host says, 'I smell a Loller [Lollard] in the wind!' and goes on to invite the 'Loller' to preach, 'for God's noble passion'.[6] Three 'sinful swearings' in a very short exchange. The imminent danger of a sermon by the Parson is cut short by the Shipman, and the

Wife of Bath takes centre stage instead. But this gentle mockery of the habit of 'taking the Lord's name in vain', as John Wesley and his followers would describe it some centuries later, invites us to conclude that Chaucer might, as Mine Host suspected, have been a Lollard, a follower of Wycliffe, in his heart.

The Holy Oil

While Henry, duke of Lancaster (see Appendix A) was campaigning in France, he must have heard about the miraculous holy oil that 'the Blessed Mary, Mother of God, once entrusted to the keeping of the Blessed Thomas, martyr, archbishop of Canterbury, when he was in exile, prophesying to him that the kings of England who should be anointed with this oil would be defenders and friends of the Church'. St Thomas did as the Virgin directed, burying the oil, with a parchment recording the prophesy, in a church in Poitiers, where it stayed for many years after his murder in 1170. This oil, kept in a phial inside a golden eagle, was hidden for a long time, but at last was miraculously revealed to a certain holy man, who handed it to the Black Prince as the heir apparent to the English throne. He accepted it, no doubt planning to use it in due course. Meanwhile he put it in a chest in his lodging in the Tower of London and forgot about it. He died in 1376, never having succeeded to the throne. Twenty-one years later, in 1397, his son, King Richard II, happened to find it. Reading the prophecy, he must have thought he was on to a good thing, since his possession of the Crown was becoming increasingly shaky. He took it to the then archbishop of Canterbury but the archbishop refused to anoint him with it, on the ground that he had already been anointed when he had been crowned in 1377 and couldn't be 'done' again. But it was duly used at the coronation of Henry IV in 1399, the first king of England to be anointed with such a precious liquid.

The whole story reeks of propaganda. Its source, Thomas Walsingham, could be charitably described as a creative historian. Henry needed all the support he could get when he invaded England, deposed Richard and assumed the throne. Miraculous holy oil was a definite help.

Pictures and Legends

What did 'the common man' believe? How can we tell, since he was unlikely to put his religious musings into writing? But we know a little about the visual aids he saw every time he came to his parish church. In varying degrees of artistic ability but unvarying sincerity, the walls were covered with paintings of angels and sinners, stories from the Old and New Testaments, God and Satan, and the last day of judgement, when devils would herd sinners towards the hideous mouth of hell while angels welcomed the virtuous to heaven. In the more prosperous churches, stained glass in the windows portrayed saints, often with the donor of the window, in glowing colours, brighter, when the sun shone through them, than the gentle natural pigments of the wall paintings.

And then there was a wealth of legends, more intriguing, sometimes, than the mysteries of the Gospels.[7] The *Protoevangelium of James* relates how Mary was born to Anna, wife of Joachim, although she had long been barren. On Mary's third birthday, Joachim gave her to the temple. When she was twelve 'the trumpet of the Lord sounded', and all widowers round about Judea were summoned by the high priest. Joseph was chosen by lot to receive Mary as his ward. When she was sixteen an angel told her that she would conceive, which she did. Joseph was angry. Poor Mary said – surely this has been heard so often since, from frightened teenagers – that she didn't know 'whence it has come to me'. The priests condemned both of them, and 'sent them into the hill-country'. Then came the order that 'all those in Bethlehem should be enrolled'. On their way there, Mary went into labour. Joseph left her in a convenient cave, and – surely optimistically – went to look for a midwife. Now 'all of creation stood still, and there was a great light'. Jesus was born. Joseph reappeared with Salome, a midwife, who examined Mary and found that she was still a virgin. She announced that 'a great king has been born to Israel'.

The *Infancy Gospel of Thomas* filled in the spaces left in the

Gospels about the childhood of Jesus. At five, he made twelve sparrows out of clay, which flew away when he clapped his hands. But sometimes he sounds rather a nasty child. He quarrelled with one child and 'withered' another, in a fit of bad temper. A teacher found him such an irritating know-all that he hit him. Jesus cursed him, and the teacher fainted. But another teacher came, Jesus was pacified, and said that the other teacher would be cured, as he was. He was once playing with some other children and one of them died; Jesus, still not yet seven, revived him. He later revived another child who had been bitten by a viper.

One anecdote rings so true. Joseph was a carpenter, specializing in ploughs and yokes, both, at that time, made of wood. He had an order for a bed, but he managed to get the two main beams an unequal length. Jesus applied his miraculous powers and 'stretched' the short one so that they matched. A really useful person to have around, just as long as he didn't 'wither' anyone.

The *Gospel of Pseudo-Matthew* was possibly compiled as early as the eighth or ninth century. The oldest extant manuscript of it dates from the eleventh century. It contains much the same collection of stories, with some additions. Three days after her remarkable labour in the cave, Mary emerged and went into a stable. She put her baby in a manger, where the ox and the ass 'adored' him. Jesus was able to drive away dragons from another cave, or was it his natal cave? Lions and panthers in the desert 'adored' him, too. When he was eight, he went into a cave where a lioness had just given birth – surely a dangerous thing to do – but the lion whelps played with him and the older lions 'worshipped him and fawned upon him with their tails'.

The *Gospel of Nicodemus*, which was very popular in the Middle Ages, tells the story of Pontius Pilate more fully than it appears in the New Testament. A telling detail that again rings true: while he is debating his judgment on Jesus, the subjects of Jesus's miracles appear before him to give evidence for Jesus, which seems the least they could do.

The *Assumption of the Virgin* was current from the fourth century. Seven months after her death, Jesus appeared 'on the chariot of the cherubim, with thousands of angels, and David the sweet singer', to 'take to himself' his mother.

All of these make the figures in the Bible so much more human. Surely Jesus, a good Jewish boy, would have helped his father out, and looked after his mother?

THE ARMED SERVICES

XX THE KNIGHT

> ...From the time that he first began
> To ride out, he loved chivalry,
> Truth and honour, freedom and courtesy.[1]

Chivalry

'Chivalry' was the code of mounted soldiers, who could perhaps be described as the medieval officer class. 'Truth' included fidelity. 'Honour' included showing proper respect. 'Freedom' meant generosity, the opposite of niggardlyness, rather than liberation; it would spill over to the poor at the rich man's back door, hoping for his largesse. 'Courtesy' meant courtly behaviour. These were high ideals for any man to sustain.

As Chaucer's audience settled themselves to hear the Knight and his Tale, they must have nodded approvingly. Many may have served in the army in their youth, and looked forward to swapping old soldiers' reminiscences. They were to be disappointed, despite his being, according to Chaucer, a 'very perfect gentle Knight'.

The Roman Empire in the west of Europe had faltered to a close by the fourth century. Continental tribes were gradually coming out of the mists of the 'Dark Ages', to coalesce into nations with defined territories and jurisdictions. In 800 the pope crowned Charles the Great – usually known as Charlemagne – Emperor of the Roman Empire, with these subject tribes or nations as his vassals. The Holy Roman Empire lasted for a millennium.

England stood apart from that hegemony. It needed a mythical figurehead as a rallying point. There was some support for the idea that the English monarchy had been founded by Brutus, great-grandson of Aeneas of Troy, but the legend somehow failed to arouse much partisanship. Another contender was Joseph of Arimathea, in whose unused tomb the body of Jesus had lain after his crucifixion (Matthew 27:57–60). A mass of legends grew up round him, relating how he came to England to preach Christianity. He arrived at Avalon, tired out. He wearily stuck his staff into the earth before he went to sleep. Behold, by the next morning it had grown and was covered with flowers – the miraculous Thorn of Glastonbury, a reliable source of income for the monks for many centuries. In some versions, Joseph brought with him the drinking cup that Jesus had used at the Last Supper, which had been used again to catch his blood as he died on the Cross. It was called the Holy Grail. Joseph buried it, and it has never been found.

Then there was Alfred, king of Wessex from 871 to 899, who famously burned some cakes because he was too busy inventing the English navy. In fact he did a great deal more, and should be revered as a great innovator and visionary, but he somehow failed to ignite the flame of legendary chivalry.

So we come to Arthur, the king who never was. He, or someone like him, may have provided a shaky factual basis for his subsequent reputation by perhaps resisting the incursions of some Anglo-Saxons in about the seventh century, in Wales or thereabouts. But his real strength lay in the legends that accrued around him as an ideal king, a leader of his people, whoever they were, against tyrants and oppressors, whoever they were. The idea of a round table, where no one knight could claim precedence, was not new: the earliest known example dates from 1223, in Cyprus. The knights seated at Arthur's Round Table vowed to seek the Holy Grail, and, while 'questing' for it, to do good, rescue maidens in distress, and so on. In 1139 Geoffrey of Monmouth, a creative historian, gave substance to this vague figure in his *History of the Kings of Britain*. Arthur turned out to have been the equal of Alexander and Charlemagne. His court had been a focus of chivalry, courtliness and high fashion. With those credentials, what British king could resist trying on Arthur's persona to see if it fitted? In 1190 Richard I set off on Crusade brandishing Excalibur, the sword that had belonged to Arthur. Edward III was described by his admirers as unmatched since the days of Arthur.

The Medieval Army

The feudal system imposed on his new kingdom by William the Conqueror in 1066, as described in Chapter XI, was unwieldy, and became more so as the centuries passed. Edward III attempted to modernize it, without much success. Local 'commissions of array', amounting to local conscription, were another way of raising an army when needed, but they were deeply unpopular, and conscripts were probably obliged to serve only in the event of a foreign invasion. They might refuse to go overseas, which was where Edward wanted them.

So a royal commission was appointed to list everyone who had an annual income above 100 shillings. Someone with that amount or more had to provide a mounted archer. Twice that amount, a lightly armed horseman. At £25 or more, a fully equipped man-at-arms. At £1,000, an improbable amount in those days, forty men-at-arms. The men were led in battle by their lord, or added to the 'retinue' of another lord. A retinue was the group of 'retained' men contracted to serve under one lord. The contract would specify the period – either a defined term, or the whole of a campaign. It was a formal document, agreed by both sides, detailing the soldier's pay, even specifying the currency in which it would be paid, and the soldier's rights to a share in any booty and ransom. In 1380, for example, Sir Hugh Hastings contracted to serve the earl of Buckingham in war, 'sufficiently arrayed and mounted', with a retinue, a mixed force of seven other knights, sixty men-at-arms and sixty archers. He sub-contracted almost all of the retinue he had contracted for, remaining personally responsible for only seven men. Chaucer's Knight was part of a lord's retinue, but had personally a retinue of two – his son the Squire, and his Yeoman.

Some landowners preferred to commute their duty to supply soldiers into a cash payment. This gave the Crown a welcome source of revenue, alleviating the severe cash flow problem which bedevilled royal affairs throughout the period.

In our time we have seen how strongly soldiers rely on their brothers-in-arms to support them in danger, as members of the same family. The same loyalty bound together the English army in the fourteenth-century war against the French. The retinues trained and fought together as coherent bodies, archers and foot soldiers and esquires and knights all relying on each other, and with strong territorial links. The French did not adopt this system, keeping their aristocratic mounted knights together, well away from mere foot soldiers. This may have contributed to the crushing defeats they suffered at Crécy (1346) and Poitiers (1356).

Hastiludes

In peace, 'hastiludes', upper-class war games (the word is derived from the Latin *hasta*, a spear or lance, and *ludus*, a game) included both tournaments and jousts. They strengthened the network linking the territorial magnates to the Crown. They also provided a safety valve for those testosterone-fuelled young men who had nothing particular to do during the sporadic truces punctuating the French War. Although nationalist feelings were beginning to knit nations together vertically, there were still strong bonds linking the upper echelons of society horizontally across the various nations of Europe. Henry of Grosmont (see Appendix A) habitually received into his household boys from the noble houses of Spain, Aragon, Portugal, Navarre and France, to be 'brought up in his noble court in [the] school of arms and for to see noblesse, courtesy and worship'. The solidarity among European aristocracies even extended to a series of jousts between the English and the French knights to while away the eleven months that it took for Calais to fall to the English in 1347. The high-ranking French prisoners joined in the hastiludes of 1348 celebrating their own defeat at Crécy.

There were two kinds of hastilude: a tournament, or tourney, and a joust.

Tournaments

A tournament was a vast armoured free-for-all. In the previous century it could involve two hundred knights or more on each side. By the fourteenth century this had come down to a more manageable number, but the combatants still fought on foot as well as on horseback, and used any available weapon, maces, swords, daggers and axes as well as lances. There had been a 'great tournament' at Dunstable 'of all the chivalry and gentles of England' in 1345. Twelve judges watched the proceedings, and gave a prize to the contestant who had performed best. Edward III fought in tournaments himself, in 1342, 1343 and 1348, usually incognito, although surely his disguise was easily penetrated by those in the know, who must have alerted any possible adversary not to damage the ruling monarch.

Chaucer gives a description of a tournament in the Knight's Tale. The Knight could be supposed, by Chaucer's audience as well as by us, to know what he was talking about, so if due allowance is made for the elaboration of the Knight's story-telling style, we have a first-hand account of a fourteenth-century tournament.[2]

Palamon and Arcite are both in love with Emily, the daughter of King Theseus of Athens. They stoop to fighting each other 'without judge or other officer' in a most unknightly way. This is interrupted by Theseus, who gives each of them fifty weeks in which to collect a hundred armed knights, and then fight it out properly in a tournament – and may the better man win, and marry Emily. The great day dawns, the opposing teams make their way to the lists, a herald calls for silence and Theseus states the rules. Only one mounted charge, with a sharp lance, is allowed. The combatants may go on fighting on foot, with long swords (i.e. not short, stabbing swords) and maces. Any knight who loses is out of the battle and has to retire. The tournament will stop if either leader is killed or captured.

The pace quickens (not before time). The heralds stop riding up and down. Trumpets blare. They're off.

> In go the lances full sadly [firmly] in arest [see p. 245,
>   under 'armour'];
> In goes the sharp spur into the [horse's] side.
> There [are] seen men who kan [know how to] joust and
>   who kan ride;
> Shafts are shivered on thick shields ...
> Up spring [the broken] spears twenty foot on high;
> Out go the swords ...
> The helmets they hew to pieces and cut to shreds;
> Out bursts the blood in sterne [terrible] red streams.
> With mighty maces they shatter the bones[.][3]

A horse trips and falls, the rider goes on fighting on foot but has to retire, according to the rules. The noise is inconceivable.

At this juncture Theseus calls a halt for much-needed refreshments, like the lemon slices in the interval at a local cricket match. After which Arcite, with twenty others, manages to capture Palamon, so the fight is over and Arcite gets Emily. (I need hardly say that the story doesn't end with Arcite and Emily living happily ever after. Palamon gets the girl after all.)

Jousts

Jousts were quite different. They were contests between pairs of knights. The technique of jousting needed impeccable horsemanship, physical strength and sheer courage, as well as a perfectly trained horse. The object was not to kill your opponent, only to win on points – to hit him squarely and break your lance on his body armour. The horses had to charge full-tilt at each other. Not until the 1420s was a barrier put between them. The natural impulse of a horse, let alone its rider, would be to swerve away from this oncoming attack, which was where the training came in. If your opponent fell off his horse, it counted as two broken lances. But what with their helmets restricting their view and their horses swerving at the last moment, the jousters quite often missed each other completely. By the end of the fourteenth century 'frog-mouthed' helmets (looking indeed like caricatures of

Mr Toad in *The Wind in the Willows*) had been designed so that the wearer had a clear view only when he was leaning forwards in the correct position for couching the lance and taking aim. At the moment of impact the jouster would straighten up to receive the blow of his opponent and in doing so his eyes were protected, though the same action also rendered him virtually blind.

Hastiludes grew ever more spectacular under Edward III. He himself jousted and was much respected for his prowess. Women did not take an active part in them, but could be relied on to supply glamour. In 1344 all ladies of noble birth, and the wives of the burghers of London, were summoned to Windsor to mark the royal foundation of the Round Table. This can't have been the most relaxed social occasion. Undeterred, Edward repeated it in 1358, dropping the London ladies but summoning the noble ladies of England '*les plus belles et mieux habillées*' (the prettiest and best dressed) to be feasted by his queen. By 1374 Edward was growing senile, under the sway of his notorious mistress Alice Perrers. Dressed as the 'lady of the sun' (think bling and gold), she led the procession through London from the Tower to Smithfield, 'always a lady leading a lord's bridle. And then began the great joust in Smithfield which endured seven nights.'

To celebrate the English victory of Poitiers jousts were held in Smithfield in 1357 attended by three kings, King Edward of England and his captives, the kings of France and Scotland. Smithfield was again used for jousting in 1389 and 1390, when picked champions of the nobility of England and Scotland fought each other, watched by the sumptuously dressed ladies of England from a grandstand erected under the supervision of Geoffrey Chaucer, as clerk of the king's works. Surely his wife Philippa, as part of the queen's household, was one of the ladies.

No special seating was probably needed in 1390 when Lord John de Welles, for England, fought Sir David Lindsay, a Scotsman, on London Bridge and lost, in front of all the onlookers at the crowded windows. But jousts were always subject to that bugbear of outdoor English sports – rain. The jousts planned for Cheapside in 1362 were rained off.

John Stow, writing in 1558 but with access to earlier sources, describes Cheapside:

> in 1331 ... the stone pavement being covered with sand, that the horses might not slide when they strongly set their feet to the ground, the king held a tournament three days together, with the nobility, valiant men of the realm, and other some strange [foreign] knights. And to the end [so that] the beholders might with the better ease see the same, there was a wooden scaffold erected across the street, like unto a tower, wherein Queen Philippa and many other ladies, richly attired, and assembled from all parts of the realm, did stand to behold the jousts; but the higher frame, in which the ladies were placed, brake in sunder, whereby they were with some shame forced to fall down, by reason whereof the knights, and such as were underneath, were grievously hurt ... After which time the king caused a shed to be strongly made of stone, for himself, the queen, and other estates to stand on and behold the joustings and other shows at their pleasure.

The 'shed' was built along the side of St Mary at Bow, 'which greatly darkeneth the said church'; it was used as a royal grandstand until 1420, when it gave way to a commercial development.

Participants had to be at least of knightly rank, although after 1363 esquires who were the eldest sons of knights were allowed in. Knighthood was not hereditary. It could be conferred by a king or a noble as an honour to celebrate some feat of arms or simply to demonstrate approval. An esquire who shone in the jousting lists might hope to be dubbed (knighted) by the patron of the lists. The patron was usually the king, since no one else could afford to put on a full-scale jousting programme, but it might strike a magnate that a young esquire had done well and deserved to be knighted. Esquires could also be knighted on the field of battle by their commander if they had caught his attention.

Armour

The leader of Arcite's team was an Indian king; even his horse was covered in steel armour, under a covering of cloth of gold. Its saddle was of gold, and its rider wore a cote-armour, a light surcoat over his armour embroidered with huge pearls, and a cloak covered with rubies. Palamon's team leader wore a black bearskin with gilded claws over his armour. As the preparations for the tournament grew,

> There you could see workmanship of armour...
> Of goldsmith's work, embroidery and steel,
> The bright shields, testers [headpieces] and trappings,
> Helmets inlaid with gold, hauberks, cote-armours,
> Lords in rich clothing on their battle-horses,
> Knights of retinue, and also squires,
> Nailing the lances, and buckling the helmets,
> Fitting the straps and fastening the thongs of shields...
> ...the armourers quickly
> Going to and fro with files and hammers.[4]

The 'embroidering' may refer to the damascening patterns inset in gold, or to the embroidered velvet or exotic silks covering the larger pieces. The Black Prince may have been so called because his armour was enamelled black.

There was a significant advance in the design of jousting armour in the 1380s. A metal bracket called the *arrêt de la cuirasse* was fixed to the right of the breastplate which engaged by a series of cogs with projections on the lance, shifting the weight of the lance to both shoulders and the chest, and enabling the jouster to take more accurate aim. This admirable device seems to me a bit unfair if a jouster so equipped met another who was still carrying his lance on his arm. Palamon's team also had heavy leather shields from Prussia, and leg armour, and carried axes and maces.

Armour for war service was less sumptuous. As soon as a battle was over the heralds hastened onto the field to identify any important casualties, but on their heels scavengers or 'pilers' would arrive, looking for corpses to despoil of their armour and valuables. If a casualty was not yet quite dead, that could be quickly cured. They were supposed to wait until they heard the 'cry of havoc', the permission to plunder, but this was not always obeyed. The armour they looted might have passed through several owners until its final destination; there was a thriving market in second-hand pieces.

The most expensive armour came from Milan. It was not usual to buy a full set at once because the cost, between £10 and £12, would be exorbitant for most men. According to Froissart, when the earl of Derby wanted an impressive suit of armour in a hurry, he 'sent messengers urgently to the Duke of Milan in Lombardy to obtain armour of his size and choice. The Duke welcomed his request and allowed a knight whom the Earl had sent... to make a choice among his entire collection of armour.' Not content with that, 'after the knight had inspected the plate and mail and picked out all the pieces he wanted, the Duke of Milan... sent four of the best armourers in Lombardy back to England with the knight to ensure that the Earl of Derby was fitted to his exact size'.

'Testers' (from the French *tête*, the head) varied almost from year to year, from plain pot shapes to the frog-mouthed version referred to above. An unforgettable picture from a slightly earlier age: a famous jouster, Sir William Marshal (1147–1219) had had his usual success in the lists, and was wanted for the prize-giving ceremony. He couldn't be found anywhere, until someone noticed him kneeling with his head on an anvil while the blacksmith tried to beat his helmet back into shape so that it could be removed.

Coats of mail (hauberks or habergeons) had been known to the Romans, and were still being worn; the duke of Milan still stocked them. The best were astonishingly light, like thin steel knitting. The heavier they were, the more effective as protection from arrows, but the more cumbersome to wear. A coat of mail could be handed down from father to son, or traded; it could be mended, and adjusted for size. A complete 'suit of harness' could include a pair of jambes for the legs, a habergeon, a basinet or helmet with an aventail, a fan-shaped extension protecting the back of the neck, a pair of vambras and a pair of rerebras for the front and back of the arms, a breastplate and a backplate and a pair of 'gloves of plate'.

Simon Wynchecombe left six such suits of harness to his servant in his will, presumably as his stock in trade since he was an armourer.

Mobility had to be weighed against protection. Parts of the body that couldn't easily be covered with plate could have some protection from a piece of chain mail, for instance at the neck, the groin and the armpits.

Le Livre de Seyntz Medicines

Le Livre de Seyntz Medicines (the Book of the Holy Medicines) is an anguished plea to God, written in 1354 in Anglo-Norman by Henry Grosmont while he was Edward III's most important general in the war against the French. This exposé of his innermost soul still has the power to move a modern reader. Looking back to his youth, he remembers how helmets caused broken or bruised noses. Then he begins an elaborate scheme of prayers, giving incidental glimpses of the physical and mental traumas likely to afflict a medieval soldier.

'If a man is poisoned, he must have a medicine or he will die. Nothing is as good as the triacle.' Put a scorpion into the triacle and kill it there. 'The scorpion is the devil, the venom is his temptations.' Wounds should be washed, and an ointment applied called 'gratia dei' (the grace of God), which represented the blood of Jesus Christ. The wounded man must have hoped that his army surgeon had a supply of such an efficient ointment.

'People drink, as a tonic, goat's milk in May. The grass that the goat eats then takes the strength of the sun, and of God.' For 'frenzy': 'often when a man has been so weakened by illness or a wound that he is out of his mind ... [The physician] will take a red cock and split it and open it all up and will place it, still warm, with feathers, blood and all, on the head of the frenzied man, and by this medicine a man is often cured of his frenzy.'

A seriously ill patient needs three things: a remedy to purge and strengthen him, another to bring his temperature down and a bath to cleanse him and make him perspire. The bath must be in running water, like the blood that flowed from Jesus Christ's side, 'neither too warm, since you were already dead, nor too cold, since you had been dead a short time only'. It would be a fortunate soldier who could call on the camp resources for a hot bath.

> A thing which is very strengthening for a very feeble patient is for a man to take a capon and place it in a little earthenware pot, which is tightly closed so no air can get in or out; and then it is put in another vessel full of water, and placed on the fire and cooked as long as may be necessary; and the broth which is produced is taken and given to the invalid, and this liquid is very sustaining. Very sweet Lord, I have great need of this medicine. The capon enclosed in the pot was the fear that the flesh has of earthly torments; and the vessel full of water was the world full of tribulations... and the fire on which the vessel full of water was put is the fire of hell... Good Lord God, you are the capon who produced the broth.

Quite how an army cook was to produce this consommé is hard to imagine, but Henry was a practical soldier at heart.

'I have often heard that a bad leg needs rest. When a weak man rises from his bed he needs three supports, his two legs and a stick. With them may I be preserved from succumbing to temptations and walk steadfastly along the road to Paradise.' And he ends: 'This book was begun and finished in the year of our Lord Jesus Christ 1354 and it was written by a foolish wretched sinner who calls himself ERTSACNAL EDCUD YRNEH. May God pardon his misdeeds.'

He adds his 'reasonable excuses' for the faults in this book: that he isn't capable of undertaking 'high' things; that if the French is poor it is because he is English and unaccustomed to the French language; and lastly that he isn't good at writing because he was self-taught, too late. He asks anyone who has read to the end to please say three Pater Nosters and three Ave Marias, so despite his modest disclaimer he was expecting his book to have some circulation.

His signature, read backwards, is of course Henry, duke of Lancaster. So at least one famous soldier was a most devout Christian.

Conditions in the Field

Knights might be wearing trusses under their armour – not romantic, but often needed. A physician qualified at Montpellier recommended that a knight in armour should wear one, 'especially for those that are heavy eaters... even those who did not suffer from hernia wore one as a precaution, particularly when they put on heavy armour and indulged in strenuous exercise'. In cases of dislocation of the vertebrae in the neck, which could easily happen when the iron helmet was jarred by the opponent's lance, the physician advised the patient to lie down on the ground or on a bench. 'Then heavy blows are administered to the sole of the foot, and this puts the bone back in place. The knights of Provence, who often suffer from this on their tournaments, always do this to one another when it happens.'⁵

Horses that could carry a knight in full armour were specially bred, massive and expensive. A good 'courser' or charger could cost up to £20, and a knight would need several, as well as ordinary steeds for day-to-day use.

A mounted knight in full armour would function like a one-man armoured tank. Once set in motion he would be impossible to stop. He and his horse would gather speed and meet the enemy with an appalling, victorious crash. That was, at least, the theory. But as Crécy showed, there were more modern ways of deploying the cavalry. Another disadvantage was that although a horse could be made to swerve left or right, as long as the order was clear, it certainly had no reverse gear, unlike a tank. If the traditional fighting order was disrupted and the ranks fell into confusion, horses fell under the archers' fire and could not rise, nor could their riders.

Meanwhile the survivors went home, took off their armour and their truss with a sigh of relief, and gave the armour to their staff to be cleaned up, the dents taken out and generally refurbished. In 1405 Sir Hugh Luttrell, who had been actively campaigning in Wales, paid 'two armourers cleaning my lords armour for eleven days, at 4 pence a day apiece, 7 shillings 4 pence. In fresh lard for the same, 7 pence.' Lard, which we think of as a cookery ingredient, was used as a lubricant before the merits of mineral oil had been developed. Chain mail was cleaned by rolling it in a barrel with sand.

Heraldry

The royal household had included heralds since the reign of Edward I or even earlier, but the fourteenth century saw their function becoming widespread. As more and more armour covered the body, it became more and more impossible to recognize its wearer. The story of Arcite and Palamon began when they were lying half – but only half – dead in a heap of corpses, after a battle. The scavengers or 'pilers' must have alerted the heralds, because it was the heralds who were able to recognize the two as 'of the blood royal' by their cote-armour and their equipment. Heraldry played an increasing role in the life of the upper classes. The right to bear a specific coat of arms was jealously guarded generation after generation. In 1386 Chaucer himself gave evidence in a famous fourteenth-century case in the High Court of Chivalry between two ancient families, the Scropes and the Grosvenors, each side claiming the exclusive right to bear certain heraldic arms. If you were so entitled, you made sure that everyone who mattered knew. You put it all over your armour, as well as on your cote-armour. You put it on your tombstone, and you carved it on your castle.

The Knight's Campaigns

To return to Chaucer's Knight: 'Full worthy was he in his Lord's war'; he was part of a retinue, not a self-employed operator. Chaucer gives him an impossible list of campaigns in which he had supposedly served: Alexandria; Prussia and Lithuania; Russia; Algeciras in Grenada; Belmarye, another Moorish territory in north Africa; Lyeis in Armenia; and Satalye (now Antalya) in southern Turkey.

Alexandria was captured by Peter I of Cyprus, in 1365. But it was not a Crusade, it was a massacre. Peter had toured Europe the year before, hoping to recruit a Crusader army to capture the rich Muslim city. Most sovereigns whom he visited, including King Edward III of England, gave him a lukewarm welcome. He raised no crusading army, but individual knights joined him with an eye to the booty to be won. Perhaps here the Knight was acting independently. Cyprus was not at war with Alexandria, and the Alexandrians, immersed in the spice trade of which their city was the centre, had no reason to expect attack. They were taken completely by surprise. Peter's army was composed of lawless adventurers and desperados from the Free Companies, the companies of mercenaries who were roaming Europe, looting and terrorizing as they went. They landed on the defenceless shore of Alexandria and set about achieving their goal: plunder. Petrarch described it in a letter to Boccaccio:

> Not that Peter himself... tarnished his own glory in any way, but his troops, who all consisted of men recruited from beyond the Alps (the kind of men always keener to undertake such exploits than to finish them) left him in the thick of the battle and showed that they had followed him in the first place not out of piety but out of greed. Once they'd got their booty, they took to their heels, little caring that the King's solemn vow [to capture Alexandria for Christendom] remained unfulfilled, once their own covetous desires had been satisfied.

The city remained in Muslim hands, all bloody and defeated, and certainly not Christian. The main result of the 1365 campaign was a steep rise in the price of spices. Such was the first exploit that Chaucer attributed to the Knight.

Next, to Prussia and Lithuania, where the Knight had reised, 'no Christian man so oft, of his degree [rank]'. 'Reise' was the technical word for the winter campaigns in those countries, where bitter weather was the only feasible time to ride over the marshes, while they were frozen hard. These were the campaigns waged by the Teutonic Knights. They had begun as a religious order, crusading first against the Saracens and then against the pagan Slavs. They founded Memel and Königsberg, now Kaliningrad. By Chaucer's time they had the reputation of fighting bloodthirsty wars and killing their prisoners, rather than propagating the Gospels. Yet some genuine Crusaders joined them for the pure love of soldiering, when most campaigning had closed down for the winter. Henry Bolingbroke spent two winters with them, 1390–91 and 1392–3, enjoying the company of fellow-soldiers. He took with him his jousting equipment, as a modern holidaymaker might take a tennis racket. He certainly was not attracted to Lithuania by the hope of booty: he was already rich. But for a landless man such as Chaucer's Knight, Lithuania beckoned. Loot was there for the taking by anyone prepared to make the journey and accustomed to the sight of blood.

The lines 'full oft he had the board begun / above all nations in Prussia' seemed to signify that this humble Knight took the head of the table, an honoured place, at meetings of all the knights, who could be of several different nationalities. But it was the same disillusioning story. It was a matter of whom you knew. A contemporary described it thus:

> Now the custom is, with respect to this so-called table of honour devised by the vanity of the said friars [the members of the Teutonic Order], that, the said friars having prepared a solemn banquet for... say ten or twelve, only those persons who were selected from the knights by the heralds there present were assigned to places at the aforesaid table, those persons being such as... had traversed various parts of the world as errant [travelling] knights... and according as one individual from the number of these knights... seemed to surpass another in this respect, the places about the table were assigned.

So he wasn't at the top of a great assembly of multinational diners, he was just sitting at the head of a table for twelve – and to get there he had probably bribed those all-powerful heralds. Maybe this source was as unreliable as Chaucer's version. But the fact that there *were* two such differing versions is unsettling.

Another custom of the times shows how words that seem recognizable may be misleading. Chaucer's Knight 'never yet no villainy he said / In all his life unto no manner wight [any kind of person]'.[6] But this didn't mean that he was commendably against bad language. It was dangerous to make provocative remarks that could lead to an argument, in Richard II's multiracial army. The penalty could be hanging.

Back to Chaucer's list of the Knight's campaigns, and to Russia, another place for 'reising'. There was no obvious reason for Crusade there, since the Russians were already Christian; but it was the wrong kind of Christianity, which they called 'Orthodox', and they needed to be brought back to the proper fold. Possibly a tender conscience could be pacified by this argument. It's more likely that a wandering mercenary could spot the opportunities for loot and plunder in the border raids between Russia and its neighbour Lithuania, and make what he could from the constant boundary disputes.

Two more theatres of war are the Moorish lands of Granada and north Africa, and three cities in Anatolia. The siege of Algeciras in Granada from 1342 to 1344 resulted merely in a ten-year truce with the Moors. Belmarye in present-day Morocco was a happy hunting ground for soldiers of fortune from all over Europe. Satalye, a fabulously wealthy Turkish city, was another bloody conquest by Peter of Cyprus in 1361. Lyes in Armenia was a worthless fiasco, after a callous campaign. By now Chaucer must have felt he had made his point, without detailing fifteen more 'mortal battles'. But then we learn that the Knight had 'fought for our faith at Tramissene [Tlemcen in Algeria] / in lists thrice, and aye slain his foe'. These were real contests to the death, distinct from the gentlemanly jousting in hastiludes where only broken lances counted. So the Knight was an accomplished and courageous jouster; but whether he was a 'very perfect gentle Knight' was increasingly open to question. Chaucer's audience must have been growing restive, wondering why all these obscure battles were attributed to him while there was no mention of the glorious victories in which some of them may have fought – Crécy and Poitiers.

A Just War?

In the late thirteenth century a Dominican monk, Raymond of Penyafort, had summarized St Thomas Aquinas's teaching on warfare. War should be just –

(1) in regard to the persons engaged in it

(2) in regard to its object

(3) in regard to its cause

(4) in intention

(5) and it should be waged on valid authority.

So we need to set Chaucer's Knight against that background. Were the wars in which he fought 'just'? Sometimes, perhaps. A Crusade authorized by the pope, even for purely terrestrial reasons such as adding to the papal lands, would surely be 'just'? Whereas a war staged purely for material gain would as surely be 'unjust'?

One last touch before you decide. 'Of fustian he wore a gipoun. / All bismotered [stained] with his habergeon[.]'[7] Once more, what was Chaucer implying? Any knight who was proud of his record and wanted to show off would have his coat of arms, or at least the coat of arms of his 'lord', plastered all over him. But this 'very perfect gentle knight' just wore a grubby gipoun; there was no insignia on it by which he could have been identified. When the Russians annexed the Crimea in 2014, they began with armed men taking over various strongpoints from the native Ukrainians. They wore standard army combat gear, without any indication that they were Russian soldiers. Only later, when Russia's intentions were clear, did they display their Russian insignia. A modern corollary? Chaucer's Knight should have shown on his gipoun what army he belonged to. If he didn't, how was anyone to know he was an honest man – if he was?

So the man who initially seemed to personify probity and integrity could equally, under examination, be a materially minded, unprincipled thug. Chaucer knew exactly what he was doing. He was compelling his audience to view commonly accepted clichés in a distorting mirror – or was the mirror the true picture, and the cliché the false one?

XXI THE SQUIRE

Embroidered was he, as it were a meede [meadow],
All full of fresh flowers[,] white and red . . .
He was as fresh as is the month of May.[1]

He was the Knight's twenty-year-old son, and the second creation
of Chaucer's pen. Chaucer's audience would have no troubling
doubts about him. No need of a distorting mirror here.

Chaucer had a son called Thomas who was born in about 1367,
so he would have been about twenty when his father began the
Tales. It's pleasant to think of a loving fatherly eye contemplating Thomas, and no doubt deploring the outrageous fashions and
habits of youth, as he writes.

His Campaigns

The young Squire had already been 'in chivachye / In Flanders,
in Artois and Picardy'.[2] The military strategy of the time favoured
these cavalry sweeps through enemy territory, '*chevauchées*', not
stopping to besiege towns that refused to surrender but cutting the
enemy's lines of communication, depriving him of supplies, showing armed might to the native peasantry and encouraging them to
rebel against their French overlords. This time, Chaucer didn't test
the military recollections of his audience as he had with the Knight.
Flanders, Artois and Picardy were the three northernmost provinces
of France, and the theatre of war first chosen by Edward III when
he declared war on the French king in 1337. Campaigns there had
sputtered on, pausing for ceasefires and truces, or when the main

push switched to Aquitaine or Brittany. But the Squire had escaped the danger, as well as the obloquy, of his father's campaigns.

His Rank

The heralds had decided, after some thought, that an esquire,[3] or squire, had the right to bear heraldic arms; he was, in their language, armigerous. The Crown would have liked all squires to take up the next rank, that of knight, incurring, no doubt, increased fees and taxes; but many never did so. In 1344 the Crown decreed that anyone holding land worth £40 per annum, or rents for three years, *must* take up the order of knighthood, to which the City replied, characteristically, that the decree couldn't possibly apply to properties in the City because they were often empty, or in want of repair, which sounds just like any appeal against council tax in modern times. Chaucer himself was made an esquire in the royal household in 1367. He was promoted to being an 'esquire of the King's chamber' in 1371, and he became a knight of the shire in October 1386, but he never took up knighthood as a title.

His Appearance

The young Squire must have been a cheering sight. He was of moderate height, athletic and very strong. His hair was in locks 'crulle [curly?] as [if] they were laid in press'.[4] Perhaps his hair was not naturally curly, but curled, smoothly arranged like that of the knaves in a pack of cards. The contemporary pictures of young men and pages show them with smooth hair in a long bob, curled at the ends. Women nowadays produce their smooth manes by literally ironing them, having the advantage of electricity. Chaucer in his reference to 'laying in press' must be referring to the medieval equivalent of ironing: smoothing garments and sheets by laying them between two flat surfaces and applying pressure by winding the top one down by a hefty screw, the whole apparatus being known as a press. So one would expect the Squire to have smooth hair. But in the picture of the Squire in the Ellesmere Chaucer, produced in 1400–1410, he has two bunches of curls, one on each side of his face. He is also wearing a hat, which Chaucer doesn't mention, so whoever drew the pictures for the Ellesmere version may have added touches of his own. 'Crulle as they were laid in presse' has to remain a mystery, but an unimportant one. The only other (almost) bareheaded pilgrim was the Pardoner, who wore a small cap on his head instead of the usual hood, deceiving himself that he was thus in the vanguard of current fashion.

Clothes

Chaucer's Squire was a fashionable young man: 'Short was his gown, with sleeves long and wide.' That fashion really upset the saintly Parson, when he got a chance to tell his Tale, and there's no better place to find a description of current fashions than a diatribe against them:

> Alas, may man not see as in our days the sinful costly array of clothing, and namely in too much superfluity or else in too desordinat [inordinate] scantiness? As to the ... superfluity of clothing ... not only the cost of embroidering, the degise endentinge [fancy indentation] or barringe [ornamenting with stripes], owndinge [ornamenting with wavy lines], palinge [decorating with vertical stripes], windinge [twining with thread or silk] or bendinge [decorating with v-shaped(?) stripes], and such waste of cloth in vanity, but there is also costly furring in their gowns; so much punching with chisel to make holes, so much dagginge of sheris [cutting patterns at the edge]; forth with the superfluity in length ... trailing in the dung and in the mire, on horse[back] and also on foot, as well of man as of woman[.]

He went on to condemn too little, after too much: 'to speak of the horrible disordinat [inordinate] scantiness of clothing ... some of them show the shape and the bulge of their horrible swollen members ... in the wrapping of their hose, and also their buttocks, which look like the rear of a she-ape at the full moon'.[5]

Nowadays we are so used to machine-knitted tights and leggings that it's hard to imagine hose made of woven fabric. But think of modern jeans as worn by the young. It is apparently possible to insert the human legs and buttocks into garments made of woven material that are tighter than skin-tight, and no one thinks of she-apes at the full moon. No doubt the young Squire's legs and buttocks were similarly displayed below his 'short gown', which was probably tight over his hips and waist. With his physique he didn't need padding, but less perfect men sometimes enhanced the chests of their gowns.

But in 1340, 'the fourteenth year of our Lord King Edward the third of England, and the first year of his reign of France', the parliamentary draughtsman of the time sat back to survey his latest piece of work, known to his successors as the Statute of Apparel. After preliminary skirmishes about goldsmiths having to mark their work with their own identifying symbol, and certain exemptions for 'workwomen that do use and work all handy works', such as brewers and bakers and textile workers including silk women, the Act got down to the 'outrageous and excessive Apparel of divers people, against their Estate and Degree', which should be stopped. It began at the lowest rung of society: 'carters, ploughmen, drivers of the plough, oxherds, cowherds, shepherds, dairymen, and all other keepers of beasts, threshers of corn, and all manner of people of the estate of a groom attending to husbandry, and all other people that have not 40 shillings of goods or chattels'. The coarse wool cloth known as blanket, with linen girdles, was good enough for them.

The Act rose through the ranks of society, taking in clerics obliged by the rules of their Church or college to wear fur, squires and knights at various income levels, and 'merchants, citizens and burgesses' who were assessed on their capital value and lumped in with knights with a corresponding income from land. Where you came in the list decided what you could wear. A squire with land or rents to the value of 200 marks a year, for example, could wear 'cloth of silk and of silver ... and other apparel reasonably garnished of silver', and his wife, daughters and children could wear 'fur turned up of [trimmed with] miniver, without ermine or letuce [a kind of fur, see p. 262]'. They were forbidden to wear precious stones or jewels, except in their headdresses. Wives, daughters and children were usually 'of the same condition' as the man of the family, except at the very top of the pile, where 'Knights and Ladies which have land or rent over the value of 400 marks a year . . . shall wear at their pleasure, except ermine and letuce, and apparel of pearls and [precious] stone[s], but only for [except for] their head[dresse]s'. So a knowing eye could tell how much a man was worth from the clothes he was wearing.

But it didn't last. The Act was duly passed, but it was repealed the very next year. Perhaps the merchants resented the constriction on their trade, having to ask a customer's income before they could sell him the latest expensive fashion. Perhaps the sheer unenforceability of it became apparent. It represented an attempt to sort people into boxes, which they were unlikely to accept. The similarly organized graduated poll tax, less than twenty years later, led to the revolt of 1381.

Women's headdresses became increasingly elaborate and bejewelled as Edward's reign wore on. They usually concealed the hair in a net of gold or silk studded with precious stones, contrived to stand out from the head in a rigid shape, framing the face. The extreme version of tall steeple-shaped headdresses came in slightly later, in the next century, but in Edward's time, as the abortive apparel legislation showed, the heads of rich ladies glinted and shone with gold and jewels. Men don't seem to have spotted the potential for display on their heads: they tended to concentrate on their hips, with belts that could be just as heavily bejewelled.

Over the short gown a man might wear a voluminous robe with those trailing sleeves that the Parson so objected to. Its fullness could be caught in by a belt. Those unfortunate French nobles who disastrously lost the Battle of Poitiers in 1356 had brought with them, expecting victory, 'trunks stuffed full of belts that were weighty from their gold and silver ornaments', according to Froissart; no doubt those belts encircled English waists after the battle. More prosaically, a belt provided a way of carrying purses and knives and 'tables' – small wax tablets for note-taking – and those useful documents that physicians carried with them. Sometimes a 'pair of pockets' could be slung on a belt.

There were no ready-made garments. A visit to a tailor could be a convivial occasion. A gentry family from Cornwall came to London regularly, to be measured by their taylor; their household accounts show the cost of 'wine at the taylor's house' as well as that of the cloth. A reasonable charge for making a robe for a man would be 18 pence, or 12 pence to make a coat and hood, and 2s 6d to make a long robe for a woman.

The Merchant wore a fur hat. The usual headgear was a hood, which could end in a long, narrow liripipe wound round the head in elaborate folds. How they fared in a high wind is difficult to imagine. The peasants wore hoods with a short end, not long enough to wind round, or hats made of straw or leather, losing what shape they ever had over the years.

Medieval magnates certainly wore sumptuous garments. On state occasions they tinkled with little silver and gold bells sewn on their sleeves, a French fashion. A cloak 'embroidered with pearls' appeared in litigation in 1376. John of Gaunt had a long gown covered with jewels and other garments of impossible luxury, which contributed to the rage of the rebels who sacked his Palace of the Savoy in 1381. Richard II wore a doublet of black silk damask under a long robe of green silk damask. In 1398, according to John Stow, he 'caused a gown for himself to be made of gold, garnished with pearl and precious stones, to the value of three thousand pounds', to celebrate the completion of his repairs to Westminster Hall. Satins were often embroidered with gold or silver thread, or patterned with small motifs in gold leaf. Even a modest chandler's widow left a 'robe of gold work' to her daughter in 1348.

Chinese silk had been appearing on the European market since the eleventh century. By the fourteenth century the mystery of silk production had been solved by weavers all over Italy, in Venice, Lucca, Sicily, Calabria and Bologna. Their beautiful fabrics were marketed at the international trade fairs in Ghent and Bruges. Between 1392 and 1394 the Mercer Richard Whittington supplied £2,000 worth of silks, cloth of gold and velvets to the king. London embroiderers were famous for their embroidered silk, called *opus anglicanum*. These masterpieces survive nowadays mainly as ecclesiastical vestments, because as such they were not subjected to hard personal wear, but in their time they adorned many a rich man and woman.

The fashion for slashing – making cuts in the fabric so that the equally rich lining could be pulled through in little puffs – had caught the Parson's disapproving eye. It lasted well into Tudor times. Chaucer's translation of the *Roman de la Rose* referred to a robe elegantly 'tostlytered', or slashed.

For women, it was customary in polite circles to cover the arms, but the shoulders could be bare. The outer garment was loose and flowing, but it might be worn over another, tightly fitted so that it showed through the enlarged armholes of the outer one. Sleeves were long and tight-fitting, fastened with buttons that could – of course – be jewelled. In 1373 Philippa Chaucer, Geoffrey's wife and one of the 'demoiselles' of the queen, was issued with a 'buttoner and 6 silver-gilt buttons'.

The overall effect of medieval garments, to the modern eye, was the flowing length of them; graceful, no doubt, and giving space for those elaborate patterns so decried by the Parson, but maddening for everyday life. Try wearing a floor-length gown, without even pockets to put your hands into and lift it up; now try carrying a lit candle, or a glass of wine. The medieval fashion-conscious were accustomed to such clothes; they stood about in statuesque poses and let someone else bring the wine. The more ordinary wearers tucked their gowns up into their belts and got on with their work.

What happened to these magnificent clothes when they showed signs of wear? There was a thriving second-hand market, run by 'fripperers', in Cornhill, in the middle of the city. It was open only during the hours of daylight, which seems very sensible. If fur became tatty it could be refurbished or cleaned, or patched with other matching skins, or even dyed a good black which might pass muster for sable in a poor light. The cheaper kind could be sheared again, bringing up a new surface though somewhat shorter.

No wonder the poor peasants resented this show of wealth. They wore what they could afford, to keep out the cold as they worked in the fields. They appear in countless images of peasant life, wearing shapeless garments and bulky hose, sometimes stuffed with hay or straw as insulation. Their girdles served only to tuck their outer garments into, so that they could go about their laborious lives. Their clothes were no doubt handed down in the family until they could no longer be patched.

The Fur Trade

Medieval houses were impossible to heat up to the level that we would regard as tolerable. The only answer was to carry your own central heating with you. The ultimate could be three layers of fur-lined garments, worn one on top of the other, such as a tunic or *cote*, plus a long or knee-length *surcote*, worn indoors, and a fur cloak or mantle, called a pilch, to throw on for outdoors. Their combined weight would have brought all but the strongest to their knees in a short while, but they would certainly have been warm.

Every aspect of the fur trade was regulated by the Skinners' Company, incorporated in 1327, with the Virgin Mary as its patroness. The various kinds of fur were minutely delineated by species and place of origin, even by the season in which the animals were caught, since they grew longer and silkier fur, which more often turned white, in the cold northern winters. The white winter coats of weasels were called lettice or letuce. Miniver was a white fur with an edging of grey, from the bellies of Russian and Scandinavian squirrels; if the grey edging was trimmed off, the resulting white fur was called 'pured miniver'. In illustrations to fairy stories and pictures of peers being introduced into the House of Lords, miniver is shown as white with little black tails in it. This was known as 'powdering', an extraordinarily labour-intensive work entailing the insertion of little pieces of fur from the legs of black lambs through slits in the main fur. Vair, a kind of miniver, was what Cinderella's slipper was made of. It was mistranslated into English as 'glass', from the French *verre*, which would have been impossible for any slipper.

Sables were hunted in the far north of Europe; their finished skins should be 12 inches long and 3½ inches wide in the middle. Minks, red foxes and lynxes lived all over Europe, otters and beavers could be found by most streams. All yielded workable skins. Even dormice were caught for their skins. There was a whole vocabulary of technical terms, relating to the country of origin as well as the animal, the season it was caught and its value. Lamb skin from north Africa, for example, was called 'budge' after the Moorish country of Bougie.

Huge sums were spent on fur. Sir John Pulteney, draper and mayor of London, had sixteen robes lined with gris or miniver, and fifteen unattached fur linings. Often a cheaper fur would be used for the lining and a more luxurious one only where it showed, such as at the wrist of a long-sleeved mantle. Fur linings could be moved from one garment to another as the fashion changed or the visible outer textile became worn.

The households retained in royal and plutocratic circles were a paying proposition for their members. As well as their salary they received substantial New Year gifts. In 1343 Elizabeth de Burgh gave 'liveries' – outfits, counting as part of their annual salary – to her household of 250 men and women, of whom 160, the upper ranks of knights, squires and ladies, received a 'furred livery'. In 1369 fourteen 'demoiselles' of Queen Philippa's household, including Philippa Chaucer, Geoffrey's wife, were each given cloth and pured miniver to be made up into surcotes, the cost of doing so to be borne by the royal household. The senior staff of Westminster Abbey, apart from the monks themselves, could look forward to a new robe every year, since they might have to deal with rich visitors who could be a source of funds if sufficiently impressed. A squire or gentleman on the staff received a furred robe, lower ranks had no fur on their robes. A self-employed minstrel reflected sadly that he had 'served many lords – and few robes I obtained or furred gowns'.

In pictures of the Virgin Mary there is sometimes a glimpse of a white undergarment edged with a blue pattern. This was the conventional signal of ermine. It was meant to show how prized to the onlooker she was, not that she herself wore such a costly garment.

Whatever the rules about dress, the young Squire caused his father no anxiety on that score as they rode on towards Canterbury. I very much doubt if he was wearing a fur lining.

Footwear and Garters

Chaucer usually includes a note on footwear in his descriptions of dress, but not in the case of the Squire. There were normal riding boots, which the Squire and most of the other pilgrims were probably wearing. Hose were sometimes soled, which would be handy for clement weather. The fashionable shape of shoe was long and narrow, increasingly prolonged beyond the end of the toes so that walking naturally was impossible. The fashionable wearer had to lift each foot and give it a slight kick to get the front of the shoe facing forwards. Yet according to a fifteenth-century French illustration of a group of men and women dancing, it was possible to lift each foot shod in these elongated shoes so as to mark the rhythm of the dance. By the 1380s, in the ultra-fashionable world the shoes had become so long that the points had to be fastened up to the wearer's garters by gold chains – a remarkable sight, introduced by Anne of Bohemia who married Richard II in 1382, and called 'cracows' from a city in her native land. They were beloved by painters of the time, but impossibly impractical. Faced with a staircase, the fashionable wearer would have to mount, with difficulty, sideways, step by step.

The fashion-conscious might also wear shoes 'decoped', or slashed, so that a coloured lining shone through. For more normal folk, a pair of shoes should cost 6 pence. Profiteers after the Great Pestilence were sent to prison for charging up to 9 pence a pair.

Garters were another place for conspicuous consumption. The obvious example was the device chosen by Edward III in 1348 for his Order of the Garter with its enigmatic motto. But a less well-known source is that penitential book in Anglo-Norman French that we looked at in Chapter XX, *Le Livre de Seyntz Medicines*. Before Henry Grosmont gets down to his elaborate prayers, he looks back to what then seemed to him his misspent youth. As he labours along in unfamiliar Anglo-Norman, he describes how, as a young man, he took pride in his shoes and his armour, and his light-footed dancing, and his – and here he grinds to a standstill, and for the only time in his whole book, as far as I can see, uses an English word – 'garters'.

Underwear

Underwear is often difficult to trace in historical documents. The inventories of debtors whose goods were being seized by their creditors give some clues. In 1376 a 'clerk' owned a coverlet of foine skins (stone martins) valued at 2 shillings, a pair of top boots, with spurs, and a saddle, together valued at 5 shillings, and two pairs of drawers, or 'bracce', with a separate pocket, together valued at 6 pence. The 'separate pocket' would be slung on a belt round the waist. And for once we have a clear picture of these bracces, in the Holkham Illustrated Bible. The two thieves crucified with Christ are wearing drawers, rolled up round a hip-level belt and hanging loose above the knees. Medieval clothes, underwear included, cry out for the invention of elastic.

Both sexes wore linen smocks next to their skins, for wool, even the finest kind, could be very itchy.

Music

'Singing he was, or fluting, all the day.'[6] He surely sang more melodiously than those duettists, the Miller and the Summoner. How did he manage to play his flute on horseback? Perhaps he just sang while they were riding along, and played his flute for a change when they halted. Or his horse just followed the others, leaving him both hands for his flute. A popular member of any travelling minstrel group was the pipe-and-tambour man, playing a drum slung round his chest with one hand and his pipe with the other. Perhaps the Squire limited his flute-playing to the notes he could manage with one hand.

There was a wide variety of instruments available to him in addition to his flute, though I doubt whether he ever tried a bag-pipe. These can still be found in some peasant communities. They need only a sheep's stomach for the bag, and something long and hollow for the pipes and the chanter. Assembled, they produce a sound of which there are many aficionados among whom I am not one: I take the view that distance – as much as possible

– lends enchantment. So, perhaps, felt the unfortunate residents of villages on the way to Canterbury, as the Miller 'brought [the pilgrims] out of town', playing on his bagpipe. But bagpipes had a legendary status. When the angel came to the three shepherds and told them to follow the star, one of the shepherds was often shown as playing a bagpipe even when he entered the stable, surely waking the baby.

Other wind instruments included hunting horns and trumpets, frequently played by angels. Heaven must have been a noisy place. Organs had one or two manuals, powered by boys with bellows. Small versions could be portable, like small hurdy-gurdies, also much favoured in angelic circles.

There were various stringed instruments, such as a recognizable fiddle, played the same way as a modern violin with the instrument tucked under the chin. The bow, however, was different, being held in the middle and arched, so that it closely resembled the kind used to shoot arrows. Another version seems to have been held across the chest and plucked. A gittern was a singular violin-type instrument. There were many variants of these, and as many – or more – names for them. The strings were probably made of sheep gut, although precious metal seems to have been used for prestige instruments.

The Friar could play a 'rota', a small triangular zither with strings on both sides on which he could accompany himself as he sang. There were many versions of harps, also known as cytharas or lyres, with many heavenly sponsors.

Henry Grosmont, in his now familiar lament for his misspent youth, regrets that he used to sing seductive love songs that often gained his objective. English sacred choral music was rapidly developing into polyphony. For the first time a system of musical notation was available to ecclesiastical choirs. But the happy young Squire will not have drawn on it for his repertoire. He could write songs himself, as well as just sing. Unfortunately popular songs are by their very nature spontaneous and evanescent. The happy thought of one medieval day gave way to another melody the next day, and no one wrote it down. But perhaps you may get some faint flavour of the songs the Squire may have sung from the thirteenth-century round 'Sumer Is Icumen In'. There is one survival from the time, a ballad thought to have been sung by the peasants as they marched towards London in 1381 (see Appendix B). Bodies of men inspired by one cause do tend to burst into song; think of the 'Marseillaise', or football crowd anthems.

Other Accomplishments

He could ...
Joust and eek [also] dance, and well purtreye [draw portraits?] and write.[7]

Jousting was a necessary skill for those days.

He could dance the formal dances of the time. Froissart sketches another delightful young man who was part of the retinue of the French king when he was travelling back to captivity in England. The royal party arrived at the palace of Eltham, where the English court welcomed them. Before supper 'there was time for much dancing and merriment. The young Lord de Coucy in particular took great pains to dance and sing well when his turn came. He was much applauded by both French and English.'

Drawing was yet another accomplishment. Before the days of map-making an ability to draw a landscape could be useful to a campaigning soldier.[8] We would take it for granted that writing went with reading, but this was not necessarily so. In 1354 Duke Henry of Lancaster, who surely enjoyed all the privileges of his station, regretted his poor writing because 'he had learned too late' and had taught himself. Those beautiful books of hours, and other devotional books, had to be read, but there was no need to be able to write as there would always be a scribe handy to take dictation.

Chaucer's Squire 'carved before his father at the table'. If his father took the head of the table as the most senior, it would be for the most junior to sit at the foot of the table and carve the joints. Some dishes would arrive from the kitchen ready for the diners to spear a mouthful-sized piece or 'gobbet' with his knife, and dip it into the sauce in the separate dish ('saucer') near him. But the well-brought-up young man had to know how to carve whole birds, including peacocks with their tails spread out behind them. There was a whole vocabulary, and doubtless a whole range of techniques. He might have to:

> unlace a coney [rabbit]
> break a joint of venison
> sauce a chicken
> display a crane
> disfigure a peacock
> tame a crab
> barb a lobster
> splat a pike
> and border a pasty.

Romantic Love

The Squire had 'born himself well' on his military service 'in hope to stand well in his lady's grace'. This was a reference to the romances of the time, which we find less than engrossing but were the bestsellers of the medieval age. Chaucer himself had begun his literary career by translating from the French part of the famous *Roman de la Rose*. The ideal of romantic love was to worship from afar, but never to approach the beloved object, still less expect her to reciprocate or do anything so physical as giving him a kiss. The lover showed off his prowess in war. If there was no war handy, he could participate in jousts and tournaments, at which she might go so far as to give him a 'favour' such as a spare sleeve or a scarf that he could wear, displaying his devotion to the donor. Here lurks one of those traps which are so easy to fall into when a modern eye sees a familiar medieval word. When Chaucer describes him as a 'lusty bachelor' he does not mean that he was a sexy unmarried man, merely that he was a lively young man in knightly service.

'Courteous he was, lowly and serviceable.' The Squire must have been a joy to his father, as his son Thomas was to Chaucer, and my son is to me.

XXII THE YEOMAN

A yeoman had he [the Knight] and servants no more...
And he was clad in coat and hood of green.[1]

The Knight was himself part of an indentured retinue to which he had brought his own retainers, during those campaigns that we have looked at. By the time the Canterbury pilgrims started out from Southwark, however, his own contractual obligations to his lord had come to an end, and he was free to set out for home.

As a Retainer

The Knight's personal retinue – his son the Squire, and his yeoman – was still bound to him, so he was accompanied by them when he set out for Canterbury.[2] A yeoman might be mounted, and a valuable archer, but still inferior in rank to inexperienced young squires. In the 1347 campaign against the Scots a knight was paid 2 shillings a day, a squire 12 pence a day, but a mounted archer only 4 pence a day. Nevertheless a spell in military service might enable a yeoman on demobilization to buy himself a small cottage and enough land to keep a family in reasonable circumstances, so it was a sensible career choice. Military service as an archer could be a stage in a man's working life, or part-time work on a regular basis over a longer period.

Bows and Arrows

A sheaf of peacock arrows, bright and kene [sharp],
Under his belt he bore full thriftily [properly] . . .
And in his hand he bore a mighty bow.[3]

The bowyers' mistery, or professional body, had monopolized the craft of bow-making in London since 1371.[4] English bows were usually made of yew, using wood imported from Italy as well as from native trees. It took a hundred years for a yew tree to grow big enough to produce perhaps four bowstaves. The skill of the bowyers lay in balancing the sapwood, which was elastic, and the heartwood, which was resilient, giving the bowstave a natural spring which provided the tension necessary to propel the arrow. The centre of the stave had a grip for the left hand while the right hand drew the string. Horn pieces, or 'nocks', were usually added to the ends of the stave, to hold the string in place. The bow was probably about the same height as that of the man using it – somewhere between 5 feet 8 inches and 6 feet, tall for those times when the average height was about 5 feet 7 inches. The bowstring was usually made of animal gut, sometimes hemp or flax (linen), very occasionally silk. It would need replacing after about a hundred arrows.

The arrow shafts were usually made of ash or poplar, which were plentiful in England. Arrows were counted by the 'sheaf' of twenty-four, so the Yeoman had twenty-four long, sharp arrows in his belt. That sounds neither comfortable nor safe, until you realize that the arrows were tucked into the back of his belt. The fletching was normally of goose feathers. Peacock feathers – the bronze pinion feathers of the male bird, not the tail feathers – were highly prized as fletching since they have a close texture and cut with a good sharp edge. In 1372 John of Gaunt, who could afford the best, ordered 'forty good arrows, with heads of good steel, and well and cleanly fletched with peacock feathers'.

Archery

The longbow as developed by English archers could release ten to twenty arrows a minute, compared to the crossbow which fired only two or three bolts a minute. According to Froissart describing the Battle of Crécy, 'the English archers took one pace forward and poured out their arrows on the Genoese [the enemy crossbowmen, who were advancing towards them] so quickly and evenly that they fell like snow'; and at Poitiers, 'no one could face the rapid heavy fire of the English archers'. A modern archer has described this as 'blanket shooting', like machine-gun fire. The same modern archer has found that a professional medieval archer using a longbow for an aimed shot, like a sniper using a rifle, would need between seven and nine seconds from first nocking it to loose an arrow, and the arrow would carry 200 yards at least. It was just as well that medieval archers never had to meet the fearsome archers of Genghis Khan, a century or so earlier. They could fire at the gallop, even turning round to fire at pursuers, and hit their targets at up to 300 yards.

The French War

Froissart carefully enumerates how many archers and other men-at-arms were engaged in each battle that he described. Archers far outnumbered the others. Even for the naval Battle of Sluys in 1340, the king 'redisposed his whole fleet... placing vessels filled with archers on all the sides, and between every two shiploads of archers there was one of men-at-arms... [and] a flanking squadron made up entirely of archers'.

Crécy

The force that Edward embarked for his 1346 campaign comprised 4,000 men-at-arms and 10,000 archers.[5] He had intended to campaign in Gascony, but contrary winds drove the massive invasion fleet back to Cornwall, so Edward decided to land in Normandy instead, where he met with little opposition since the French were not expecting him there. The English made their way along the coast, pillaging and looting as they went. The French army realized that they had been outwitted, and sought to catch up with the English. Edward drove north, planning to join forces with his allies in the Low Countries. The two armies played a grim game of leapfrog. At one stage it looked as if Edward would be blocked by the River Somme; but luckily a local man knew a ford that was passable at low tide. The English army had to wait for the right moment, while the French were gaining ground. But just in time – and, according to Froissart, with considerable loss of life – the English got across, and the French, too late for the tide, could only stand and watch in frustration. As Froissart recorded, 'when the English had scattered the enemy and cleared the ground, they formed up in excellent order, assembled their supply-train and moved off in their habitual way'. It sounds so simple.

Edward divided his forces into three. His son the Black Prince had 800 men-at-arms and 2,000 archers under him, the second division comprised 500 men-at-arms and 1,200 archers, the third, led by the king himself, amounted to 700 men-at-arms and 2,000 archers. He chose the site of the eventual battle carefully, making use of every quirk in the terrain. Crucially, it had rained the night before, so that the chalky earth was slippery. Instead of doing the normal thing and deploying his troops in solid masses to receive the enemy's cavalry charge and then counter-charging, he adopted tactics which had already proved their worth in the campaign against the Scots, which the French had probably never heard of and no one thought important: he combined his archers and men-at-arms and cavalry, with devastating effect. Worse: he used carts as fortifications – humble carts such as menials used to carry goods, prisoners and manure. With these carts, linked together by chains, he created a giant corral, open at one end with inviting open wings at its mouth. He concealed archers at the approach to the mouth and stationed his cavalry, dismounted, inside the trap.

The French approached and saw nothing but some carts. They sent in their first wave, the Genoese crossbowmen. A crossbow is admirable for dispatching bolts ('quarrels') at high speed, but it has to be wound up, usually by putting one foot in a stirrup on the ground, and winding the bowstring back to get the necessary tension. Rain on chalky ground... time after time the wretched crossbow men slipped. In the end they turned tail and fled. But where could they go but back into the lines of the advancing French cavalry, who simply rode them down in a hideous mêlée of men, horses and armour? All this time the English longbowmen were firing their arrows in a continuous lethal hailstorm, wounding and killing the French cavalry horses and men and whatever wretched Genoese survived. The French still advanced, into the trap set by Edward. In the struggle that ensued, the discipline and battle experience of the English were the decisive factors, but luck, in the shape of the local man who knew the ford over the Somme at low tide, and the rain that had the Genoese crossbowmen slipping all over the place, played a part too.

The English casualties were negligible. The French suffered appallingly. According to Froissart 'eleven princes lay dead on the field, eighty bannerets [the higher rank of knights], twelve hundred ordinary knights and about thirty thousand other men'. His totals were probably fairly close to the truth, except for his 'other men' who numbered probably 10,000 or less. In the aftermath of the battle some French nobles were anxiously looking for someone to whom they could safely surrender. They recognized an English knight 'because they had campaigned together in Granada and Prussia and on other expeditions', in the way knights did meet each other. (So perhaps my judgement of Chaucer's Knight in Granada and Prussia has been unduly harsh; decent knights were there too.) Sir Thomas Holland took the count of Eu prisoner and handed him over to the English king for £12,000, a staggering sum. There was a convention that when a high-ranking enemy was taken prisoner he should be 'sold' to the monarch for use in negotiations with the enemy; Sir Thomas must have thanked his lucky stars that he had happened on such a prominent noble.

In August 1347, on his way home to England, Edward took Calais after an eleven-month siege. The inhabitants had been driven to surrender by starvation. The English king proposed to execute the six burghers who brought him the keys of their city, but his queen, Philippa, famously begged him on her knees to spare them, which he did. The English looted the city. Sitting in his monastery in St Albans, Thomas Walsingham, sourly writing his chronicles, commented on how the spoils of the French War were scattered throughout England. 'There was hardly a humble household who did not have some of it – clothes, furs, household utensils, table-cloths and household linen. The French women grieved, but the English women rejoiced.'

Poitiers

Poitiers came just nine years later. This time the English army was led by the Black Prince, aged twenty-five. Froissart gave his usual impartial and gripping account of the battle. The prince adopted the tactics that had served his father so well at Crécy, luring the French into a trap. He was hugely outnumbered – 8,000 to 50,000. Not surprisingly, the French were so confident of victory that they had come equipped with chests of jewels and silver with which to celebrate in fitting style. But their optimism was misplaced. Again, the English archers 'were a huge asset to their side and a terror to the French'. The prince had stationed them behind a hedge, with a clear field of fire to the advancing enemy cavalry. Their aim was so accurate that 'the French did not know where to turn to avoid their arrows. So the English kept advancing and slowly gaining ground', until finally the French army broke and fled. 'There died that day . . . the finest flower of French chivalry, whereby the realm of France was sorely weakened . . . With the king [John II, called 'the Good King'] and his youngest son Philip, seventeen counts were taken prisoner, besides the barons, knights and squires; while between five and seven hundred men-at-arms were killed, and six thousand men in all.'

The English army had realized by now that war could be a very paying proposition. Apart from loot – and the French treasure chests came in very handy here – there were ransoms to be gained, so it was well worth taking prisoners and keeping them safe. The French morale was so broken that they were practically queueing up to surrender. Many of them bought their liberty there and then, or were freed simply on their promise to surrender themselves later, or pay up their ransom after they got home. Being knights, their word could be trusted.

To capture the French king, however, would have been like winning the jackpot in modern terms. To avoid just that emergency eleven lookalikes impersonating the king had been fielded by the French, but where were they when they were most needed? King John was able to surrender himself formally to a knight in the English army who spoke French, but they were separated in the scrimmage. The next thing the king knew was a mob of men-at-arms, who had recognized him and were fighting each other for possession of such a valuable prize. Poor King John had never in his life been so pushed and shoved and manhandled. He had the presence of mind to promise to 'make each one of you rich' if they would take him to the English prince, but soon the brawling broke out again and they came to blows at every step they took. The uproar attracted the attention of two senior English officers, who sprang to the ground and bowed humbly before him – a king is a king, after all, even if he is an enemy – and took him to the Black Prince. He was safe.

The last days of the French king cannot have been happy. He was treated by the English court with the utmost respect due to a king. He joined his noble compatriots in the Palace of the Savoy, where he led an almost regal life. But a huge ransom was demanded which would impoverish the French peasantry for years to come. After the Peace of Brétigny in 1360 the king was allowed to go home, leaving one of his sons, Louis, and other important nobles in England as hostages, to guarantee payment of the ransom. But Louis broke the terms of his parole and escaped. His father was so shamed by this breach of the rules of chivalry that he returned voluntarily to captivity in England. The English court welcomed him warmly, and celebrated his return with much dancing and merriment. He went back to the Savoy and spent the winter there cheerfully and sociably, often going upriver to the English king's Palace of Westminster nearby. But he fell ill and died in captivity in April 1364. If he had not observed the rules of medieval chivalry he could have died in peace, at home.

Compulsory Training

To maintain such numbers of archers it was vital to have a reservoir of trained men on whom to call. Every citizen was expected to be able to handle a war bow. In 1363, for example, the king wrote to the sheriff of Kent deploring that

> Whereas the people of our realm, nobles as well as commoners, usually practiced [used to practice] in their games the art of archery... now the art is almost totally neglected and the people amuse themselves with throwing stones, wood or iron or playing handball, football or stickball [the ancestor of cricket?] or hockey or cockfighting... and now the said art is almost wholly disused, whereby the realm is likely to be kept without archers.

The sheriff was to see that every man in the shire learned archery. All the sheriffs in England duly issued proclamations that 'every able-bodied man, on feast days when he has leisure, shall in his sports use bows and arrows, pellets or bolts [from crossbows], and shall learn and practice the art of shooting... forbidding all... to attend or meddle with [the forbidden] vain games of no value'. It does seem a bit hard on Englishmen who were looking forward to the few hours they could call their own, after working all week and attending the compulsory church services on Sundays and other feast days, that they had to do military training instead of 'meddling' with a promising cockfight. And an 'able-bodied man' meant any male between the ages of twelve and sixty. As always, there is little chance of knowing how effectively this order was enforced.

The Forest Law

'A forester was he soothly [truly], as I guess.'

The word 'forest' did not mean what we think of as a forest, with trees and not much else. It related to the royal forests, the land that Norman kings from William the Conqueror onwards had set aside for their favourite pastime, hunting. By the thirteenth century, the area of royal forest covered a quarter of the land area of England. The entire county of Essex was a royal forest. Epping Forest is a remnant of this. The New Forest in Hampshire is another.

William the Conqueror had imposed a special law to protect red deer, fallow deer, roe deer, and wild boar. By 1217 this 'forest law' was recognized as part of the law of the land, and routinely confirmed by each monarch on his accession, along with the Great Charter, Magna Carta. Offences were categorized by their effect: did the alleged offence damage the 'vert' – the essential greenery, trees, grassland and so on – or the 'venison' – the animals?

An elaborate administrative system evolved. At the top was a royal appointee, a 'justice' or 'warden', who had to account to the royal treasury for any profit he made out of the post. He would be a man of substance. Below him was a network of lesser officials, from the 'wardens' down to the 'riding foresters' and the mere 'walking foresters'. The forest laws were strictly enforced, and their officers were heartily disliked. A charge was payable if you needed to drive your cart over a stretch of forest on your way to somewhere else. You could be arrested and fined for taking wind-fallen wood, or some nuts growing wild, or honey from a wild bees' nest, or a fish from a weir or a river, or if you let your pigs feed on the beech mast without a licence. If you happened on a wild hawk's nest, you must on no account disturb it; hawks belonged to the king. Even if you had a valid permission to keep your cow or a pig in the forest, all domestic animals had to be cleared from the forest during the 'fence month', the two weeks either side of midsummer, when the hinds were giving birth and must not be disturbed.

The tension between dwellers in or near a forest and the foresters could erupt into fights in which the foresters could pay with their lives. Their job was no sinecure. But sometimes they could be bought off by a judicious bribe. They were notoriously corrupt, as well as unpopular.

Under the common law that covered the rest of the realm, the clergy had a special status. They could 'plead their tonsure' or recite the 'neck verse', to prove that they were literate; it followed, since few other men were able to read at the time when the doctrine evolved, that they were clerics and subject to ecclesiastical law, which as we have seen was often more lenient than the common law. But their privileged status did not apply within the royal forests – an interesting example of the power of the king to trump the privileges of the clergy. They had to pay fines for offences against the forest law just like anyone else.

Chaucer's Yeoman fitted into this administration somewhere, but we are not told how senior he was. 'Of woodcraft well knew he all the usage', which was no less than any forester would know, even a mere walking forester. But the rest of his equipment demonstrates a fairly prosperous standard of living. He had a handsome (Chaucer's word was 'gay') bracer, an arm guard used by archers; a sword and a small shield; a dagger, also 'gay' and ornamented, and a horn on a green baldric. Quite how he managed all that as well as the equipment belonging to his other capacity as an archer, i.e. his mighty bow and those twenty-four sharp arrows in his belt, is hard to imagine. Perhaps Chaucer failed to imagine it, too. Here was no lowly walking forester.

St Christopher

A Christopher on his breast of silver sheen [bright].

Chaucer never wastes words in the details he chooses. The pity of it is that their significance so often passes us by, faded and distorted by the passage of time. So why did Chaucer attribute to the Yeoman this particular badge, popularly used in the Middle Ages, and still, as a good luck symbol for wayfarers? According to legend, St Christopher carried the Christ Child across a stream, the Christ Child representing God. Prayers to him would safeguard travellers. His image was often painted on the wall opposite the south door of a church, to greet anyone entering. The medieval faithful believed that anyone seeing that image would be safe all that day. A charming and reassuring legend; but why was it appropriate to the Yeoman? Perhaps he was just following the custom of wearing a Christopher badge like any other traveller, and there's no deeper meaning behind it.

A Medieval Joke

John of Gaunt owned extensive forests. Here is a faint echo of a medieval joke. He gave permission to a friend, whenever he happened to be passing through one of Gaunt's forests, to take a stag and a hind *and a hedgehog*. If it was during the closed season, the hedgehog had to be replaced by a female cat, 'une chate'.

XXIII THE SHIPMAN

A shipman was there, woning fer by weste [living far in the
   west] –
For aught I woot [for all I know] he was of Dartmouth.
He rode upon a rouncy [a hired horse], as he kouthe [as
   well as he could].[1]

Chaucer pokes gentle fun at the Shipman, or sea captain, who was
more used to ships than horses. His 'rouncy' was probably hired for
the trip, since he would have no need to own a horse in his seafar-
ing life. He was clearly prepared to invest a considerable sum in the
journey; hire of a horse from from Southwark to Rochester alone
cost 12 pence, and another 12 pence from Rochester to Canterbury.

Why Dartmouth? Chaucer had been sent to Dartmouth in 1373
to arrange for the restoration to its master of a wrongfully detained
Genoese merchant ship possibly captured by West Country pirates.
Perhaps he had found the experience traumatic – more exotic than
any of his travels in France and Italy? Or perhaps Chaucer was
looking further back, to 1343, when King Edward III had gathered
his invasion fleet together by the simple expedient of conscript-
ing all privately owned ships over a certain size: Dartmouth had
resisted, attracting the royal wrath and the arrest of twenty-seven
ships with their owners and masters. So perhaps the very mention
of Dartmouth warned Chaucer's audience that the Shipman should
be treated with caution in real life. It's one of those resonances with
echoes in medieval minds that, unfortunately, we can't hear.

The impression of a man who, in a later idiom, might be 'quick
on the draw' was strengthened by another odd detail:

> A dagger hanging on a laas [cord] had he,
> About his neck, down under his arm[.][2]

It was normal for a man to carry a knife, to use for cutting up his food and such domestic purposes, but he would wear it hanging from his belt, with his purse, not slung round him like a shoulder holster; and a knife was not a 'dagger'.

Medieval Shipping

Not surprisingly, 'the hot summer had made his hue [complexion] all brown'. He was probably weatherbeaten all year round. 'With many a tempest had his beard been shaken.' There was little shelter on board a medieval ship.

There were two methods of building medieval ships: carvel and clinker. The two systems hardly ever met until the fourteenth century, when each began to adopt some of the features of the other. Mediterranean shipbuilders made the frame first, and then nailed planks onto it with their edges flush: carvel-built. Shipbuilders catering for the northern European trade made the outer shell of the vessel first, of overlapping 'strakes' or planks, nailed together with iron 'clench' nails. The interior fittings, such as they were, were added later. The result was a capacious, single-masted, square-sailed, flat-bottomed 'cog', the workhorse of the Baltic and North Sea ports.

The approach to London was tricky to navigate, with its unpredictable shifting sandbanks. The 'great galleys' from Venice and Genoa with cargoes of luxury goods such as silks and spices often preferred to anchor in the safe waters of Sandwich Haven, trans-shipping their cargoes to smaller English cogs well used to the vagaries of the Thames estuary shoals.

Most cargo was carried in huge barrels called tuns, holding 216 imperial gallons, taking up about 33–40 cubic feet of space. The more valuable tuns could be padded with strips of willow – 'pantalooned'.[3] Crew and passengers lived on the single deck, with no protection from the weather save for their leather sleeping bags.

The sailing season lasted only from March to October, or possibly November. A contrary wind could delay sailing for weeks.

In September 1372 Edward III sailed out of Sandwich, bound for France with a massive invasion fleet, the trumpeters trumpeting, the flags flying. By early October he had only got as far as Winchelsea, the weather was still against him, and the whole enterprise had to be aborted. But given a fair wind, the 120 miles between the Thames estuary and the Flemish ports could be covered in two full days.

The French War didn't stop the English from normal trading with other nations. The Venetians, the Italians and the Hanse traders all had merchant shipping in the seas between England and the Continent throughout the war. But there were always pirates lurking. Any of them might attack an English vessel.

Naval Warfare

The medieval technique of sea battles, before gunpowder and cannon made long-range attack possible, was to sail up to the enemy ship, ram it, grapple it, board it and fight hand to hand. To adapt the civilian design of a cog for fighting was simple. Temporary 'castles' for the soldiers to occupy would be built high up on the mast nearest the prow – the 'forecastle' – and on the other mast or masts, to gain the advantage of height, so as to fire their arrows and crossbow bolts down onto the enemy. Long streamers or banners which hung from the mast, the painted panels of the castles and shields mounted on the gunwales, identified each ship, like flags or standards in a land battle.

The war had begun well for the English navy with the Battle of Sluys in 1340. The French had put their faith in oared galleys built and manned by Italians, especially the Genoese. Granted, they were not subject to the vagaries of the weather, but they were expensive to build and man. The French fleet of 198 ships moored in Sluys included twenty-eight oared galleys, each with a crew of a hundred men or more, and twenty-eight with crews of two hundred or more. The English fleet sailed in and captured nearly all the French ships. In 1346 the English army had been transported over the Channel in an invasion fleet of 147 ships to win the famous Battle of Crécy. Another naval victory was won off Winchelsea in 1350.

But these victories did not prevent terrifying coastal raids by enemy ships. Gravesend and Rye were burned by enemy raiders in 1377, Gravesend suffered again in 1380. The country lived in fear of invasion. Even the rebellious Kentish peasants who marched on London in 1381 told supporters who lived near the coast to stay at home, ready to defend England against another invasion. Not until the victory of Cadzand in 1387 could coastal dwellers sleep easily in their beds.

Victors of battles at sea were deprived of one advantage enjoyed by victors on land: it was rare to hold prisoners for ransom. The Shipman certainly never did:

> Of nice conscience took he no keep [he didn't bother about it]:
> If that he fought and had the higher hand,
> By water he sent them home to every land.[4]

He just threw his prisoners overboard.

But sometimes it was worth preserving an enemy sailor from a watery grave. In the Battle of Cadzand, which began off Margate and ended off the Flemish coast, the English admiral Arundel captured the enemy admiral, Jean de Bucq. Arundel set de Bucq's ransom at the huge sum of £2,666. But the French admiral was so unsporting as to die in captivity before the ransom was paid. His fleet had been carrying the whole annual wine shipment from La Rochelle in Gascony to the Low Countries. This windfall of wine severely dislocated the London wine market. The Crown took full advantage of it. Richard Whittington, for example, the future mayor of London, was owed £333 by the Crown; all he got by way of payment was 200 tuns of wine.

Navigational Skills

> ... Of his craft to rekene [skill in calculating] well his tides,
> His streams, and his dangers him bisides [near to him],
> His harbours and his moon, his lodemenage [navigational skills],
> There was no such from Hull to Carthage...
> He knew all the havens as they were
> From Gotland to the cape of Finisterre,
> And every creek in Brittany and in Spain.[5]

Medieval shipping tended to cling to the visible coastline, not venturing into open seas. Every ship's captain had to have a thorough knowledge of the hazards likely to be met, and the places where he might seek shelter if necessary. He needed to forecast the tides by the phases of the moon. He carried in his head the salient points of the coastlines where he was likely to sail. Chaucer's Shipman might go as far north as the island of Gotland off the coast of Sweden, and as far south as Cape Finisterre. Knowledge of 'every creek in Brittany and in Spain' could be vital, since what would be navigable by a small, flat-bottomed English cog would be impassable for a great enemy galley.

How did a medieval mariner know where he was? He might have access to a portolan, a description of coasts and harbours, with sailing directions and warnings about rocks and shoals, which had begun to circulate during the thirteenth century, but detailed maps and charts were yet to come. At night, if the sky was clear, he could find the north star, but if the sky was clouded over he would have to wait. By day he could use a lodestone, a piece of magnetic oxide of iron, magnetite, which would indicate north with a fair degree of accuracy. Chaucer's Shipman may have adopted the practice of wearing his in a little bag round his neck, so that he could consult it without the risk of losing it in a high sea.

Gradually the lodestone was sophisticated into what we know as a compass, said to have been invented in Amalfi early in the fourteenth century. 'Navigators have a small box, with a small wheel of light paper that rotates in the centre. This wheel has many points, and on one of them that has a star painted on it, the point of a needle is inserted. When navigators want to find where north is, they make the needle giddy with a magnet.'[6] The Amalfitans' invention took some time to appear in northern seas.

The World Picture

It was generally known that the world is round, like a ball. Plato (424–348 BC) had described the world as like 'one of those twelve-piece leather balls, variegated, a patchwork of colours'. Ptolemy (c.100–c.170 AD) is mainly known as a great astronomer, but he also wrote *Geographia*, including all that was known of the geography of the world in his time. The Arabic translation movement beginning in the ninth century (for more on this see Chapter XVIII) took Ptolemy further, and into Arabic. Al-Idrisi (*c.*1100–66) travelled widely until he settled in the Norman kingdom of Sicily, where Roger II employed him to produce a new world atlas. This *Tabula Rogeriana*, completed in 1154, remained the most accurate world map for the next three centuries. The '*mappae mundi*' were not nearly so useful; they were designed to show how Jerusalem was culturally and religiously the centre of the world, which was not geographically accurate.

The land mass of the earth was encircled by the ocean, and bounded to the east by the far coast of Cathay (China), and to the west by the coast of northern Brittany (Finis Terrae, the end of the earth) and the Straits of Gibraltar. To the north lay the cold regions, and to the south lay the hot lands. If you take a modern map of the world, cut off the Americas and, of course, Australia, and then tear off Africa along the Equator, you would have a very rough idea of the Shipman's world.

In Chaucer's time the coast of the Mediterranean – the 'sea in the middle of the earth' – had been known for centuries, but knowledge of other lands was fragmentary. A Viking ship had crossed the Atlantic and discovered the edge of the continent which would eventually be known as America, but the discovery was not followed up by settlement. Genoese galleys had sailed north round Cap Finistère and arrived in Flanders as long ago as 1277, but exploration southwards from the Straits of Gibraltar had reached only a short distance down the coast of Africa. The great age of discovery dawned in the next century.

Exotic foreigners occasionally appeared in London. 'Baldack, son of the King of India', with his entourage, made a fleeting appearance in the City records in 1366, but there was nothing known of his father.

Crusaders, and after them pilgrims, had been going to the Holy Land for many years. There were rumours of lands beyond. The terrifying Mongol armies had conquered China and its capital Beijing in the early thirteenth century, and invaded Europe and stormed

Moscow, Rostov and Kiev by 1240. Then suddenly, when Vienna was almost within their grasp, they wheeled round and disappeared in 1242, as suddenly as they had arrived.

Marco Polo

Marco Polo was born in Venice in 1254. His father Niccolò and his uncle Maffeo were both prosperous merchants belonging to a noble Venetian family. They had set out on a trading voyage to the Crimea, but their return had to be postponed because of a local war, so they went on to Bokhara, where they stayed for three years. Then they decided to join a party bound via the Silk Road for the court of Kublai Khan, in Shangdu, near modern Beijing. Kublai Khan was so impressed by their stories of life in the west that he told them to go back to their homeland and recruit a cadre of a hundred learned Christians to teach him about it. They were also to bring him some of the famous holy oil from Jerusalem. They duly got back to Venice in 1269. Two years later they set off for Cathay again, this time taking with them young Marco and some holy oil, but only two friars instead of the hundred 'learned Christians' that Kublai had asked for. The friars decided that the journey was too dangerous when they heard rumours of war on the way, and went home. The three Venetians travelled on, reaching Shangdu in 1275, where they presented Kublai Khan with letters from the newly elected pope and the holy oil.

The two older men made themselves invaluable to the khan by applying modern western technology. A certain city was resisting all attempts by the khan's army to end its rebellion. Maffeo and Niccolò were able to construct siege engines, mangonels, that threw heavy stones over the city wall, which so terrified the rebels that they immediately surrendered. They were also more skilful navigators than the Chinese, and put their seamanship at the disposal of Kublai Khan. Young Marco had a gift for languages. Kublai Khan appointed him governor of a district in southern China, so far distant from his father and uncle in Shangdu that it took him fourteen months to get there. He spent three years there, sending back regular reports to his employer of the local conditions, such as the distances between major cities, the local marketable commodities and the wildlife. (As to that, the translator of the *Travels* into English always got it wrong: there were tigers galore there, but no lions; he always used 'lions' for whatever foreign word he encountered for 'tigers', just occasionally describing them as 'striped'.)

By 1291 the three Venetians were anxious to return home. They had made huge trading profits. Marco's father and uncle were growing old, and so was Kublai; when he died there could be succession problems and the Venetians had no desire to be there then. But they had made themselves so invaluable to Kublai Khan that he was reluctant to let them go. Providentially, an embassy from Persia had come to escort a Tartar bride to the Persian court. The political situation blocked their journey back to Persia overland, and they asked Kublai Khan to allow the Venetians, with their superior knowledge of navigation and seamanship, to accompany them on their return by sea. Kublai could hardly refuse. He fitted out a magnificent fleet of junks, which left a Chinese port in 1292 bound for Persia. The fleet took two years to reach Hormuz on the Arabian Sea, after many privations. From Hormuz the Venetians were able to travel overland to Trabzon on the Black Sea, and hence home to Venice. But Marco, as a young noble, had to take part in the war then being fought between his native city and Genoa. The galleon under his command was captured, and he spent the next three years, after all his adventures, mewed up in a Genoese prison.

His fellow-prisoner was a man from Pisa called Rustichello. Marco reminisced about his epic travels, and Rustichello wrote them down in very bad French. The difference between the two men, the one a prudent Venetian merchant and the other a fiction writer by trade, must have shaped the final book. Marco occasionally mentioned notes he had taken on his journeying. He sometimes referred to other members of his company; he surely travelled with servants and probably with an armed guard, no medieval traveller would make the journey alone. But as one reads his *Travels* one is always dimly conscious of Rustichello, the fiction writer, hovering at his shoulder.

Wherever he went, Marco had noted the productions and the risks of each area they crossed – where to buy provisions, how many days until the next staging post, where best to buy pack animals. One of the major cities they saw on the way to Shangdu was Baghdad, 'the residence of the khalif or pontiff of all the Saracens'. The best dates in the world could be bought there, and 'almost all the pearls brought to Europe from India are bored here'. There was a school teaching Muslim law, magic, physics, astronomy, geomancy and physiognomy.

The district over which Marco was appointed governor was in Manji, Kublai's newly acquired territory in the south of modern China. His account of those years was a sober checklist of climate, population, distances between major cities, marketable commodities and local wildlife. (The modern reader by now has got out an atlas and has his pen poised to track Marco's travels on his map, but he will be disappointed. The transliteration into western font of the Chinese place names, and the subsequent translation into various European languages, as well as the passage of time, has made it impossible to trace Marco's travels in detail. It is better just to enjoy them as a colourful travelogue.)

The principal production of Manji, and of all Cathay, was silk, raw or woven into various textiles. These were the fabrics that embellished Kublai Khan's courts, and after long journeys turned up in the English court as well – satins and velvets, embroidered in gold with animals and birds, woven with gold thread, bejewelled and heavy with pearls. There doesn't seem to have been a wool industry in China, although Marco does occasionally mention sheep. In Prester John's land (also mentioned by Mandeville; see p. 295) there were 'a variety of woolen cloths', but we are not clear where that was. Cotton does appear, but only as the finest muslin, sometimes interwoven with gold.

Other commodities that Marco regularly records are 'spices and drugs', including rhubarb, regarded as a medicinal drug in the medieval West and exported all over the world from China, and the ginger used in so many recipes. Sugar was also listed as a spice, improved on the advice of some merchants from Cairo who had taught the method of refining it. Pepper was the most important spice of all. In Canton 'many vessels from India', according to Marco, traded their jewels and pearls for pepper. The trade in pepper was 'so considerable, that what is carried to Alexandria to supply the demand of the western parts of the world is trifling, perhaps not more than a hundredth part' of the demand for it in China. Bengal was the place to go for eunuchs, available after every minor skirmish when all prisoners of war were emasculated and put up for sale.

Marco gives a detailed description of his employer's magnificent palace. Vast courtyards, exquisite buildings decorated in gold and silver, tame animals in lovely parks . . . and, of course, '300 maidens', as well as his four empress wives. There was an annual beauty contest to choose these maidens, where the tests were even more rigorous than any western parade: they must not snore, nor smell, and they must have sweet breath. Kublai 'observed equally the festivals of Jews, Muslims, Christians and "idolators "'. When he referred to 'idolaters' Marco may sometimes have meant Buddhists, prostrating themselves before statues of the Buddha, or simply the conjurors who managed to make Kublai's wine cup mysteriously float from the middle of his hall to his mouth without apparent human intervention, the secret lying in cunningly concealed wires.

The three Venetians were far from the only western merchants in Kublai's domain. In the suburbs outside his main palace there was a caravanserai for 'Lombards' from north Italy, such as Genoese and Venetians, another for 'Germans' and a third for French. Marco sometimes refers to other Venetians, but clearly felt no compulsion to spend any time with them. He was intrigued by the paper money with which the Chinese emperors had solved the problem that beset western rulers – how to finance an increasingly expensive government: just print more. Alternatively, import cowrie shells, valueless in themselves but accepted widely as effective currency.

By now Rustichello was probably urging Marco to tell more 'human interest' stories. So Marco duly describes the strange marriage customs of some tribes, often to the advantage of visiting foreigners; for example, 'travellers can have the wives of their hosts', which was reckoned, probably rightly, to increase the birth rate. 'While the stranger is in the house, he places a signal at the window, [such] as his hat or something . . . by such an act of kindness [to the visitor] a blessing is obtained [by the host].' Marco also dwells on the gruesome funeral ways of some tribes, cooking and eating the dead man's body.

In 1280 Marco went to Siam, conquered by Kublai Khan in 1268, where the king had 326 children. He then went on to Sumatra, where he visited six of the eight kingdoms into which it was divided. It was here that he heard of 'men with tails a span in length but not covered with hair' (possibly some kind of baboon or orangutan). He was stuck there for five months 'because of contrary winds', i.e. the monsoon. For the first time we see how far from being a lone traveller he was – he describes how he 'established himself on shore, with a party of about 2,000 men'.

Next he went to Malabar, where among other oddities he saw a mosquito net, which the sleeper can 'draw close about them by pulling a string'. Here was where St Thomas the Apostle was martyred, shot by accident by a man who only meant to kill a peacock. Christian pilgrims flocked to the site of his death and collected the miracle-working red earth from it.

Marco went twice to Taprobane, also named Zeilan (Ceylon, now Sri Lanka), across what we call the Indian Ocean. The main commodities there were rubies, sapphires and other precious stones, and gold.

For diamonds it was worth visiting the mountains of India, but they are infested with snakes, which attract eagles. So diamond-hunters throw bits of meat from the rocks above, to where the diamonds lie on the ground and the eagles fly down, pick up the meat and take it up to the top of the rocks to eat it. The hunters are waiting there. They drive the eagles away, and check the bits of meat. There are often diamonds stuck to them or in the eagles' droppings.

As Marco says at about this point in his *Travels*, 'should we attempt to treat of all the cities of India the account would be prolix and tiresome'. So, reluctantly passing over Gujarat, where there are 'pirates of the most desperate character', and Socotra, where whales are harpooned to get ambergris and spermaceti oil, and Zanzibar where 'the women are the most ill-favoured of the world', and Abyssinia, where the king is Christian, we arrive at Aden, where ships from India unload into smaller ships that 'navigate an arm of the sea for twenty days', then load their cargoes onto camels for the thirty-day journey to the Nile, where the cargoes are loaded onto small boats that reach the final destination of Alexandria.

It seems an anticlimax to be told about 'the northern parts of the world', with its sledges and polar bears, where Marco never went, nor did he go to Russia, where 'the inhabitants are Christians and follow the Greek ritual. North of there is the Region of Darkness. I have been assured that it extends as far as the Northern Ocean.'

Marco's *Travels* came out in about 1300, to a mixed reception. Though incredulous at some of the stories, people were eager to read them. It was a bestseller, flying off the copyists' desks as fast as they could write. Their many scribal errors were magnified as the book was translated into several European languages. But it was sufficiently well thought of for a copy, in Latin, to appear on the austere bookshelves of Merton College, Oxford. Marco died in 1324, never having left Venice again.

Mandeville's Travels

The *Travels* of Sir John Mandeville were also in Merton College library, beside a copy of the Koran.[7] He wrote it as a guide for those who want to visit the Holy Land, 'for I have very often been there'. Indeed his accounts of the pilgrim routes to Palestine and even to the tomb of St Catherine in Sinai, and the way to Constantinople, read tolerably credibly. After all, as he said, 'the way is common and is known of many nations'. But from there on he often relied on second-hand sources and his imagination. It's almost impossible to choose from the wealth of exoticisms he spreads before the reader, all with a straight face.

He does sometimes pause for a brief moment of reality in a fog of fancy. He mentions the phenomenon of the Nile's seasonal flood, but locates its source in 'paradise terrestrial'. He describes with equal interest and accuracy incubating hens' and ducks' eggs in horse dung, and selling 'men and women of other laws [nationalities] as we do here [sell] beasts in the market'.

'Also in Egypt be gardens that have trees and herbs the which bear fruits seven times in the year... and in that country and in others also, men find long apples to sell, and men call them apples of paradise ... and though ye cut them in never so many gobbets ... evermore ye shall find in the midst the figure of the Holy Cross of our Lord Jesu ... they will rot within eight days [so they can't be exported] ... they have great leaves of a foot and a half of length.'[8] Another noteworthy fruit tree was 'the apple tree of Adam, that have a bite at one of the sides', such as Adam left on the apple he bit into in the Garden of Eden.

The Pyramids were

the garners [barns for storing grain] of Joseph, that he let [ordered] made to keep the grains for the peril of the dear years. And they be made of stone, full well made of masons' craft; of which the two be marvelously great and high, and the other two be not so great. And every garner hath a door to enter within, a little high from the earth; for the land is wasted and fallen since the garners were made. And within they be all full of serpents ... And above the garners be many scriptures of divers languages. And some men say, that they be sepultures of great lords that were some time, but that is not true

– everyone knew they were Joseph's garners.

Then he turns to Sicily, where 'there is a manner of a serpent, by the which men may assay and prove whether their children be bastards or no ... if they be born in adultery the serpents bite them and envenom them'.

A quick tour around the lands of the Old Testament follows, including Hebron, and the 'cave in the rock, where Adam and Eve dwelt when they were put out of paradise; and there they got their children ... From Hebron men go to Bethlehem in half a day, for it is but five mile.'

By now Mandeville has reverted to the role of guide to the Holy Land, describing the church containing

the place where Our Lord was born. That is full well dight [decorated] of marble, and full richly painted with gold, silver, azure and other colours. And three paces beside is the crib of the ox

and the ass. And beside that is the place where the star fell, that
led the three kings, Jaspar, Melchior and Balthazar . . . This land
of Jerusalem hath been in many divers nations' hands, and often,
therefore, hath the country suffered much tribulation for the sin
of the people that dwell there.

He adds a pious hope that it would soon be in Christian ownership again. His description of the Church of the Holy Sepulchre
and the other pilgrimage sites in Jerusalem would be useful to any
intending pilgrim.

He recounts the history and appearance of the Temple of the
Lord, where Charlemagne was 'when the angel brought him the
prepuce [foreskin] of Our Lord Christ'. So many other fascinating
relics could be seen, such as the rock 'where sat Our Lady, and
learned her psalter'. Nearby is 'a well, in manner of a cistern, that is
clept [called] Probatica Piscina, that hath five entries. Into that well
angels were wont to come from heaven and bathe them within.
And what[ever] man, that first bathed him after the moving of the
water, was made whole of whatever manner of sickness he had'. He
gave his readers a good run for their money all over the holy sites,
including the River Jordan, where Jesus was baptized 'and the Holy
Ghost alighted on him in the likeness of a culver [pigeon]'.

Mandeville was fascinated by the Muslim faith. The sultan ruled
Egypt, Jerusalem, Syria, Aleppo and Arabia 'and many other lands'
from his throne in Babylon, near Cairo. Mandeville served in his
army for a period, and reminisces about a long private conversation with him. The sultan professed to be shocked by the loose
living of Christians. (One suspects that Mandeville is using this
to get his own disapproval off his chest.) The sultan explained his
detailed knowledge of Christian habits through his 'messengers
that he sent to all lands, in manner as [if] they were merchants of
precious stones, of cloths of gold and of other things, for to know
the manner of every country among Christian men . . . they spake
French right well, and the Sultan also: wherof I had great marvel' –
and the French-speaking diamond seller from the east would never
be viewed in quite the same light again.

Then to (modern) Turkey, where 'near Erzerum is mount Ararat, where Noah's ship rested, and yet is upon that mountain. And men may see it afar in clear weather.'

Even Mandeville is tiring by now. 'After[wards] men go by many cities and great countries that it were too long to tell.' In Ethiopia live the 'folk that have but one foot... so large that it shadoweth all the body against the sun, when they will lie and rest them'. Thence to India, and diamonds again; they can be induced to produce offspring if a male diamond is juxtaposed to a female one, which 'I have often-times assayed'. A diamond will keep its wearer safe in war, 'if his cause be rightful' – a large proviso.

Two merchants from Venice and Genoa who had travelled as far south as an island in the great ocean – which shows just how far the citizens of those cities travelled – found that the tropical heat there caused 'men's ballocks [to] hang down to their knees... men of that country bind them up, and anoint them with ointments'. After a realistic description of 'cockodrills' (crocodiles) he strains our credulity again, with 'wild geese that have two heads' and giants with only one eye in the middle of their foreheads, and men with their eyes in their shoulders, and men with upper lips 'so great that when they sleep in the sun they cover all the face with that lip'. But it's only fair to say that these strange beings had been tucked into the corners of maps for many years; they were only to be expected by his readers.

'Cathay is a great country and a fair... merchants that come from Genoa or from Venice or from Romania or other parts of Lombardy, they go by sea and by land eleven months or twelve... or [before] they come to the isle of Cathay... and it is of the great Chan.' ('Isle' seems to be used as a synonym for 'realm'.) Mandeville really lets himself go in describing the riches of the Great Chan's court. 'My fellows and I with our yeomen [the first time he has mentioned them] served this emperor and were his soldiers fifteen months... And truly we found it [the emperor's kingdom] more noble, and richer and more marvelous, than ever we heard speak of, inasmuch as we would never have believed it had we not seen it.' Mandeville devotes four whole chapters to the Great Chan. Again, he seems to have been there, although he may well have exaggerated – a fault not unknown in travel writers.

'Under the firmament is not so great a lord, nor so mighty, nor so rich, as is the great Chan; not Prester John, that is emperor of the high Inde, nor the Soltan of Babylon, nor the Emperor of Persia.' Prester, or Presbyter (Bishop) John had been around for a very long time in legend. According to Mandeville he 'had under him many kings and many isles and many divers folk... And this land is full good and rich, but not so rich as the great Chan.' The two emperors exchanged daughters as brides, being 'the greatest lords under the firmament'. 'The Emperor Prester John is Christian, and a great part of his country also. But yet they have not all the articles of faith as we have.' When the emperor goes into battle 'he hath three golden crosses' carried in front of him; in peacetime a simple wooden cross preceded him, 'in remembrance that Christ suffered death upon a cross of tree [a wooden cross]'. His kingdom was even more distant than Cathay, 'by many dreadful journeys' – but quite where, Mandeville still leaves us in doubt.

Mandeville tells his own version of the Old Man of the Mountains, who ran the Assassins. An old man had an impregnable castle where there was every imaginable delight, including fifteen-year-old virgins, that he said were angels, in his garden, that he said was paradise. Whenever a 'brave young knight' came to see this famous sight, he would drug him into a hashish-induced dream of an even more perfect paradise. Still under the effect of the drug, the young man was sent to kill one of the Old Man's enemies, his promised reward being a return to paradise, where he could play with the maidens and see God. Death was not to be feared, since it was the portal to an even better paradise where he could play with the maidens evermore. 'And thus went many [young men] to slay great lords in divers countries, and made themselves to be slain, in hope to have that paradise.' But finally the Old Man was rumbled by the local worthies – you would think they might have noticed before – who attacked his castle and slew him. 'And it is not long gone, since that place was destroyed.'

In Taprobane [Sri Lanka] there are great hills of gold, which ants, a kind of animal, look after... The ants are as big as our hounds are here. No one dares go there for fear of these foul beasts. But men often get that gold by cunning. The ants' nature is that when the weather is hot they stay underground from mid-morning until noon. Then the men of that district come with camels and horses and load them with the gold, and go home fast and eagerly before the ants come out.

Herodotus has much the same story: Mandeville probably used him as one of his many sources.

Mandeville tells another anecdote about a 'Valley Perilous' said to be one of the entries to hell. 'In that vale is great plenty of gold and silver.' Although it is guarded by fierce devils, Christians would be safe. 'There were with us two worthy men, friars minors, that were of Lombardy, that said if any man would enter they would go in with us.' So after celebrating Mass, and confessing their sins and receiving absolution, in they went, all fourteen of them – but only nine came out. 'We saw [the missing men] never after, and those were two men of Greece, and three of Spain.'

Beyond that valley there is 'an isle where the folk be great giants of twenty-eight feet long [tall]', who catch any passing ship and eat its crew. 'And men have seen, many times, those giants take men in the sea out of their ships and brought them back to land, two in one hand and two in another, eating them going, all raw and quick [living].' To give him his due, Mandeville 'saw none of those, for I had no lust [desire] to go to those parts'.

After a few more isles, we arrive back at Prester John. The emperor, presumably already Christian, went into a Christian church in Egypt and listened carefully to the service that was going on. He asked one of his entourage, a Christian knight, who it was that conducted the service. He was told 'priests', i.e. presbyters. He said he would take the name of the first priest who came out of the church, who happened to be called John – hence 'Prester, short for presbyter, John'.

'Of Paradise can I not speak properly. For I was not there,' says Mandeville. But he's very happy to tell of what he has heard 'as wise men say'. Paradise is the highest place on earth, so high that Noah's flood failed to reach it. In its centre is a well from which flow four rivers: the Ganges, which runs through India, rich in precious stones and gold; the Nile, which runs through Ethiopia and Egypt; the Tigris, called after a tiger, which runs fast; and the Euphrates, 'that is to say, well-bearing'. Many men have tried to row up the rivers to reach their origin but have been defeated by the noise and huge waves, and many have died, or become blind or deaf by the noise of the water.

As soon as he got home he showed the book of his *Travels* to the pope, who had it examined by his council and approved it. So Sir John Mandeville could go home and rest, being disabled by gout and arthritis 'that define the end of my labour'. I know how he felt. I suspect that His Holiness gave his seal of approval only to the first part of the book, a reasonable account of how to get to the Holy Land and what to see when you got there – although His Holiness's eyebrows may have been raised by the angelic bathers in Jerusalem. But perhaps he was never shown, or anyway never read as far as, the second part, where Mandeville regales his readers with marvels.

Both books had a wide circulation. The Shipman's own Tale strays no further than Paris and Bruges, but he must surely have heard from fellow-mariners about the marvels recounted by Polo and Mandeville. Any English ship's captain would be bound to meet those ubiquitous Venetians and Genoese somewhere along the coast, and they would pass the time together when the weather was too stormy for sailing, exchanging stories of foreign lands.

EPILOGUE

In Chaucer's Prologue we met the pilgrims setting out for Canterbury. They had two days' ride ahead of them through the Kentish countryside, by the old Roman road, Watling Street. His pilgrims never did reach their goal in the *Tales*. They were a motley bunch, from the loud-mouthed Wife of Bath to the humble Parson, from the overbearing lawyer to the minor court official with his eye on the main chance. They were escorted by the Host of the Tabard Inn where they had gathered, and by Chaucer himself.

What would they have seen if they had arrived in Canterbury?

In Chaucer's time the only structures competing with cathedrals in bulk, height and permanence were the castles which William the Conqueror had built as soon as he occupied England, from 1066 onwards. Castles were designed to frown down on the native population, ready to fire on it from the arrow slits in the walls. They guarded strongpoints such as bridges. They were solid, rigid, vertical, intimidating, uncompromisingly alien. Many have survived, such as the Tower of London guarding the crossing of the Thames, and Rochester Castle guarding the crossing of the Medway.

Cathedrals were different. They welcomed lay people, who could use them for daily human business. But their main purpose was to house the priests who had direct communication with heaven. Their towers and spires soared upwards, taking the prayers of the devout with them.

The Norman cathedral of Christchurch in Canterbury was begun in 1070 by a Benedictine archbishop, Lanfranc, who came over from his abbey in Caen, in the heart of William's ducal territory.[1] The quarry near Caen that had provided the beautiful creamy yellow stone for his abbey there was used for his English cathedral, since there was no English stone as suitable for cathedral-building within easy transporting distance overland. By 1070 the sea passage between the English coast and France had been thoroughly organized by those efficient Normans, and stone from Caen began to arrive in Canterbury. The new cathedral was dedicated in 1077.

Lanfranc inherited a stock of holy relics from the Anglo-Saxon cathedral that had stood on the site for decades before the Normans came. They included miscellaneous holy bones, three whole holy Anglo-Saxons and another foreign one. Plegmund, archbishop between 891 and 923, had 'journeyed to Rome [already the main market for relics] and bought the blessed martyr Blase with much money of gold and silver, and he brought him home with him when he returned to Canterbury and placed him in Christchurch'.[2] Lanfranc's building survived in the crypt, but above ground it was soon obliterated by successive rebuildings. His choice of the creamy stone from Caen was adopted by his successors, and is still used in the current restoration. Lanfranc died in 1089, to be succeeded by Archbishop Anselm, who began a huge programme of rebuilding and expansion, nearly doubling the size of the cathedral.

The vast church served two purposes. It was the headquarters of the senior priest of England, the archbishop, whose 'cathedra' (Greek for throne, chair) still stands there. It was also the heart of the Priory of Christchurch, a community of Benedictine monks living under the Rule of their founder. St Benedict's insistence on spells of manual labour interspersed with the holy offices meant that where there was space, most Benedictine abbeys and priories were surrounded by workshops and farms. At Canterbury, however, there was little room. The Archbishop's Palace and grounds took up a wide area to the south-west of the church, and the township crowded close, to the south-east. As the fame of the cathedral's treasury of holy relics spread, crowds of pilgrims arrived. Their horses needed stables and farriers and blacksmiths. The community needed its own brewhouse, granary and bakery. The new faculty of canon and civil law being taught there needed premises. The priory officials needed space for their records and accounts. A big pond had to supply the monks with fresh fish, since meat was forbidden them. An orchard provided fruit, and beehives honey and wax for candles – a valuable commodity in those days.

The complexity of the priory's domestic organization can be gathered from the duties of the obedientiaries, or heads of department, under the prior.[3] The precentor was responsible for the music and the library. He saw to the provision of parchment and other materials used for copying manuscripts. His staff included a choirmaster and a novice-master, who taught the young entrants not only Latin but also the usages and discipline of Benedictine life. The sacrist, with four assistants, looked after every aspect of the physical buildings, from providing and lighting candles and keeping the floor of the cathedral carpeted with rushes or sweet-smelling hay to ensuring that the buildings were in good repair and guarding the abbey's many treasures. The cellarer purveyed all food supplies, including wine and beer, for the priory and its visitors. The chamberlain looked after the monks' clothes and their washing and shaving arrangements, including their three-weekly tonsuring and regular blood-letting. The penitentiary maintained discipline within the priory. The two treasurers dealt with the financial affairs of the community, including exchanging the foreign coins left by pilgrims into bullion or coin of the realm, and collecting the rents from the many properties scattered over England that had been given or bequeathed to the priory. The prior even owned a ship that had taken part in the Battle of Sluys in 1340.[4] Then there was the almoner, distributing the charity that was the sole recourse of the destitute, and the infirmarer, who looked after the sick. His spacious quarters included a herb garden for the simples he dispensed.

Wibert, prior from about 1150 until his death in 1167, transformed the layout of the priory grounds and buildings. In 1165 he created an elaborate water system, distributing piped water under pressure throughout the monastic buildings from springs half a mile distant. He also installed sewers to dispose of the community's waste.[5] Another achievement, equally far-sighted, was the acquisition of three acres just to the north of the monastic enclosure, known as the Green Court, where the occupations presenting fire hazards, such as baking and brewing, could be segregated. To reach the monastery and the cathedral, all visitors crossed the Green Court to the gatehouse leading into the monastic enclosure.

In 1170 the archbishop, Thomas Becket, was assassinated in his cathedral. The news of his terrible death spread like wildfire over England and Europe. The pope took only three years to canonize him. The cathedral became an even more venerated – and profitable – pilgrimage site. The monks took fifty years to create a setting worthy of their saint, but in 1220 Becket's remains were reverently laid in an elaborate tomb in the Trinity Chapel dedicated to his memory at the east end of the great building. There are still marble slabs in the pavement leading to the Trinity Chapel, worn away by the countless pilgrims kneeling at his shrine.[6] The pilgrim trade was looking up.

One of the Benedictine order's rules was to give hospitality to visitors, extending from royalty down to the poorest supplicant, each rank of society to be housed as they lived in the outside world. When pilgrims arrived at the Green Court gate it was the job of the gatehouse-keeper to sort them out according to their status – a task generating, one imagines, occasional stress. He would know the regular visitors who came on priory business. Royal and aristocratic visitors, with their impressive entourages, were easily identifiable.[7] As guests of the prior they were deferentially escorted to luxurious accommodation that even had an ensuite bath, and their servants were sent to a building within call of their masters. Appropriate provision was made for the poor. Between these extremes there was plenty of room for visitors such as the pilgrims.

As they approached Canterbury, they caught occasional glimpses of the cathedral towers, gilded by the sunlight. They may have heard the voice of 'Bell Harry', the great bell that had hung in the central tower for a hundred years.[8] They crossed the Green Court and dismounted. Their horses were taken away to the stables, and they waited by the gatehouse to be allocated sleeping quarters. Probably the women – the Wife of Bath and the Prioress and her nuns – made their own arrangements. I can't imagine that the Wife, that well-travelled lady very conscious of her status, would submit to the scrutiny of a mere gatehouse-keeper. She will have found herself a comfortable inn, of which there were many in Canterbury, perhaps aided in her choice by the Host, who would know most of his fellow-innkeepers. Similarly the Prioress will surely have called on a relation or friend who ruled over a nearby convent of nuns. They too were bound to extend hospitality to visitors, including the priests who were with the Prioress, but they had clearer ideas of feminine comfort than the Benedictine monks, and they could exchange the kind of gossip which was forbidden to monks.

At last Chaucer's pilgrims entered the great building.

The Gothic cathedral was a miracle of soaring pillars and flooding light. Gone were the heavy, robust Norman pillars. Instead, delicate stone arcades, tracery and fan-vaulted ceilings embroidered every surface, and vertiginous slender pillars defied gravity. The walls were painted with lively illustrations of Holy Writ. The immense windows were filled with stained glass dating from the thirteenth century.[9] High up in the clerestory of the quire, a series of eighty-six figures, each 55 inches tall, showed the genealogy of Christ. Here were Methuselah (Genesis 5:27), thoughtfully pondering his long life, one hand stroking his beard: and Adam, wearing a sheepskin round his loins, hooves and all, digging with a wooden spade with a pointed metal tip, a shape still familiar as the 'spade' in a pack of playing cards. King Hezekiah sat with one leg over the other knee, a pose proper to a thirteenth-century authority. He was holding a sundial, because God changed the time in his reign (2 Kings 20:8–11). All the figures are realized with a fluency and sophistication unexpected by twenty-first-century eyes. Their meticulous detailing is invisible from ground level. They were created not to delight the human eye but to glorify God.

On High Days and Holy Days in the church calendar, the archbishop sometimes came to his cathedral. Then the brown habits of the monks gave way to an explosion of colour, as the archiepiscopal procession moved round the church. Some of Lanfranc's vestments had been so heavily encrusted with gold embroidery that when they finally wore out, in 1371, they were burned, so that the precious metal could be retrieved.[10] But there were others from his time, of dark-blue silk embroidered in gold with stars and beasts, and red silk embroidered with eagles.[11] Edward I had given a red silk cope embroidered with the story of Joseph, probably in the *Opus*

Anglicanum technique that was famous throughout Europe.[12] Those vestments must have been heavy on the shoulders for the older clergy. On a man strong enough to bear their weight without effort they would have looked magnificent, but it has to be said that no matter how splendid the vestment, it could make an elderly stooping figure resemble a surprisingly painted tortoise. The hangings of black tapestry embroidered with the Black Prince's badge of white ostrich feathers, bordered in red with swans with women's heads, bequeathed by him in 1376, were still new. They had dressed his royal hall in his lifetime, and now made frontals for the High Altar and other altars.[13]

As the pilgrims moved through the great building, they glimpsed precious reliquaries containing the holy relics for which the cathedral had been famed even before St Thomas's death. St Blase seems to have been a good investment. His body rested in a shrine behind the High Altar, except for his head, which was kept in a separate silver-gilt head-shaped reliquary; one of his arms; and one of his teeth, which was tucked into a golden cross alongside a piece of the Holy Cross, St Paul's staff and some other bits of saints. Another silver-gilt cross enshrined fragments of Jesus's tomb and of his cradle, some of his sweat and Moses' staff.[14] Including St Blase's, there were eleven holy arms, each enclosed in its silver-gilt reliquary, and many, many other holy relics.

But their guide halted them in front of another series of twelve windows in the quire, this time clearly visible from the ground. He took as his theme that the Old Testament 'proved' Christ's incarnation: a subtle message that could be understood on many levels.[15] Here were the Three Magi, on beautiful horses, pointing to a large star in the sky. A little further down that window, there they were again, on foot but still wearing their crowns, being ordered by Herod to come back and tell him where the Christ child had been born. Further on still, they were being advised by an angel, in a dream, to go straight home instead. There they were, tucked up together in one bed as was the medieval fashion, still wearing their crowns.

At last, their minds full of the immense majesty of God, the pilgrims moved up a flight of steps, some of them on their knees, to the Trinity Chapel, where lay the tomb of St Thomas, 'the holy blissful martyr . . . that had helped them when they were sick'.[16] The windows surrounding the tomb were just as brilliantly coloured as those in the quire, but the stories they told were on a different scale, a human scale, about people whom the pilgrims might have known: a blind woman, a shepherd lad with leprosy, a woman in the grip of some mental ailment, another in an epileptic fit, a man who was just plain 'mad', a household whose sons were smitten with a deadly disease, a carpenter who wounded his leg with his own axe – all were cured by the blood of the Martyr. The windows told these stories, and many more, in instalments, sometimes in two panels, sometimes in as many as nine. The blood was mixed with water – surely to an almost homeopathic degree – and administered by a monk. The cure could not be expected immediately. It might be delayed until the supplicant returned home, but once it happened the supplicant or his family had a duty to thank the saint by an appropriate offering to the monastery.

The pilgrims emerged, dazed and blinking, into the sunlight.

The Prioress dismissed her yapping dogs and her fractious sisters from her mind, and for a moment rested in God. The Knight resolved to find a better cause to lay down his life for. His son looked at the beauty of the Blessed Virgin, and thought of his lady love. The Yeoman sturdily bore himself, as ever, in the service of God. The Monk and the Friar each were reminded of the ideals of their founders, and considered how to amend their lives. The Merchant brought to his mind the policy of his house on usury, and decided to have another look at it when he returned to his counting house. The Doctor of Physic saw again how his potions and salves were nothing if not applied with love for the patient and for God. The Parson and his brother the Plowman smiled to see their world so translated into the beauty of God. The Guildsmen and their Cook considered for a moment how to bring God into the busy life of the city. The Shipman thought of far-distant lands, where even there God reigned. The Pardoner was ashamed. The Summoner gave up his scheme to adjust the list of hearings to his own advantage. The Miller resolved to put away his deceptive measures. The Reeve and the Franklin thought how God could improve life for the poorest on their lands. Mine Host, who had been here before, was humbled, and Geoffrey Chaucer smiled benevolently on his creations.

The last to emerge was the Wife of Bath. Contrary to her habit of many years, she had stood back to let her fellow pilgrims precede her. She needed time to think. Did she really want another husband? They were so predictable in their wants and demands. She was growing older, and someone to look after her in old age would be useful. In spite of all her different partners, she had never had children who could be leant on when she was old, so how should she plan best?

Why not change her ways altogether, and take the veil? Then make a trip over to Ghent and Ypres, to see how the weavers there arranged their businesses. They were more likely to show her around if she were a nun than if she went as a commercial competitor. There was bound to be some holy shrine somewhere near that could serve as the pretext for the trip. And when she joined her chosen community of nuns she would rise to the top fast and easily, by sheer force of character – she saw no difficulty there; she was far more able than that foolish Madame Eglantine.

Indeed the occupation of running a large establishment would be an enjoyable challenge. She would have an amenable work force at hand, to produce whatever the market indicated. The only snag would be all that getting out of bed at inhuman times of the night. But being married had involved a certain amount of that, anyway. Then when at last old age did come to claim her, she could be sure of a comfortable life being looked after, with no danger that, like a husband, her carers might die or abscond and leave her helpless.

The idea was definitely worth considering.

She might even, along the way, find God.

Perhaps.

APPENDIX A

Grosmont, Gaunt and Bolingbroke

HENRY OF GROSMONT

1310 Born in Grosmont Castle, Monmouthshire. Parents Henry, 3rd earl of Lancaster and Maud Chaworth.

1330 Knighted. Marries Isabella, daughter of Henry, Lord Beaumont, by whom he has two daughters, one of whom, Blanche, later marries Edward III's son John of Gaunt.

1337 Becomes earl of Derby.

(1337 War with the French begins.)

1345 On his father's death he becomes 4th earl of Lancaster and Leicester. Leads a campaign through France to Aquitaine, won the Battle of Auberoche, captured Poitiers.

1347 Participates in siege of Calais.

1348 Made a founding knight of the Order of the Garter.

1351 Becomes duke of Lancaster.

1351–2 Crusades in Prussia.

1359–60 Participates in Rheims campaign.

1352 Co-founds Corpus Christi Colllege, Cambridge.

1354 Writes *Le Livre de Seyntz Medicines*.

1360 Negotiates the Treaty of Brétigny with the French.

1361 Dies in Leicester Castle, probably of plague.

JOHN OF GAUNT

1340 Born in Ghent (pronounced Gaunt), Flanders, to Edward III and Philippa of Hainault.

1359 Marries Blanche, daughter of Henry of Grosmont.

1361 On the death of his father-in-law Henry Grosmont, becomes earl of Lancaster.

1362 Becomes duke of Lancaster.

1368 Blanche dies.

(1369 War against the French resumes.)

1369 Campaigns in northern France.

1370 Goes to Aquitaine to reinforce his brother the Black Prince; takes part in the siege of Limoges.

1371 Marries Constance of Castile.

1372 Assumes the title of king of Castile.

(1377 Edward III dies; his grandson Richard ascends the throne aged ten.)

1380 De facto ruler of England during Richard's minority. Imposes unpopular taxes that lead to the rebellion of 1381.

1386 Takes an army to Spain to enforce his claim to the throne of Castile, but fails. He gives up his claim in return for an annual payment. Moves to Aquitaine.

1389 Returns to England.

1394 Constance of Castile dies.

1396 Marries Katherine Swynford, his long-standing mistress. Their four children were legitimized as 'Beaufort'. Katherine's sister was Philippa, Chaucer's wife.

1399 Dies in Leicester Castle.

HENRY BOLINGBROKE

1367 Born in Bolingbroke Castle, Lincolnshire. Son of John of Gaunt and Blanche of Lancaster.

1377 Becomes earl of Derby.

1380 Marries Mary de Bohun, co-heiress of the earldom of Hereford.

1390 Campaigns in Lithuania, at the unsuccessful siege of Vilnius.

1392 Again crusading in Lithuania; also visits the Holy Land.

1397 Becomes duke of Hereford.

1398 Banished by Richard II.

1399 Richard II disinherits him. He protests, and returns to England to pursue his claim. With popular support he deposes Richard II and becomes king as Henry IV.

1413 Dies in Westminster Palace, possibly of leprosy. Buried in Canterbury Cathedral.

APPENDIX B

'THE CUTTY WREN'

O where are you going? said Milder to Moulder
O we may not tell you, said Festel to Fose
We're off to the woods, said John the Red Nose
We're off to the woods, said John the Red Nose.

And what will you do there? said Milder to Moulder
We'll shoot the Cutty Wren, said John the Red Nose
And how will you shoot us? said Milder to Moulder
With bows and with arrows, said John the Red Nose.

Oh that will not do, said Milder to Moulder
Oh what will you do then? said Festel to Fose
Great guns and great cannon, said John the Red Nose
Great guns and great cannon, said John the Red Nose.

And how will you fetch her? said Milder to Moulder
Oh we may not tell you, said Festel to Fose
On four strong men's shoulders, said John the Red Nose
On four strong men's shoulders, said John the Red Nose.

Ah that will not do, said Milder to Moulder
Oh what will you do then? said Festel to Fose
Great carts and great wagons, said John the Red Nose
Great carts and great wagons, said John the Red Nose.

Oh how will you cut her up? said Milder to Moulder
With knives and with forks, said John the Red Nose
Oh that will not do, said Milder to Moulder
Great hatchets and cleavers, said John the Red Nose.

Oh how will you boil her? said Milder to Moulder
In pots and in kettles, said John the Red Nose
Oh that will not do, said Milder to Moulder
Great pans and large cauldrons, said John the Red Nose.

Oh who'll get the spare ribs? said Milder to Moulder
Oh we may not tell you, said Festel to Fose
We'll give 'em all to the poor, said John the Red Nose
We'll give 'em all to the poor, said John the Red Nose.

This song is said to have been sung by the insurgents during the Peasants' Revolt of 1381. It dates from pre-Christian times, and seems to have originally celebrated a midwinter ritual. The 'cutty', or tiny, wren, which was the King of All Birds, represented, by folklore irony, a huge bird that was difficult to dismember, perhaps the king. The 'forks' in the sixth verse were of course pitchforks. It is not possible to identify the various characters. In 1381 the singers were intent on their plan to dismember some large bird – the state? The Church? John of Gaunt? – and use the proceeds to feed the poor.

APPENDIX C

One penny would buy eight red herrings or four larks...

4 farthings = 1 penny (d, from Latin denarius*), 1 groat = 4 pence, 12 pence = 1 shilling (s), 20 shillings = 1 pound (£).*

1 mark = 13s 4d, often used as money of account. Half a mark, 6s 8d, was the value of the English noble (coin).

16 ounces (oz) = 1 pound (lb).

2 pints = 1 quart, 4 quarts = 1 (imperial) gallon = 4½ litres.

1 farthing was the maximum to be paid to a priest for a Mass in 1382.

1d was the controlled price for eight red herrings. It would buy a snipe, four larks or a dozen finches, or six pigeons after a good harvest. It was the controlled price that a cook might charge to put a capon or a rabbit in a crust of pastry.

1½d was the controlled price of a gallon of best ale.

2d would buy a pullet or a teal (a kind of duck), or a pound of candles.

2½d would buy a tame mallard, or pay for hay for a horse for a night and a day.

3d would buy a rabbit without the skin, a wild mallard, a woodcock or a plover. It was the daily pay of an unmounted archer in the 1350s, and a gardener and a sailor in 1387. It was the weekly toll on carts bringing sand and gravel, or corn and flour, into London.

It was the daily wage for enforced labour paid to 'sturdy vagrants' in 1343.

4d would buy a cygnet, a rabbit with the skin, or a partridge, or two hens, or twelve eggs. It was payable by everyone over fourteen, under the first poll tax of 1377. It was the assessment on every married man, including his wife, not otherwise assessed, to the 1379 poll tax. It was the annual rent for an acre of land demanded in the Peasants' Revolt of 1381. A mounted archer was paid 4d a day in the war against the Scots, 1347.

6d would buy a curlew, a dozen thrushes, or a lamb, or 1 ounce of cloves. It was the valuation of a backgammon board with its pieces. It was the controlled price per gallon for red wine and 'Rhenish' wine. It was the daily pay of a mounted archer in the 1350s and the weekly allowance of some students at Oxford and Cambridge. It would buy twelve pigeons, or a hundred Spanish coney skins.

1s would buy a pheasant or a hundred English coney skins. It was the controlled price per gallon for Cretan and Provencal wine; the daily pay of esquires who went on a pilgrimage to Prussia in 1390; the flat rate payable under the second and third poll taxes; the valuation of a beaver hat; and the permitted charge for making a man's coat and hood.

1s 2d was the sickness benefit payable to a paid-up member of a fraternity.

1s 4d would buy a heron; or four pairs of shoes for a boy, or two pairs of hose. It was the controlled price per gallon for 'Malvesie' (Malmsey), a Greek wine.

1s 6d would buy a bittern or an egret and was the permitted charge for making a man's robe.

2s was the controlled price per gallon for Vernage, a Tuscan red wine. The knights who went on a pilgrimage to Prussia in 1390 were paid 2s per day, as were the knights who fought the Scots in 1347. Membership of a fraternity to encourage the reform of its members cost 2s.

2s 6d was the permitted charge for making a woman's long robe.

3s 6d would buy a conger eel or twenty-four doves, for a feast.

3s 8d would buy 2lb of pepper.

4s was the value of a woman's saddle. It was the daily expense allowance for a knight of the shire.

5s was the controlled price for 1,000 grey-work skins (the back of the squirrel in spring), or 1,000 tiles, or the value of a 'counting board' (a type of abacus).

5s 6p was the controlled price of 1,000 Polish dark squirrel skins.

7s a week was the pay of a master mason or a master carpenter.*

9s 5d would buy a plough horse in the 1340s.

13s 6d would buy a plough horse in the 1380s.

13s 9d would buy a sheaf (24) of arrows in 1390.

£1 was the assessment to the 1379 poll tax on a 'great merchant'.

£1 6s was the cost to a mounted archer of his equipment, i.e. a bow, a sheaf of arrows, a sword, a strong coat and a horse.

£1 6s 8d was the highest cost of a carved angel in the roof of Westminster Hall. It was the annual wage of a 'yeoman cook' in a nunnery.

---

*The wages of those employed in the building trades, such as stonemasons, carpenters and plasterers, varied with the hours of daylight. The employer could choose whether to pay 'for everything' or at a lower rate but providing food, their 'table'. For example, from 11 November to 2 February the rate was 3d, or 1d and their table, rising to 5d/2d in the summer months. A later ordinance gives the top rate of these skilled artificers as 6d a day in the summer, 5d a day in the winter months.

'Controlled prices' of labour were imposed by the Ordinance, later Statute, of Labourers after the Black Death in 1349, in an attempt to maintain pre-1349 levels. It was, however, impossible to enforce them, so different amounts may appear in the above list.

£1 10s was the prize money paid to ships' boys in 1387. It would buy two young oxen and three cows.

£2 was the assessment to the 1379 poll tax on a serjeant-at-law or senior barrister, and an alderman of London.

£3 was the fee payable for becoming a freeman of London by redemption in 1364.

£2 13s would buy a jousting helmet.

£4 was the assessment to the 1379 poll tax on an earl or a widowed countess.

£5 would buy a battle helmet. It was the prize money won by ships' captains in 1387.

£6 1s 4d was the assessment on the duke of Lancaster under the second (graduated) poll tax of 1379.

£8 would buy 12 yards of best wool cloth, 'scarlet'.

£10 was the salary, for life, of John of Gaunt's physician, plus 3s a day while actually attending him. It was the amount of the annuity John of Gaunt paid to Geoffrey Chaucer and his wife in 1374; and the annual rent of a shop on London Bridge.

£15–£30 would buy an adequate warhorse, or a suit of armour.

£16 was the ransom paid to the French to free Geoffrey Chaucer in 1359.

£20 per annum was the pension paid to Edward III's surgeon until 1361. It was the yearly pay during peacetime (doubled in wartime) of a knight in John of Gaunt's retinue in the 1370s.

£25 (10 marks) was the premium a goldsmith could charge for an apprenticeship. It was paid by John of Gaunt for a saddle covered in cloth of gold.

£40 was the salary, for life, of a physician of Richard II, and of the royal judges.

£50 (20 marks) was what an esquire was paid annually in John of Gaunt's retinue.

£51-plus was the dowry John of Gaunt paid for Elizabeth Chaucy (Chaucer?) to become a nun.

£100 would buy a good warhorse. It was the fee a top-flight surgeon could charge for performing an operation; and the annual fee of one of Edward III's physicians. William Walworth, the mayor of London in 1381, was granted £100 worth of land as a reward.

£858 was the prize money won by Admiral Arundel in 1387.

£1,000 was the value of the velvets and cloth of gold Dick Whittington supplied to the king in one year.

£2,666 was the ransom of the French admiral in 1387.

£12,000 was paid for a French noble captured at Crécy.

£35,000 was spent by John of Gaunt on refurbishing his Palace of the Savoy, 1357.

The ransom of the king of France, captured at Poitiers, was fixed at 3 million gold écus. Only half was ever paid since he died in captivity.

NOTES

I *The Wife of Bath*

1 Geoffrey Chaucer, *The Canterbury Tales*, ed. Jill Mann (London, 2005; hereafter Mann), General Prologue 458, p. 20.
2 Ibid., 456.
3 Ibid., 457, 471–2.
4 Ibid., 448.
5 Ibid., 460–61.
6 Ibid., WB 45, p. 212. I have here broken the rule I observe elsewhere, by which I confine myself to the description of each pilgrim in the General Prologue. Her hopeful notice that she's looking for a sixth husband comes from the Prologue introducing her Tale.
7 Ibid., 196–7, p. 218.
8 Ibid., 453–6, p. 227.
9 Ibid., 527, 526, p. 229.
10 Ibid., 597–9, p. 232.
11 Ibid., 79, p. 214.
12 Ibid., 615–8, p. 233.
13 Ibid., 131–2, p. 215.
14 R. N. Swanson, *Religion and Devotion in Europe 1215–1515* (Cambridge, 1995), p. 144.
15 Mann, GP 463–6, p. 20.
16 W. M. Rossetti (ed.), *The Stacions of Rome*, Early English Text Society no. 25 (London, 1867).
17 Francis Davey (ed. and trans.), *The Itineraries of William Wey* (Oxford, 2010), p. 25.
18 Mann, GP 464, 467, p. 20.

II The Ploughman

[1] Mann, GP 529–30, p. 23. A 'fother' of lead weighed 2,184 pounds, according to Christopher Dyer in *Standards of Living in the Later Middle Ages* (Cambridge, 1989), p. 103. I don't know whether the same measure applied to dung.

[2] Mann, GP 15, p. 3.

[3] Ibid., 536, p. 23.

[4] Joan Thirsk (ed.), *The Agrarian History of England and Wales Vol. III, 1348–1500* (Cambridge, 1991), p. 484.

[5] V. H. Galbraith (ed.), *The Anonimalle Chronicle 1333–1381* (Manchester, 1927), pp. 133–52. This chronicle gives a vivid account of the events, but is not always consistent with other chronicles; in particular, dates may vary for a few days one way or the other. It was a very confused time! The following account is based on the *Anonimalle Chronicle*, with additions from other chronicles.

[6] A. R. Myers (ed.), *English Historical Documents Vol. IV, 1327–1485* (London, 1969), p. 128.

[7] John Stow, *A Survey of London* (Stroud, 2005), p. 364.

[8] The palace had been built on a site originally owned by a monastic order based in Savoie. In 1270 it came into royal ownership, and between 1345 and 1370 the mansion on the site was rebuilt by Henry, 1st duke of Lancaster from the proceeds of his French campaigns. In 1361 the palace was inherited by John of Gaunt, Henry of Lancaster's son-in-law, who filled it with lavish furnishings and objets d'art of gold and silver. He was hated by the peasantry, who blamed him for their poverty and for the detested poll tax. They missed John of Gaunt but demolished his palace.

[9] Myers (ed.), *English Historical Documents Vol. IV*, p. 129.

[10] Anon. ('Nicolas'), *A Chronicle of London from 1089 to 1483; written in the fifteenth century, and now for the first time printed from Mss. in the British Museum*, ed. E. Tyrell (London, 1829), p. 73.

[11] Stow, *Survey of London*, p. 372. 'Plate' was of course silver.

12 Myers (ed.), *English Historical Documents Vol. IV*, p. 135.

13 Ibid., p. 73.

14 Ibid. Not surprisingly, there were various accounts of these events, often differing depending on the sympathy and bias of the writer. But I have tried to sift the most authentic story. The details are arguable.

15 *Anonimalle Chronicle*, quoted in Helen Lacey, *The Royal Pardon* (Woodbridge, 2009), p. 131.

16 Myers (ed.), *English Historical Documents Vol. IV*, p. 139.

17 Mann, GP 539–40, p. 23.

18 Ibid., 537–8.

III The Miller

1 Mann, GP 546–59, pp. 23–4.

2 Edith Rickert (ed.), *The Babees Book* (London, 1908), p. 93.

3 Mann, GP 563, p. 24.

4 Richard L. Hills, *Power from Wind* (Cambridge, 1994), p. 1.

5 Ibid., p. 62, note at p. 424.

IV The Reeve

1 Mann, GP 587–92, p. 25.

2 P. D. A. Harvey (ed.), *Manorial Records of Cuxham, Oxfordshire, circa 1200–1359* (London, 1976), p. 12 *passim*.

3 For tallies, see p. 174.

4 Edward Miller (ed.), *The Agrarian History of England and Wales Vol. III, 1348–1500* (Cambridge, 1991), p. 465.

5 H. G. Richardson, 'Business Training in Medieval Oxford', *American Historical Review* Vol. XLVI (January 1941), pp. 259–80.

6 D. Oschinsky, 'Medieval Treatises on Estate Accounting', *Economic Historical Review*, first series, XVII (1947).

7 Chaucer gave the Reeve thirty-six lines (Mann, GP 587–622, pp. 25–6). I have given a translation which is readable and clear, I hope, but I found it impossible to do a word-for-word translation, as I usually do. My own fault, not Chaucer's.

8 Mann, GP 609, p. 26.

V The Franklin

1   Mann, GP 332–3, 357–8, p. 15.
2   William Langland, *The Vision of Piers Plowman*, ed. A. V. C. Schmidt (London, 1978), X 96–101, p. 146.
3   Mann, GP 355, p. 16.
4   Anthony Musson (ed. and trans.), *Crime, Law and Society in the Later Middle Ages* (Manchester, 2009), p. 231.
5   Mann, GP 359–60, p. 16.

VI 'Mine Host'

1   Mann, GP 747–54, p. 31.
2   Mann, 15–16, p. 3.
3   E. J. Burford, *Bawds and Lodgings: A History of the London Bankside Brothels c.100–1675* (London, 1976), p. 57. I have drawn on this source for much of what follows about medieval prostitutes.
4   Sylvia Thrupp, *The Merchant Class of Medieval London* (Chicago, 1948), p. 168.
5   *The Vision of Piers Plowman*, ed. Schmidt, V 308–18, p. 78.

VII The Merchant

1   Mann, GP 274–5, p. 13.
2   Eileen Power, *Medieval English Nunneries* (Cambridge, 1922), pp. 26–7.
3   *The Vision of Piers Plowman*, ed. Schmidt, XIII 390–98, p. 224.
4   Mann, GP 276–7, p. 13.
5   Peter Spufford, *Power and Profit* (London, 2002), p. 204.
6   *The Vision of Piers Plowman*, ed. Schmidt, V 247–8, p. 74.
7   Lucy Toulmin-Smith (ed.), *Expeditions to Prussia and the Holy Land by Henry Earl of Derby 1390–1391, 1392–1393* (London, 1894), p. xcviii.
8   *The Vision of Piers Plowman*, ed. Schmidt, XV 348–9, p. 263.
9   I have taken the information on the Mercers from Lisa

Jefferson, *The Medieval Account Books of the Mercers of London,
Vol. I* (Farnham, 2009), and Anne F. Sutton, *The Mercery of
London: Trade, Goods and People 1130–1578* (Aldershot, 2005).

VIII The Five Guildsmen

1 Sutton, *The Mercery of London*, p. 118.
2 Juliet Barker, *England, Arise: The People, the King and the Great
  Revolt of 1381* (London, 2014), p. 267.
3 Richard Mabey, *Flora Britannica* (London, 1996), p. 144.
4 Mann, GP 365–8, p. 16.
5 Ibid., 363–4.
6 Ibid., 376–8, p. 17.

IX The Cook

1 Mann, GP 379–83, p. 17.
2 The Tale breaks off unfinished. See Mann, Notes to Co, p. 857.
3 Mann, Co 4346–52, p. 160.
4 *The Vision of Piers Plowman*, ed. Schmidt, Prologue 226–7,
  p. 13.
5 E. J. Arnold (ed.), *Le Livre de Seyntz Medicines* (Oxford, 1940),
  p. 194.
6 *The Vision of Piers Plowman*, ed. Schmidt, XIX 400–405,
  p. 342.
7 Constance B. Hieatt and Sharon Butler, *Curye on Inglysch*,
  Early English Text Society (London, 1985), p. 145.
8 Ibid., p. 150.
9 Ibid., p. 148.
10 Ibid., p. 563.
11 Clarissa Dickson Wright, *A History of English Food* (London,
   2012), p. 58.
12 Terence Scully, *The Art of Cookery in the Late Middle Ages*
   (Woodbridge, 1995), p. 30.
13 Mann, GP 421, p. 19.
14 Scully, *The Art of Cookery in the Late Middle Ages*, pp. 42, 49.

X *The Doctor of Physic*

1   Mann, GP 411–14, p. 18.
2   Ibid., 419–21, p. 19.
3   Ibid., 429–34.
4   Ibid., Notes to GP, p. 816, citing T. J. Garbaty, *Medical History*, 7 (1963), p. 350.
5   Remarkably, the same treatment was followed when Queen Elizabeth I caught the same disease, with the same happy result. She was wrapped in red flannel.
6   Mann, GP 525–8, p. 18. An electuary was a paste of drugs mixed with water or honey that could be taken orally.
7   In Tanganyika in the 1950s a man thought to be casting evil spells by *mumiani*, Swahili for mummy, was lynched by a mob.
8   Robert S. Gottried, *Doctors and Medicine in Medieval England 1340–1530* (Princeton, 1986), p. 18.
9   E. J. Arnould (ed.), *Le Livre de Seyntz Medicines* (Oxford, 1940), p. 161.
10 For all that follows from the Trotula I am indebted to Monica H. Green (ed. and trans.), *The Trotula: A Medieval Compendium of Women's Medicine* (Philadelphia, 2001).

XI *The Sergeant of the Law*

1   Mann, GP 309–15, p. 14.
2   Ibid., 328–9, p. 15.
3   In the very early days there was a movable bar, a wooden barrier, in court, dividing 'utter' or outer barristers from the senior barristers who had 'taken silk' and wore silk gowns. I am only an utter barrister.
4   Mann, GP 316–17, p. 14.
5   William Langland, *The Vision of Piers Plowman*, 'Rendered into modern English by Henry W. Wells' (London, 1959), 211–16, p. 9.
6   Mann, 314–15, p. 14.
7   Ibid., 318–20.

8   Ibid., 325–6, p. 15.

9   Psalm 51 was always known as 'the neck verse', but it is not clear whether just one verse was enough, or more might be needed.

10 Anthony Musson (ed. and trans.), *Crime, Law and Society in the Later Middle Ages* (Manchester, 1999), p. 179.

11 Alan Harding, *The Law Courts of Medieval England* (London, 1978), p. 104.

12 Mann, GP 321–2, p. 15.

XII The Summoner

1   Mann, Fri 1304–10, p. 257.

2   Ibid., GP 647–8, p. 27.

3   Ibid., Note to GP 625–35, p. 821.

4   Ibid., GP 663–5, p. 28.

XIII The Manciple

1   Mann, GP 567, p. 24.

2   Quoted from a contemporary chronicle in Barker, *England, Arise*, p. 61.

3   Some Oxford and Cambridge colleges still have Manciples. In Oxford he is the accountant to the steward (or domestic bursar) and at Corpus Christi College, Cambridge, he is the head chef.

4   Mann, GP 576–81, p. 24.

5   Ibid., 569.

6   Ibid., 571–2.

7   A. H. Thomas (ed.), *Calendar of Pleas and Memoranda Rolls of the City of London: Volume 2, 1364–1381* (Cambridge 1929), p. 205.

8   Mann, GP 573–5, 586, pp. 24–5.

XIV The Monk

1   Mann, GP 167–204, pp. 9–10.

2   Ibid., 184–8, p. 9.

XV The Prioress

1 Mann, GP 118–121, p. 7.
2 Ibid., 128–35.
3 Ibid., 139–41, p. 8.
4 Power, *Medieval English Nunneries*, p. 11.
5 Ibid., p. 19.
6 *The Vision of Piers Plowman*, ed. Schmidt, V 155–9, p. 69.

XVI The Friar

1 Mann, GP 208–11, p. 10. I have taken various bits of this chapter from different places in Chaucer's description of him.
2 I have quoted from the version of the New Testament translated by Wycliffe's followers in 1388, and edited in modern spelling by W. R. Cooper (London, 2002).
3 It is included in a collection of medieval manuscripts possessed by the Honourable Society of Gray's Inn.
4 Power, *Medieval English Nunneries*, p. 509. The same regret seems to have pervaded nunneries as well.
5 Mann, GP 252, p. 12.
6 Ibid., 221–6, p. 11.

XVII The Pardoner

1 Mann, GP 669–714, pp. 28–9.
2 Ibid., 689, 691, p. 29.
3 Ibid., 705–6.

XVIII The Clerk of Oxenford

1 Mann, GP 285–308, pp. 13–4.
2 G. H. Martin and J. R. L. Highfield, *A History of Merton College, Oxford* (Oxford, 1997), p. 11.
3 Jim Al-Khalili, *Pathfinders: The Golden Age of Arabic Science* (London, 2010), p. 6.

⁴ I have had the enormous advantage of a conversation with Paul Wright, of William Cowley, makers of parchment and vellum, on which this section is based.

⁵ Stella Panayotova, *The Macclesfield Psalter* (London, 2008), p. 30.

⁶ The Master of Gray's Inn Library has kindly allowed me to refer to these documents and to quote from the catalogue. I am indebted to the Inn's librarian, Theresa Thom, now retired, whose scholarly wisdom illuminated medieval manuscripts for me.

⁷ Al-Khalili, *Pathfinders*, p. 6.

⁸ Mann, CY 702, p. 648.

XIX The Poor Parson

¹ Mann, GP 525–8, p. 22.

² Ibid., 507–14.

³ Myers (ed.), *English Historical Documents Vol. IV*, p. 89.

⁴ Swanson, *Religion and Devotion in Europe*, p. 233.

⁵ An edition of Wycliffe's New Testament in modern spelling with an Introduction on which I have drawn was published by the British Library in 2002.

⁶ Mann, ML 1166–77, pp. 209–10.

⁷ This and the following excerpts are from J. K. Elliott, *The Apocryphal New Testament* (Oxford, 1993).

XX The Knight

¹ Mann, GP 44–6, p. 4.

² But the allowance has to be generous. Try Mann, Kn 1845–54, pp. 69–70, then plough through 'Part Four', as far as l. 2673, pp. 92–9.

³ Mann, Kn 2602–11, pp. 96–7.

⁴ Ibid., 2496–508, pp. 92–3.

⁵ C. H. Talbot, *Medicine in Medieval England* (London, 1967), p. 93.

⁶ Mann, GP 70–71, p. 5.

⁷ Ibid., 75–6.

XXI *The Squire*

1   Mann, GP 89–90, 92, p. 6.
2   Ibid., 85–6.
3   Until recently it was middle-class etiquette to add 'Esq.', standing for Esquire, after the name of a male to whom you were addressing a letter. The custom was decried as sexist, and had fallen into desuetude by the beginning of the twenty-first century.
4   Mann, GP 81, p. 6.
5   Mann, Pars 415–24, pp. 720–22.
6   Ibid., GP 91, p. 91.
7   Ibid., 95–6.
8   My grandfather fought in the Afghan War as a Victorian soldier, before the days of cameras, let alone satellite pictures. He took his drawing kit with him to sketch the enemy lines and possible avenues of attack.

XXII *The Yeoman*

1   Mann, GP 101, 103, p. 6.
2   This is what sense I can make of the two phrases 'in his lord's war', applying to the Knight, and 'A yeoman had he [i.e. the Knight] and servants no more / At that time, for him liste [it pleased him] to ride so': prime examples of what would have been a perfectly simple relationship to Chaucer's audience, but fraught with meanings for the modern reader.
3   Mann, GP 104–5, 107, p. 6.
4   I have drawn for this section on Richard Wadge, *The World of the Archer in the Hundred Years War* (Stroud, 2009), made even more enlightening by the author's own expertise as an archer, and Jim Bradbury, *The Medieval Archer* (Woodbridge, 1985).
5   The Battle of Crécy is well described by Richard Barber, 'Edward III and the Battle of Crécy', *History Today*, Vol. 63 (October 2013), pp. 33–8, as well as by Froissart.

XXIII The Shipman

1 Mann, GP 388–90, p. 17.
2 Ibid., 392–3, pp. 17–18.
3 Peter Spufford, *Power and Profit* (London, 2002), p. 162.
4 Mann, GP 398–400, p. 18.
5 Ibid., 401–9.
6 Description by Giovanni da Buti, Chiara Frugoni, *Inventions of the Middle Ages* (London, 2007), p. 142.
7 M. C. Seymour (ed.), *The Bodley Version of Mandeville's Travels* (London, 1969).
8 They must have been bananas. My mother, born in 1890, when a very small child in Jamaica remembered how no Jamaican would use a knife to cut a banana because there was a picture of the Cross inside it. Next time you eat a banana, check; there's a faint triangle at its centre.

Epilogue

1 Jonathan Foyle, *Architecture of Canterbury Cathedral* (London, 2013), p. 32.
2 J. Wickham Legg and W. H. St John Hope, *Inventories of Christchurch, Canterbury* (London, 1902), p. 29 quoting Gervase of Canterbury, who was of course writing in Latin.
3 C. Eveleigh Woodruff and William Danks, *Memorials of the Cathedral and Priory of Christ in Canterbury* (London, 1912), pp. 222–64.
4 Myers (ed.), *English Historical Documents Vol. IV*, p. 19.
5 Recorded in the famous 'waterworks drawing' of *c*.1165, shown in Foyle, *Architecture of Canterbury Cathedral*, p. 40, fig. 33.
6 Ibid., p. 110 and fig. 106.
7 Peter Fergusson, *Canterbury Cathedral and Priory in the Age of Becket* (New Haven and London, 2001), p. 62.
8 Woodruff and Danks, *Memorials of the Cathedral and Priory of Christ in Canterbury*, p. 473.
9 M. A. Michael, *Stained Glass of Canterbury Cathedral* (London,

2014), p. 32 *et seq.* Some of the windows have been lost and destroyed over time, and moved around the cathedral as successive priors thought best. I have referred to them in their original places. The Ancestors can now be seen in the south-west transept window. Much of the stained glass was unfortunately 'restored' by a Victorian whose own efforts are so meticulously like the originals that to an uneducated eye it's hard to tell them apart.

[10] Legg and Hope, *Inventories of Christchurch, Canterbury*, p. 13.

[11] Ibid., p. 17.

[12] Ibid., p. 14.

[13] Ibid., p. 97. The learned authors noted that the inventory made when Henry VIII took over the cathedral with all its treasures listed 'one old hanging of six pieces of ostrich feathers'. These were probably the remains of some of the Black Prince's bequest.

[14] Ibid., p. 81.

[15] Michael, *Stained Glass of Canterbury Cathedral*, p. 32 *et seq.*

[16] Mann, GP 17–18, p. 3.

INDEX

Liza Picard

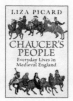